Critical Edition of the Complete Works

of

*Saint Thérèse of the Child Jesus
and of the Holy Face*

Centenary Edition
(1873–1973)

The Poetry
of
Saint Thérèse of Lisieux

Complete Edition
Texts and Introductions

Translated by
Donald Kinney, O.C.D.

ICS Publications
Institute of Carmelite Studies
Washington, DC
1996

A critical edition of all the poems written by St. Thérèse according to the autographs and different copies.

This edition was prepared by Sister Cécile of the Carmel of Lisieux and Jacques Lonchampt, with the assistance of Sister Geneviève, O.P., of the Clairefontaine Monastery, Jeanne Lonchampt, Fr. Bernard Bro, O.P., and Fr. Guy Gaucher, O.C.D.

POETRY OF ST. THÉRÈSE OF LISIEUX is a translation of volume I of *Poésies,* with selected passages from volume II (Les Éditions du Cerf / Desclée de Brouwer, 1979). Photos used with permission of Office Central de Lisieux.

Cover design by Nancy Gurganus of Grey Coat Graphics.

ICS Publications
2131 Lincoln Road, N.E.
Washington, D.C. 20002

Library of Congress Cataloging-in-Publication Data

Thérèse, de Lisieux, Saint, 1873–1897
  [Poems. English]
  The poetry of Saint Thérèse of Lisieux / translated by Donald Kinney. — Complete ed.
    p. cm. —(Critical edition of the complete works of Saint Thérèse of Lisieux)
  Includes bibliographical references and index.
  Contents: [1] Texts and introductions.
  ISBN 0-935216-56-1 (v. 1)
  1. Thérèse, de Lisieux, Saint, 1873–1897—Translations into English. 2. Christian poetry, French—Translations into English. I. Title. II. Series: Thérèse, de Lisieux, Saint, 1873–1897. Works. English. 1982.
PQ2450.TZZ16A25 1995
841'.8—dc20
                                           95–295
                                           CIP

Contents

Translator's Note 7
Abbreviations 9
Preface by Jean Guitton of the Académie française 11
General Introduction 15

The Poems

PN 1   The Divine Dew 35
PN 2   To Mother Marie de Gonzague
         for Her Sixtieth Birthday 39
PN 3   Saint Cecilia 41
PN 4   Canticle to Obtain the Canonization of Joan of Arc 46
PN 5   My Song for Today 50
PN 6   The Portrait of a Soul I Love 54
PN 7   Song of Gratitude to Our Lady of Mount Carmel 56
PN 8   Prayer of the Child of a Saint 59
PN 9   Prayer of an Exiled Child 64
PN 10   Story of a Shepherdess Who Became a Queen 65
PN 11   The Time of Tears Has Passed at Last 71
PN 12   It's Close to You, Virgin Mary 74
PN 13   The Queen of Heaven to Her Beloved Child 76
PN 14   To Our Father Saint Joseph 80
PN 15   The Atom of the Sacred Heart 82
PN 16   Song of Gratitude of Jesus' Fiancée 84
PN 17   Living on Love 87
PN 18   The Canticle of Céline 93
PN 18a   He Who Has Jesus Has Everything 103
PN 19   The Atom of Jesus-Host 106
PN 20   My Heaven on Earth (Canticle to the Holy Face) 108
PN 21   Canticle of a Soul Having Found the Place of Its Rest 111
PN 22   To My Dear Mother, the Fair Angel of My Childhood 113
PN 23   To the Sacred Heart of Jesus 117
PN 24   Jesus, My Beloved, Remember 121
PN 25   My Desires Near Jesus Hidden in His Prison of Love 132
PN 26   The Responses of Saint Agnes 136
PN 27   Remembrance of February 24, 1896 139
PN 28   The Eternal Canticle Sung Even in Exile 142

PN 29   How Sweet It Is for Us 144
PN 30   A Gloss on the Divine 147
PN 31   The Canticle of Sister Marie of the Trinity 149
PN 32   Heaven for Me 152
PN 33   What I'll Soon See for the First Time 155
PN 34   Strewing Flowers 158
PN 35   To Our Lady of Victories 160
PN 36   Jesus Alone 163
PN 37   These Worthless Quatrains 166
PN 38   Confidential Message from Jesus to Thérèse 167
PN 39   A Holy and Famous Doctor 168
PN 40   The Sacristans of Carmel 169
PN 41   How I Want to Love 172
PN 42   Child, You Know My Name 174
PN 43   The Aviary of the Child Jesus 176
PN 44   To My Little Brothers in Heaven 179
PN 45   My Joy 184
PN 46   To My Guardian Angel 187
PN 47   To Théophane Vénard 190
PN 48   My Weapons 193
PN 49   To Our Lady of Perpetual Help 197
PN 50   To Joan of Arc 199
PN 51   An Unpetalled Rose 201
PN 52   Abandonment Is the Sweet Fruit of Love 205
PN 53   For Sister Marie of the Trinity 209
PN 54   Why I Love You, O Mary 211

Supplementary Poems
PS 1   O Hidden God 223
PS 2   In the Orient 224
PS 3   For Fifty Years 225
PS 4   Heaven's the Reward 226
PS 5   For a Feast of Saint Martha 229
PS 6   To Mother Marie de Gonzague 231
PS 7   Silence Is the Sweet Language 232
PS 8   You Who Know My Extreme Littleness 233

The Poems in French 236
Index 331

Translator's Note

The complete edition of the works of St. Thérèse is the remarkable achievement of twenty-five years of close collaboration by a team of eminent specialists: Jacques Lonchampt, Sr. Cécile of the Lisieux Carmel, Sr. Geneviève, O.P., Jeanne Lonchampt, Fr. Bernard Bro, O.P., and Fr. (now Bishop) Guy Gaucher, O.C.D. In 1992 their edition was reprinted in eight volumes, and that same year the Académie française awarded it its "Cardinal Grente Prize" for excellence in a critical edition.

The team named above spent five of those twenty-five years meticulously preparing the original edition of St. Thérèse's poetry, which was first published in two volumes in 1979. The editors of the Institute of Carmelite Studies and I decided to include in this English version only selected passages of the second volume, because the original contains very specialized material which would be of little interest to most readers.

In my translation, I have tried to retain the same key words and phrases as Fr. John Clarke used in his fine translations of *Story of a Soul, Her Last Conversations,* and the (two-volume) *Letters.* I have left the melody titles for each poem in French, however, since it is often impossible to translate them accurately out of context.

In an appendix I have provided the poems in French for those who wish to read St. Thérèse's originals.

Translating poetry means taking a risk. The poetry of St. Thérèse, so simple, fresh, and pure, is particularly challenging to render into another language. But I have wanted to take this risk because her poetry reveals wonderful new aspects of her life and thought, which English-speaking readers might otherwise miss.

My goal in this book has been to remain faithful to St. Thérèse's vocabulary, style, and message. This unfortunately has meant sacrificing the meter and rhyme, but I hope that a certain lyric quality lingers still.

In one of St. Thérèse's most beautiful poems, "Living on Love" (PN 17), she writes that her love for God is "a great treasure in an earthen vase" (st. 7) and that in dying of love she is "shattering the vase to anoint [his] Sweet Face" (st. 12). We can also say that St. Thérèse's poetry is "a great treasure in an earthen vase." Translating it is like shattering the vase! Yet I hope that the essence of its precious perfume still wafts out to us, and, especially, that it consoles his Holy Face.

I would like to express my gratitude to all those who so generously helped me with this book: Fr. Daniel Chowning, O.C.D., first began this translation with the Institute of Carmelite Studies, but he had to give it up because of new responsibilities in his Province. He and I have collaborated on this book, and he translated the General Introduction. Fr. Kieran Kavanaugh, O.C.D., kindly advised me on translating poetry. Mlle. Claudette Tricoire and the Carmelite nuns allowed me to research the poetry at the "Centre de documentation thérésienne" at the Carmel of Lisieux. Profs. Janine and Robert Kreiter of the University of the Pacific and Helen Taylor are long-time friends who, in different ways, have been instrumental in my Carmelite vocation. They each proved their friendship once more by proofreading and correcting my manuscript. Wendy-Marie Teichert, and Theresa Thomas, O.C.D.S., read and made suggestions for improving the final draft. Sr. Marie-Cécile, O.C.D., of the Carmelite Monastery in Carmel-by-the-Sea, helped me render difficult Carmelite monastic vocabulary into English. Terry Schack gave me much-needed computer assistance. I also wish to thank my Provincial, Fr. Gerald Werner, O.C.D., and my superiors, Fr. Bernard Perkins, O.C.D., and Fr. William Fenton, O.C.D., for their continuing support.

At the ICS, I am indebted to Fr. Regis Jordan, O.C.D., and Jude Langsam, O.C.D.S., for their editing of the manuscript. Fr. Steven Payne, O.C.D., has especially encouraged me all during this project.

Prof. Joyce Rogers, outstanding Secular Order Carmelite, teacher, author, and scholar of St. Thérèse, first suggested that I take on this translation. She was a source of inspiration throughout. Joyce died very suddenly just a few weeks after I completed my work. I would like to dedicate this book to her memory.

Donald Kinney, O.C.D.

Abbreviations

PN   The "New Poetry" classification for each of the poems. Established in the 1979 French "Centenary Edition" and used in this translation.

PS   "Supplementary Poems." Some are incomplete fragments, others are copied in Thérèse's handwriting.

These four abbreviations are frequently used in this volume. All refer to the ICS translations by Fr. John Clarke, O.C.D.:

SS   *Story of a Soul* (1976)
HLC   *Her Last Conversations* (1977)
GCI   *General Correspondence, vol. I* (1982)
GCII   *General Correspondence, vol. II* (1988)

The following abbreviations refer either to poetry terminology or to French titles cited in the complete critical edition of the *Poésies*, from which this volume is translated:

C.   Couplet

CE I, etc.   Copie des Ecrits, 1910 (CE I, II, III, IV)
              (Copy of the Writings, 1910)

CGI, CGII   *Correspondance générale*, 1972-1973, 2 vols.
              (French edition of the *General Correspondence* above)

CMG I, etc. Carnets manuscrits de Soeur Geneviève (CMG I-IV)
              (Manuscript notebooks of Sister Geneviève)

CRM   "Carnet rouge" de Soeur Marie de la Trinité = déposition au Procès ("Red Notebook" of Sister Marie of the Trinity = testimony at the Process)

CSG   *Conseils et Souvenirs*, publiés par Soeur Geneviève, 1973 *(Counsels and Reminiscences,* published by Sister Geneviève, 1973)

DE   *Derniers Entretiens*, 1971. (Original French edition of *Her Last Conversations* above)

Ms A   Manuscrit autobiographique dédié à Mère Agnès
de Jésus, 1896 (Autobiographical manuscript
dedicated to Mother Agnes of Jesus, 1896)

Ms B   Lettre à Soeur Marie du Sacré-Coeur, manuscrit
autobiographique, 1896 (Letter to Sister Marie of
the Sacred Heart, Autobiographical manuscript,
1896)

Ms C   Manuscrit autobiographique dédié à Mère Marie
de Gonzague, 1897 (Autobiographical manuscript
dedicated to Mother Marie de Gonzague, 1897)

NPPO   Notes préparatoires pour le Procès de l'Ordinaire
(Preparatory notes for the Ordinary Process)

PA   Procès Apostolique, 1915–1917 (Rome, 1976)
(Apostolic Process)

PO   Procès de l'Ordinaire, 1910–1911 (Rome, 1973)
(Ordinary Process)

Pri   *Prières* de Sainte Thérèse de l'Enfant-Jésus, 1988
(*Prayers* by Saint Thérèse of the Child Jesus
[ICS translation forthcoming])

Refr. or R.   Refrain

RP   *Théâtre au Carmel: Récréations Pieuses* de Sainte
Thérèse de l'Enfant-Jésus, 1985 (*The Plays of St.
Thérèse of Lisieux: Pious Recreations* [ICS translation
forthcoming])

St., sts.   Stanza, stanzas

V.   Verse

Preface

by Jean Guitton
of the Académie française

Among the many varied vocations Thérèse of Lisieux had to synthesize, I think that, without her suspecting it, she had a poetic vocation. At the threshold of this book, I would like to justify these feelings.

Considered in its essence, what is the poetic act? It is a certain use of common language, more concentrated, more dense, more intimate—singing, melodious, and rhythmic—and often subject to strict conventions. Thus the ordinary, uncontrolled chattering we call "prose" changes its nature, like coal becoming incandescent. Poetry resembles music. But its difficulty lies in using the words of language, which, contrary to musical tones, have a definite meaning. Rare are the poets who have the good fortune of uniting *sounds* and *meaning* through a kind of continual miracle. When that happens, we are led to a state of quiet delight, analogous to the ecstasy of the mystics, to "pure prayer." I needed this detour to explain the poetry of Thérèse.

How easy it is to belittle the poems of this child! They are childlike exercises, often written on request and (I dare say, "in a devil of a hurry") by a young girl with no academic background. Did she have good taste? Did she know how to discern what is insipid and what is powerful? Did she know how to separate the wheat from the chaff? Her prose is often colorless; if it were not illuminated by conviction, it would be banal. We cannot compare her style to that of the great Teresa, who recreated the Spanish language.

But in the French tradition there exist two types of expression for poetry as well as for prose. The one, more Latin, more Roman, closer to eloquence than to the literal word, aims at a certain effect, at magic. The other, more Greek, more Hellenistic, seeks transparency flowing from the source. Compare Bossuet to Fénelon, and you will sense the difference between these two genres. In poetry, compare Corneille to Racine and La Fontaine. Compare Hugo to Lamartine; Leconte de Lisle to Verlaine.... Our young Thérèse is part of this second line of descent.

In these two schools (and more in the second) we notice much failure. How many flat, fabricated, and monotonous verses are necessary to merit the grace of one inspired verse: that fragment which stands alone in the memory and makes up for everything else, like a woman's smile, a single word in a book, one line of a drawing. When an author, as dull or as affected as he or she may be, leaves in my memory a few eternal verses, then (with Bremond, Thierry Maulnier, and Pompidou) I crown that author a poet in my heart.

Open this collection of poetry. Pay no attention to the banality, the awkwardness, and the way the material is put together. Keep only the flower, and beyond the flower, the fragrance.

*

* *

While studying Simone Weil, a sister of Thérèse in the world, I wondered what makes her prose sparkle. Certainly its literary quality, but also, from what I know of Simone, that relentless act of her will that incarnated her thought in action. Total poetry demands the incarnation of being in life. Would we love Pascal if we did not know his effort toward sanctity? The subtle Valéry distinguished poetic art from *poiétic* art. I translate that: fabrication and inspiration. Even more, the latter is pure poetry and that even purer *Poiesis* which is the consecration of oneself in sacrifice.

> My God, who can disturb the peace
> Of a heart that loves you?
> It seeks your supreme will in all things
> And never seeks itself.
> On earth, even in heaven,
> Is there any other happiness
> Than the tranquil peace
> Of a heart that loves you?

These verses, almost childish, were not written by Thérèse Martin but by Jean Racine. Thérèse composed some that are comparable to them, but she did it more naturally than the elderly Racine. And did Racine experience that peace he celebrated, that identity of temporal and eternal love? The value of Thérèse's compositions lies in the splendor that creates within the reader the memory of her sacrifice.

> You wasted not your time
> You remain so light
> After your fair abandonment
> (Paul Valéry in *Palms*)

I imagine that after having written these prayer-poems, Thérèse felt even lighter, more ready for abandonment, as if she had been playing.

*
* *

I have sketched out these few thoughts on the unfulfilled poetic vocation of "little Thérèse" before examining this work and its remarkable commentaries. I once said to myself on reading Thérèse's poetry: May there arise a critic, both poet and theologian, and endowed with scholarly erudition, who can give us a "critical apparatus" able to confirm what I vaguely feel. Here it is, this exhaustive commentary, this edition compiled according to strict modern requirements.

Perhaps what taught me most in these presentations of each poem is the joint development of poetic art and mystical depth. In the first poem of February 2, 1893, on "The Divine Dew," we already breathe in Theresian themes. And when we know that on her deathbed Thérèse wanted to keep near her a painting by her sister Céline that was an artistic translation of the subject of her first poem, we are reminded that the deep life of the consciousness expresses itself in the symbolic language of the arts. An exegesis of her poems reveals to us Thérèse's predestination, the resemblance of the *alpha* and the *omega*, of "Cana" and "Calvary," so perceptible in the Gospel of St. John.

All this happened as if Thérèse had "put a mirror to her life," as Lamartine says. Poetry was this mirror in which we can discern, thanks to this edition, both the stages of her talent and the progress of her soul. The more skillful she became in writing, the more she rose to mystical heights. I do not know if she knew Racine's rule: "to write easy verses with difficulty." But wasn't that her entire spiritual method?

Jean Guitton

General Introduction

The poetry of Thérèse of Lisieux undoubtedly remains the most unknown part of her work. It seems to confirm a number of prejudices and commonplace ideas about her, and it has contributed to the reputation of insipid charm surrounding her whom Pius X nevertheless saw as "the greatest saint of modern times." Certainly the exegetes of her thought, Msgr. André Combes, Fr. François de Sainte-Marie, Hans Urs von Balthasar, Jean Guitton, Jean-François Six and, from the beginning, Fr. Godefroid Madelaine[1] have emphasized the importance of her poetry to understanding and interpreting her message: "She had to write in verse to give shape to her most original and delicate ideas."[2] But it is not certain that these scholars all measured the full dimension of her little-educated genius, which many have considered secondary, but which nevertheless gives an exceptional stature to Thérèse the writer and spiritual guide.

If we examine the poems of Thérèse of Lisieux at all, they reveal themselves richer than we first thought. And this is the problem with her poetry: We have to go beyond the simple style, which is naturally and deliberately artless—as is fitting for a "Carmelite poem"—to discover the treasures it conceals. Thus Jean Guitton wrote, "in order to gain access to the mystery of a great life or a great work, we have to know how to cross a foggy zone. In poetry, for example, there are two types of fog: that of difficulty as in Mallarmé and that of facileness as in Jean de La Fontaine. And the fog of facileness takes longer to dissipate."[3]

Not merely unappreciated, Thérèse's poetry is above all

---

[1] Letter-Preface written April 4, 1898, for the first edition of *Story of a Soul.*
[2] Abbé Combes, *Theresiana* (Paris: Vrin, 1970).
[3] Conference on Thérèse of Lisieux at Notre Dame Cathedral, March 6, 1973. Special issue of *Nouvelles de l'Institut catholique de Paris,* May 1973, p. 30.

barely known. Until this edition, fifteen poems were unpublished (PN 2, 6, 7, 9, 11, 12, 15, 19, 22, 29, 37, 38, 39, 49, 50).[4] All the others appeared in the early editions of *Story of a Soul*, in versions corrected by Mother Agnes of Jesus, who most often distorted—and sometimes even disfigured—Thérèse's poetry and thought. Moreover, these poems have not been re-edited since 1953, which, for Theresian scholars, has meant a "doctrinal deficit," as Abbé Combes put it.[5]

With this Centenary Edition presenting the complete critical texts of the poetry, it is at last possible to make up this "deficit" and to discover new aspects of Thérèse's spiritual genius.

Poetry for Thérèse of Lisieux

For Thérèse, poetry was not "art for amusement," because she did not write for her own satisfaction but out of duty, or at least with a concern to serve, to help, and to encourage.[6] She followed a tradition, that of Carmel. She had to use the little gifts that others recognized in her. For her first try at writing verse, in February 1893, she responded to a request by a sister in her convent, but she did not come back to this kind of expression for a year—and then only for a banal greeting for the prioress' birthday (PN 2). But at the end of 1893 she wrote her first play, or "pious recreation," in prose: 381 lines long. In April of that year, she wrote her first poem for herself, "Saint Cecilia" (PN 3), of astonishing dignity. Something had clicked: Thérèse continued writing poetry, and poetry played a more and more important role in her life, without ever being a goal in itself.

---

[4] PN 22 was first published in Mother Agnes's death circular. Added to this list of unedited poems are eight "Supplementary Poems," included at the end of this collection.

[5] *Theresiana*, p. 240.

[6] "Since the canticle on love pleased you, our good Mother told me to copy out several other poems for you... These poor poems will reveal to you not what I am but what I would like to be and should be... When composing them, I have looked more at the substance than at the form, so the rules of versification are not always respected; my purpose was to translate my sentiments (or rather the sentiments of the Carmelite) in order to respond to my Sisters' desires" (CGII, p. 1059).

In order to appreciate her poetic work, we should not forget that these fifty-four poems were written between February 1893 and May 1897 (fifty-three between February 1894 and May 1897, that is, in three years and three months) by a young woman between twenty and twenty-four years of age with no literary training. We will see what "giant steps" she took in this area as in others, at an age when many poets are hardly even beginning to spread their wings. Her poetic background was indeed quite mediocre, like her spelling and overall education. Her sister Céline recounted some interesting "Precise details on the poetic compositions of Sister Thérèse of the Child Jesus to respond to questions we have been asked on this subject"[7]:

1. Sister Thérèse of the Child did not learn the rules of versification from anyone, and she was unaware of them. She only benefited from what she absorbed in the traditional education she received. For instance, she remembered some passages from Boileau's *l'Art poétique.*

2. She never used a "dictionary of rhymes," because there was none in Carmel.

3. She did not write any poetry before she entered the convent, and only did so in Carmel to respond, most often, to requests from the sisters.

4. She often composed her poems during the day, while she worked or during certain moments of recollection. But apart from free days, like Sundays, she had to wait for the hour of free time in the evenings to *write them down.*[8] She did not have any favorite poets, but she did enjoy certain poems she had read as excerpts in anthologies. She also liked to read the *Fables* of La Fontaine, and she knew several by heart.

5. She usually wrote out a rough draft of her first inspiration, and she worked on it until she was satisfied with it. But for her,

---

[7] Recorded by Sister Marie-Henriette about 1953 (unedited).

[8] "God did not let Mother Agnes tell me to write down my poems while I was composing them, and I would not have wanted to ask her to do so, for fear of commiting a fault against poverty. So I would wait until our free hour and it was not without great difficulty that I remembered, at eight o'clock in the evening, what I had composed that morning" (*Conseils et Souvenirs, recueillis par Soeur Geneviève de la Sainte Face* (Lisieux: Office Central de Lisieux, 1952). Cf. also the introduction to PN 17.

obviously, the deep ideas of her subject counted more than the poetic form she gave them, and she said that often she felt hindered at expressing exactly just what she wanted to say.

This statement is confirmed in a letter from Sister Marie of the Trinity to Mother Agnes in 1932:

> The other day you were saying you were sorry that our saintly little Thérèse didn't learn the rules of versification so as to avoid mistakes in her poetry. Alas! my little Mother, her ignorance was voluntary. When I entered Carmel in June of 1894, I brought along a treatise on versification. She glanced at it and quickly gave it back to me, saying: "I prefer not to know all those rules; my poems are an outpouring from the heart, an inspiration I wouldn't know how to subject to a work of the intellect, to study. If it cost me that, I'd prefer to give up writing poetry." [9]

As a matter of fact, aside from several Romantic poets, such as Lamartine (PN 5, 26, 43), Musset (PN 8, 24), and Chateaubriand (PN 18), Thérèse's "poetic models" were the canticles the sisters sang in Carmel, the pious images around her, the fairly mediocre poetry of her sisters (notably Mother Agnes of Jesus) and the texts—generally quite poor—of songs on which she based her poems.[10] Knowing that, if we read poems such as "Living on Love" (PN 17), "To the Sacred Heart" (PN 23), "Jesus Alone" (PN 36), "My Weapons" (PN 48) or "An Unpetalled Rose" (PN 51), we notice to what extent they testify to spontaneous genius, where the poetic material is sublimated by spiritual intensity. But Thérèse was especially inspired by the biblical and liturgical texts that were her daily nourishment, as well as by the works of St. John of the Cross.[11] It was mainly from them that she drew her inspiration.

---

[9] Letter to Mother Agnes, February 28, 1932.
[10] [Readers who know French could consult the introduction to Vol. II of the *Poésies* for more information on Thérèse's poetic models—Trans.]
[11] Thérèse knew the main poems of St. John of the Cross by heart. This provided her with a great wealth of images and vision.

Literary Genres

All of Thérèse's poems are not of equal value, far from it. Her sisters collected them all and submitted them to the Bishop's Process (1910), except PN 50, "To Joan of Arc," one of the most beautiful ones, and six of the "Supplementary Poems." It is this complete collection that the reader will find here. But Thérèse herself had made a selection from this abundant output born haphazardly from convent life, most notably for her "spiritual brothers," Maurice Bellière and Adolphe Roulland. And at the end of her life she agreed to allow some of them to be published (for a final chapter of her autobiography). These poems have quite different destinations.[12] Some are just unpretentious "compliments" (PN 2, 9, 37, 38, 39) in which Thérèse, for different reasons, gives little of herself. Others were written for a special occasion (PN 4, 11, 27, 28, 30) or for the community (PN 12, 29, 40, 43), and at times they have their charm. Many were commissioned by different sisters.[13] Sometimes she would docilely conform to the inspiration of the sister who made the request (PN 14, 15, 19, 49). Sometimes she would reveal a little about herself (PN 1, 32, 42, 52, 53). And sometimes she would open up completely (PN 5, 23, 24, 25, 31, 33, 41, 45), without however forgetting the recipient in the process.[14]

Very much related to these are the poems she intended for one sister or another (PN 3, 7, 13, 16, 20, 21, etc.), though the distinction between the two categories is sometimes difficult (PN 6, 46). Frequently Thérèse took advantage of a special occasion to teach a lesson (PN 24) or to give encouragement (PN 10), nuanced with great care. Such poems require a delicate exegesis, for we have to avoid interpreting them only in terms of the author (PN 32).

Finally, there are poems in which Thérèse expresses herself freely (even if they are in answer to a request or are dedicated to

---

[12] For more specific details, see the introduction to vol. II of the French *Poésies*.
[13] "Almost all the poems were written at the request of the Sisters, following their own personal devotions; and some were written to encourage the novices in the practice of the virtues, and for their Entrance, Clothing, Profession, etc., the custom being, in Carmel, to sing on these feasts." (Note in red by the copyist, Sister Madeleine of Jesus, at the beginning of vol. III of the "Copy of the Writings.")
[14] Cf. "Jesus Alone" (PN 36), with its two possible interpretations.

someone else). These are likewise written in different genres:

- childhood remembrances, with which her blood sisters are associated (especially PN 8, 18, 22);
- liturgically inspired hymns (PN 25, 34), poems praising the saints she feels close to and who are models for her (PN 3, 26, 44, 47, 50), and poems about the Blessed Virgin Mary (PN 54);
- poems about combat and the apostolate (PN 35, 48);
- and especially poems about contemplation and the love of Jesus, the Holy Face, the Sacred Heart, and a whole gamut of love and espousal poems that are more luminous and tragic as the night of faith closes in on her (PN 17, 23, 24, 26, 31, 33, 36, 41, 45, 51).

The Itinerary of Her Poetry

If we examine Thérèse's poetry in chronological order, we notice an undeniable evolution, despite the shortness of its course. Along with her "Pious Recreations," which make up 1,820 of the total 3,083 verses of her poetry, this evolution corroborates the spiritual evolution we find in *Story of a Soul*, but especially what we find from one day to the next in her letters. As in any evolution, however, the stages intermingle, with regressions as well as advances heralding future features. Perhaps it would be useful to paint a panorama of the poetry in its entirety now, before the reader begins considering each individual poem. That long journey will reveal so much wealth (and poverty as well) that he or she risks perceiving the main features with difficulty then.

First Period: PN 1–15 (February 1893–December 1894)

In February of 1893 Thérèse was asked to help with the formation of her companions in the novitiate. This is also the time of the beginning of her own illness, the death of her father, and Céline's entrance into Carmel.

Even with "The Divine Dew" (PN 1), Thérèse shows unmistakable gifts. Despite her obvious inexperience, she proves herself capable of translating mysterious and barely expressible realities through a blending of images. The themes she uses in this poem are already as complex as her mature ones.

A year later, with her poem for the prioress' birthday (PN 2), we fall back to the lowest level of convent compliments. Her writing seems to have no art to it.[15] But every poet needs to be carried along by a theme: Two months later, Thérèse spontaneously wrote one of her most complete poems, "Saint Cecilia" (PN 3). This vast composition in long stanzas, of somewhat noble Lamartinian style, is remarkable for its overlapping themes. Here Thérèse's poetic ambition is undeniable, but she expresses it through an abundance of images that are a bit clumsy. Nevertheless, the general movement is smooth and somewhat impressive. Thérèse could have continued in this direction, as certain incidental oratorical turns that give great strength to her verse show (PN 23, sts. 3 and 4, for example). But her poetry, like herself, becomes pared down with time. "Saint Cecilia" is a "symphony," more or less unique for her. Nevertheless, Thérèse did not create art for art's sake. She went to so much trouble in writing this poem in order to convince Céline of her religious vocation by a picture more edifying and persuasive than a letter.

If Joan of Arc did not bring out her talents much at this time (PN 4), "My Song for Today" (PN 5), in contrast, seems very characteristic of her and shows considerable progress. Almost from the beginning of this poem she finds her craft, and we do not sense the affectation of "Saint Cecilia." Through poetry, she successfully incarnates a spiritual attitude, that of leaving behind weakness through grace. Even the elegiac, Lamartinian tone is transformed into positive strength.

PN 6 ("The Portrait of a Soul I Love"), despite its flourishes, and PN 7 ("Song of Thanksgiving to Our Lady of Mount Carmel") testify only to the ease with which Thérèse would rhyme from then on. "The Prayer of the Child of a Saint" (PN 8) shows that she could mold her style without much difficulty to the outlines of Musset's irregular rhythms. Besides, an essential trait of her personality comes out here: remembering the past as a source of life for today. Thanks to this ability to integrate the past, Thérèse lived the present moment intensely.

After the acrostic poem for Fr. Pichon (PN 9), which is devoid of interest, PN 10 to 13 form a little cycle (November 20 to December 25, 1894) that we could call "the cycle of Mary and the Lamb."

---

[15] Even though she had written the sizable play "The Mission of Joan of Arc" (RP 1) just one month before.

These fresh songs addressed to the novices sing of the hidden life and of a plan for living out the little way. This plan is charming, but also demanding and of extreme delicacy. The tone is soft and tender, but the teaching is firm and deep. Both the unoriginal poem to St. Joseph (PN 14) and "The Atom of the Sacred Heart" (PN 15) are about the hidden life. Not forgetting the 304 verses of the play "The Angels at the Crèche" (RP 2), with these poems we can say that Thérèse's "first style" comes to a close.

Second Period: PN 16–30 (February 1895–April 1896)

During this period, Thérèse wrote the first part of her autobiography (Manuscript A) and made her "Oblation to Merciful Love." In April of 1896 she coughed up blood for the first time, and at Easter she entered the dark night of faith.

Thérèse's "Song of Gratitude of Jesus' Fiancée" (PN 16), from February 5, 1895, already has a totally different emphasis. "A new horizon" opened up for her at the time she began to write her autobiography. "Living on Love" (PN 17), written twenty-one days later, is the first summit of her poetry. In it are allied theological thought, contemplative ardor, and a poetic beat that grows stronger as it becomes starker. This poem shows us an "aesthetic" understanding of theological charity.

"The Canticle of Céline" (PN 18) does not contradict this interior maturation, despite its somewhat banal abundance of expressions in a different register: that of nature, understood from memories joyously fulfilled in the Beloved. In Jesus, Thérèse has all these marvels of creation, and she enumerates them without any sentimentality. But the verbosity of this poem can be irritating. We find a more concentrated expression of it in the choice of verses she made for Abbé Bellière (PN 18a).

After the insipid "The Atom of Jesus-Host" (PN 19), the next two poems, "My Heaven on Earth" (PN 20) and "Canticle of a Soul Having Found the Place of Its Rest" (PN 21), develop with unequal success some important themes that will stand out later in a different way. "The Fair Angel of My Childhood" (PN 22) takes us back in some ways to "the cycle of Mary and the Lamb." To please Mother Agnes of Jesus, Thérèse put herself back for a moment into that climate of childhood dependency regarding her little mother.

But we reach the heights again with "To the Sacred Heart of Jesus" (PN 23). Never has Thérèse appeared so passionate, so near to Jesus. (In "Living on Love" she was perhaps not so close to the humanity of Christ.) This poem—rich, contemplative, intense, dynamic, and related to the "Act of Oblation to Merciful Love" (SS, pp. 276–277)—is perhaps the starting point on the way that leads to "An Unpetalled Rose" (PN 51).

"Remember" (PN 24) is a long meditation on the life of Jesus, in which the most tender adoration sometimes brings forth great poetic beauty. These thirty-three stanzas are animated by an increasingly passionate inspiration. In a simpler register, "My Desires Near Jesus Hidden in His Prison of Love" (PN 25) seems more traditional, although concentrated and burning with fervor. "The Responses of Saint Agnes" (PN 26), a poem about spiritual espousals that is full of calm assurance and great harmony, offers the most beautiful example of liturgical inspiration for Thérèse. This is where we could best study all the finesse of her poetic work from her sources.

Then there is a pause in Thérèse's inspiration (PN 27, 28). Her poems for the profession of Marie of the Trinity (PN 29, 30), though very polished, cannot stand with her most important poems. This is the end of an extraordinary period of spiritual and poetic blossoming for her.[16] Her trial of faith will give an entirely new emphasis to her poetry.

Third Period: PN 31–44 (May–December 1896)

Thérèse entered into the dark night of faith in April of 1896. If the two profession poems for Marie of the Trinity (PN 29, 30) hardly bear a trace of it, a third poem, "The Canticle of Sister Marie of the Trinity" (PN 31) shows how much her trial had begun to work on her. Here we see the relentless nakedness of "My Weapons" (PN 48) breaking through, and the holocaust of "An Unpetalled Rose" (PN 51). "Heaven for Me" (PN 32) is of a gentler tone. Nevertheless, it expresses a melancholy rare until now for

---

[16] Besides her poems, during this period Thérèse wrote four plays (RP 3-6) with some 1,045 verses, almost as many as the 1,195 verses of poems PN 16 through PN 30.

Thérèse. This is the only one of her poems that mentions "the trial of faith," like a secret clue. Reading it, we sense that she has lost sensible contact with Jesus. The following poems confirm this, try as she may to hide it. "What I Shall Soon See" (PN 33), the third of these poems written in thirteen days, sings with trembling fervor of the "life beyond" that she is afraid to question.

"Strewing Flowers" (PN 34), despite its disappointing form, is central to Theresian lyricism. In it we clearly grasp the limits of aesthetic judgment in and of itself. But devotees of Thérèse and lovers of poetry will undoubtedly be reconciled with "An Unpetalled Rose" (PN 51). Could we say that missionary activity is somehow substituted here for the sensible consolations escaping Thérèse at this time? Discovering her more urgent missionary vocation also helps her to rise above her trial in "To Our Lady of Victories" (PN 35), which is akin to the inspiration of Manuscript B in *Story of a Soul*, although it does not come up to the same level. She rises above her trial poetically too as she reaches new heights in "Jesus Alone" (PN 36). Here she becomes even more loving and passionate, with a fighting ardor that announces "My Weapons," because we have to fight to love and then surrender to him who "begs for our love."

We can quickly pass over the affectionate verses for the La Néele couple (PN 37, 38, 39). The tone of "The Sacristans of Carmel" (PN 40) harkens back to the poems of 1894. Without confiding anything personal about Thérèse, "How I Want to Love" (PN 41) is one of her most characteristic and perfect poems. Nevertheless, it is one of the poems most disfigured by Mother Agnes's corrections. Nor does she tell much about herself in the three poems that follow. "Child, You Know My Name" (PN 42), is a lullaby with a charming turn. "The Aviary of the Child Jesus" (PN 43) is a Christmas poem for the community with some art and depth. In "To My Little Brothers in Heaven" (PN 44), the doctrinal content is richer, despite some affectation.

Fourth Period: PN 45–54 (January–May 1897)

With "My Joy" (PN 45), Thérèse crosses a last threshold and at the same time begins the last year of her life. She settles into an unshakeable faith, devoid of all sensible consolation. This faith is

fortified by her will as she surrenders little by little to total aban-
donment and outwardly shows a serene face.[17] Only a few poems
(and rare secrets with others, notably in *Her Last Conversations*) re-
veal the bitterness of her mystical combat.

"To My Guardian Angel" (PN 46), in a minor genre, undeni-
ably bears the mark of this last period. "To Théophane Vénard"
(PN 47) seems too heavy and flowery, despite some very beautiful
images. "My Weapons" (PN 48), is a "warrior poem" in one surging
movement that develops some allegories, but is branded with the
red-hot iron of suffering overcome with difficulty. Each verse in this
poem is a cry in which the poetic meter is refined and expression
stripped down as never before. One wonders how, in the same
month, Thérèse could write "To Our Lady of Perpetual Help" (PN
49), where nothing draws attention to the poet.

Four months before her death, Thérèse concludes her work
with five poems of varying degrees of strength in which she sum-
maries all her poetry:[18] "Abandonment Is the Sweet Fruit of Love"
(PN 52), written with great transparency, represents what Thérèse
was living out before her sisters, refusing any tragic or grandiose
expression. "For Sister Marie of the Trinity" (PN 53) calls to mind
the Lamartinian tone of her first poems (PN 3) and lets us mea-
sure her poetic evolution at the time when her life is coming to a
close.

The last poem of all is a song of gratitude, "Why I Love You,
O Mary" (PN 54). Its ultimate message is a song of thanksgiving, a
liturgical hymn, a prayer. Here the almost total absence of allusions
to her physical trials has something of the heroic: Thérèse is dress-
ing her ravaged being, not in some miserable disguise, but in a
sumptuous, flowery habit, just as she would be laid out in the coffin
after her death. This is an expression of her faith in the resurrec-
tion, to which the last stanza of the poem testifies with its distress-
ing signature, "little Thérèse."

---

[17] "If you are judging according to the sentiments I express in my little poems com-
posed this year, I must appear to you as a soul filled with consolations and one for
whom the veil of faith is almost torn aside; and yet it is no longer a veil for me, it is a
wall that reaches right up to the heavens and covers the starry firmament. When I
sing of the happiness of heaven and of the eternal possession of God, I feel no joy in
this, for I sing simply what I WANT TO BELIEVE" (SS, p. 214).
[18] Along with PS 6, 7, and 8 written at this time.

But before this, she speaks her last word in the two poems in which she went the furthest. In "To Joan of Arc" (PN 50), a powerful, stark poem, she identifies with one of her favorite heroines, "at the bottom of a black dungeon, laden with heavy chains," to acknowledge that with Jesus, crucified and put to death, the worst suffering has become a "treasure." "An Unpetalled Rose" (PN 51) is undoubtedly the most extraordinary of these fifty-four poems and expresses the highest point of Thérèse's mystical abandonment.

Thérèse's Poetic Skills

If Thérèse had no real guide for her poetry and at first rhymed unpretentiously, she still tried to respect the conventional rules for rhyming. Besides, Mother Agnes would always remind her of them, and the latter's numerous—and often unfortunate—corrections bear out this honorable concern.[19] Although Thérèse was more interested in ideas than in the form they took, she worked assiduously to make her poetic craft more supple, knowing that what she wanted to say would be more forceful if she expressed it well. The numerous rough drafts for most of her poems illustrate this.[20]

Musical Support

When Sister Geneviève sent Brother Simeon in Rome a selection of her sister's "most typical" poetry, she took care to indicate the melodies that went with them, since, she said, "they are prettier sung."[21] No doubt this was Thérèse's opinion too, and for each poem she generally provides the melody she selected to go with it.[22]

---

[19] In Thérèse's authentic texts, we find a number of stylistic and syntactic mistakes.
[20] These drafts are studied in vol. II of the French *Poésies*.
[21] Letter of February 11, 1897, quoted in CGII, p. 1160.
[22] Of the 62 poems (54 PN + 8 PS), 8 are not meant to be sung (PN 6, 9, 37, 38, 39, PS 6 and no doubt PN 2 and PS 7). For 17 poems, Thérèse does not give an accompanying melody (PN 7, 12, 15, 22, 30, 31, 33, 35, 40, 42, 49, 50, 52, 53; PS 2, 3, 5). Nevertheless, an oral tradition at the Carmel has kept melody titles for 7 of these (PN 30, 31, 33, 40, 42, 52, 53). We can surmise that the others would have been adapted to music, except perhaps PN 22, but certainly not PS 5. All in all, we have been able to identify 39 different melodies for the poems. Other melodies introduced in the *Pious Recreations* would bring the total to 65. For more information on this subject, the reader could consult the "Centre de documentation" at the Carmel of Lisieux.

It is difficult for us today to agree with this judgment, because the difference between our cultural world and that of a very closed provincial circle a century ago is so great. Almost all the melodies Thérèse chose for her poems are badly dated now, like ladies' hats in old family photos. It is the face that is important, not the hat. Far from enhancing Thérèse's poetry, the "music" she chose can even make them seem ridiculous, like an old-fashioned garment. Thérèse was not too concerned with adapting her poetry to the rhythm of these songs. The mute syllables she used often fall on strong beats of the music, and vice versa. Probably once she chose the melody for a poem, she forgot about it and only kept in mind the number of syllables, after which the rhythm and melody followed somehow or other.

However, we should correct this negative evaluation on two counts. First, the *Pious Recreations* show that "the author" was usually better inspired by the dramatic needs of her plays in choosing the parts to be sung. Second, for the poetry itself, Thérèse was able to find the right music in more than one case. The melodies she used were from her favorite tunes. Undoubtedly she saw in them something of her own "melody." They offered her ample rhythm and a fervent or nostalgic expression that matched her own feelings. She spontaneously chose these tunes for her most personal creations. Then, except for a few blunders, the text really corresponds to the music. But we have to admit that these cases are rare.

Above all, harmony for her was *spiritual,* as we see from the way she uses the words "melody" and "harmony." For example, in *Story of a Soul* Thérèse writes that "if she could express what she understands, you would hear a heavenly melody" (SS, p. 233) that transcends anything that could be written. The "melodies" that touch her most are "the silence of Jesus" in his passion (GCII, p. 808), "the eloquent silence" of Mary after the Annunciation (PN 54,8), the "sublime abandonment" of Cecilia (PN 3). And in the play "The Angels at the Crèche" (RP 2), she writes of the silent language of flowers.

What Thérèse of Lisieux Sings

Thérèse's life was a love song. Even on the first page of her autobiography, she announced, "I'm going to be doing only one thing: I shall begin to sing what I must sing eternally: "*The Mercies of the Lord*" (SS, p. 13). We also find this quotation from Psalm 89 at the top of the "coat of arms of Jesus and Thérèse" where, near the Holy Face, there is a harp with this inscription: "The harp represents Thérèse who wants to sing melodies of love to Jesus unceasingly."[23] This is how her sisters remembered her before the image of Thérèse with roses was imposed on her: Mother Agnes had chosen "A Canticle of Love" for the first title of *Story of a Soul*. Marie of the Sacred Heart said of her sister, as early as July 14, 1897, "her life was just one celestial melody" (DE, p. 703). And Céline's first portrait of Thérèse (in 1899) after her death depicted her holding the Gospel over her heart as she plucked the chords of a harp (a Carmelite Saint Cecilia).

Thérèse's song is eminently "Christian." When we sing, we sing *for* someone, *in the name of* someone, *to* someone. The presentations and notes for each poem will have much to say about the importance these poems had for those who received them. Thérèse's song is never egotistical. It is addressed to her family, her sisters, her missionary brothers, the saints of heaven, the Blessed Virgin Mary, and to God. Her song is especially a spiritual or mystical conversation with Jesus.

Thus Thérèse makes heaven and earth converse unceasingly. Her poetry is fundamentally a "song of exile" (the word "exile" recurs twenty-two times in her poetry) in a foreign land on the bank of a "river," with frequent references to Psalm 137 ("By the streams of Babylon"). [24] Her poetry is a song addressed to heaven (the "Homeland"), or it speaks of "Heaven" (used 163 times). That is why there is so often a back-and-forth movement between heaven and earth (cf. PN 21, 22, 33, 46) and why she so often refers to "angels" (fifty-four times), and to "flight" and "wings."

This "Jacob's ladder," this "celestial bridge" that she establishes between heaven and earth exalts "the mercies of the Lord." Thérèse's poetry sings her perpetual amazement and her thanksgiving before the All-Powerful who became human and made a

---

[23] [This fine drawing is not reproduced in the English version of *Story of a Soul*—Trans.]

[24] Cf. *La Bible avec Thérèse de Lisieux* (Paris: Cerf/DDB, 1979).

covenant with humble humanity. Thus we have numerous images or alliances of paradoxical words. These give a real "leap of faith" to so many poems. For instance, note the admirable progression of word and feeling in: "My only love, Jesus, Eternal Word" (PN 36).

What Thérèse marvels most at, the inexhaustible subject of her poetry, is the love of Jesus (sometimes identified with the Trinity), the Lord of the world who is her fiancé, her spouse. She responds to this love with a passionate love that is more and more focused and burning, martyred and fighting, until the absolute oblation of "An Unpetalled Rose." Her poetry is the song of a great lover, who is almost "possessive" (as early as PN 1 she wrote, "*For me* you will leave your mother"). This note, already so strongly present in Saint Paul and Pascal, will be constant in her poetry, with a daring that at times made her sisters, especially Mother Agnes, back away. This explains, moreover, a certain number of corrections she asked Thérèse to make or made herself in *Story of a Soul*. For instance in "To the Sacred Heart of Jesus" (PN 23), the first version of st. 5,1–3 declared:

> You heard me, Creator of the world,
> *For my love alone* you became man.

These lines were changed to:

> You heard me, only Friend whom I love.
> To ravish my heart, you became man.

A remarkable "joy" (felt or not) further refines Thérèse's happiness in loving and accentuates the resonance of her poetry. She sees physical or moral suffering, the abnegation of an austere life, and even her trial of faith in a fundamentally positive perspective, because behind them is God's love, to which Thérèse's love simply responds.

From this angle, these poems are even more revealing of the great movement of Thérèse's *prayer*. The familiar "You [Tu]" (and inversely the divine "I") are constants. Thérèse the contemplative, who never lived more than three minutes without explicitly thinking "of God,"[25] prayed while composing her poems all during the course of her work day. Using "Tu" with Jesus set free the need

---

[25] CSG, p. 77.

locked up within her for familiarity. According to what she con-
fided to Céline, she addressed Jesus in the familiar "Tu" when she
prayed.[26] Though she did not dare do this when she spoke or wrote,
she did dare do so in her poetry.

Poetry enabled Thérèse to express all the tenderness of her
being as a woman and as a spouse. How many times we see her in
the "arms" of her Beloved (PN 24, 32, 36, 48, 52), resting on his
Heart (PN 3, 5, 24, 32, 52), studying the look in his eyes, caressing
his Face, yearning to receive a kiss from him! Very few people have
believed so profoundly, so carnally, we could say, in the Incarna-
tion of the Son of God. The "natural satisfaction" she still found in
this love was completely purified by her trial of faith, as she wrote
in *Story of a Soul* just after speaking of her poetry.[27] The Risen Jesus
helped this other Magdalene's innate tenderness to grow and be-
come "more pure and more divine" (SS, p. 216).

Importance of the Poetry

The more we read the poetry of Thérèse of Lisieux, the more
we realize how irreplaceable it is for knowing her. Poetry, with its
appeal to music, to sensitivity, to the unconscious, and even to the
difficulty of searching for rhythm and rhyme, neutralized in a way
her control over her ideas. It compelled her to say certain things,
to use certain images, and to reveal the depths of her being in a
way that prose more easily dispels or hides. It also allowed her, in
the poems addressed to her sisters, to break through certain barri-
ers (PN 10) and to pass along much advice, many truths that would
be difficult for her to express in everyday life without hurting. But
even more, her poetry tells us about Thérèse's interior evolution:
how she blossomed, radiated, loved, and—and perhaps more than
anything else—about the bitterness of her combat in her trial of
faith.

Finally, as Fr. Fl. Jubaru—who wrote the preface to the first
edition of the *Poetry*—rightly saw even in 1907, we discover Thérèse
"entirely" in her poetry, as in *Story of a Soul*:

---

[26] *Ibid.*, p. 82.
[27] Cf. above, note 17.

It is the same childlike candor, with an astonishing, profound sense of spiritual things. It is the same total abandonment to the Divine Beloved with unremitting initiatives to 'capture' him. It is the same tranquillity of seraphic contemplation with immense apostolic desires for unbelievers and sinners. It is the same complete detachment from herself with an affectionate tenderness for her family. But most of all, it is a love for God 'that has become an abyss, the depths of which she cannot fathom.' She desired 'to love God as he had never been loved.'[28] In fact, she loved him in a way no one else had.

At the end of this introduction, it might seem that we have made these "poor verses"[29] of a Carmelite too beautiful. The images she uses are often conventional. But what at first seems insignificant reveals unknown riches and strength drawn from her sanctity. Thérèse knew how to transfigure, by a great dream of love, the most humble gestures of everyday life and expand the limits of her human horizon to a cosmic scale.

Jacques Lonchampt

Translated by Daniel Chowning, O.C.D.

---

[28] Cf. CGI, P. 500 ("I would so much like to love Him!... Love Him more than He has ever been loved!...") and SS, p. 256.
[29] Thérèse spoke modestly of her "little poems" (GCII, p. 850), and she even called them her "poor poems" (GCII, p. 1059).

The Poems

PN 1 – The Divine Dew
(February 2, 1893)

A rosebud opening up a little at the first rays of sunshine, under the effect of the morning dew: We should not be surprised to find such a Theresian symbol on the first page of the *Poetry* of the Saint from Lisieux.

And when the "tender flower" undergoes a metamorphosis, becoming a radiant little boy on his mother's breast—which is his "sun"—suckling his own dew: That is an original idea truly worthy of a young person very attached to her childhood.

But Thérèse's ingenuity really becomes daring when she tries her skill at translating barely expressible mysterious realities into poetic images, for the baby in question descends from a "heavenly dwelling": he is the Son of God. The dew that his Mother offers him is also "heavenly," for she is a virgin.

And there is more. With the calm boldness of a child at home with mystery, Thérèse takes it upon herself to follow the development of this "heavenly dew." She discovers its "morning fragrance" in the bleeding Flower on Calvary. She recognizes its taste in "the Bread of Angels," the eucharistic Body of the Lord, "the Word made Host" that was made flesh through the mediation of Mary.

In a style all her own, even if a stammering one, Thérèse finally sings the same *Ave verum* as St. Thomas Aquinas. "Under the veil" of the sacrament that the "Eternal Priest" offers her, she takes part in the "banquet of love" (PN 24, 4) offered to her "divine little brother," "under the veil" of the Virgin Mother.

Our modern tastes run the risk of being put off by these strong doctrinal images. Passed down from the first Fathers of the Church, they were familiar to Thérèse thanks to Dom Guéranger in particular.[1] In his commentary on the Feast of Corpus Christi, the Abbot of Solesmes brought together several texts from Clement of Alexandria, Zeno of Verona, and above all Saint Augustine. These gave a full faith dimension to the attraction felt by our Carmelite—as for Sister Mary of St. Peter from Tours[2]—for this mystery of the childhood of Jesus. To understand better the doctrinal background of this poem, we need to quote the following text from Saint Augustine on the Incarnation of the Word. Thérèse read it in Dom Gueranger's *The Liturgical Year.*

> Men do not live on one food, and angels on another: truth, divine Wisdom, is the one food of every intelligence. The Angels, the Powers, the heavenly spirits feed on it; they eat of it; they grow upon it, and yet the mysterious food lessens not. In the beginning was the Word, and the Word was with God, and the

Word was God; take it, if you can; eat it; it is food. Perhaps you will say to me: "Oh! yes, it is verily food; but I—I am a babe; what I must have is milk; else I cannot reach that Word you tell me of." Well! since it is milk you require, and yet there is no other food for you save this of heaven (the Word), He will pass through the flesh, that He may thus be brought within reach of your lips; for food does not become milk, except by its passing through flesh. This is what a mother does. What the mother eats is what the child drinks; but the little one not being, as yet, strong enough to take the bread as it is, the mother eats it, and then gives it to her child under a form that very sweetly suits the babe. He does not receive the food such as it lay upon the table, but after it has passed through the flesh, and is thus made suitable to the child. Therefore was the Word made Flesh, and dwelt among us; and man hath eaten thus the bread of angels. Eternal Wisdom came down even to us, by the Flesh and Blood of Him who was our Savior; He came as milk, which was full of blessing to us.[3]

More than Augustine, Thérèse lingers on Mary, "the Mother who incarnates" the Word of God for us, who makes the divine substance assimilable for us weak creatures. *Story of a Soul* will sing, "You desire to nourish me with Your divine substance" (p. 199). Her first poem is a Marian one, just as her last great composition will be: "Why I Love You, O Mary!" (PN 54).

Still another personal feature of the poem is that Thérèse interprets this doctrine with a floral symbolism totally absent in her sources.

It was a daring undertaking for someone who had never written poetry to start so soon with such a difficult subject. We owe this to Sister Teresa of Saint Augustine, who insisted that Thérèse write it. In 1898, a few months after our Saint's death, she wrote down how "The Divine Dew" came to be:

One day I asked her to write a canticle on our favorite subject, the Holy Infancy of Jesus. "That's impossible," she replied, "I don't know anything about poetry." I answered, "What does that matter? We're not going to send it to the Académie française. This is just to make me happy and to satisfy a desire of my soul." Sister Thérèse replied, "I still hesitate a little because I don't know if this is God's will." I then said, "Oh! I'll give you some advice about that: Before you start to write, ask Our Lord: 'My God, if this is not your will, I ask you for the grace not to be able to succeed at it. But if this is for your glory, help me.' I believe that after that you will not have to worry." She followed my advice and that is how she wrote her first poem.[4]

So, "to make her happy," Thérèse set to work. Despite the lack of encouragement from Sister Agnes of Jesus, who received her effort coolly,[5] she could depend on that of Sister Marie of the Angels, her novice mistress, who was also a fervent reader of Sister Mary of Saint Peter.

Thérèse gave the poem to Sister Teresa of Saint Augustine on February 2, 1893.

There is no denying that it has real naive beauty. Behind Thérèse's inexperience, especially in the continuity and adaptation of her images, we see true poetic gifts revealed: an ability to create access to "more hidden mysteries of a superior order" through images (GCII, p. 748). Already in this attempt we find a whole Theresian thematic: the flower, blood, the rose, and dew [In French, note the play on words: *la rose*—the rose—and *la rosée*—dew], the seraphim, love, the brotherhood of Jesus, the Eucharist, etc.

[1] [Thérèse had known Abbot Guéranger's *The Liturgical Year* since childhood, when Marie or Pauline used to read passages to the family at Les Buissonnets. cf. SS, p. 43n.— Trans.]

[2] [The young Carmelite nun (1816–1848) from Tours, France, who received revelations on devotion to the Holy Face. This devotion was particularly strong at the Carmel of Lisieux. Thérèse added the title "of the Holy Face" to her religious name at her clothing, January 10, 1889.—Trans.]

[3] Abbot Guéranger, OSB, *The Liturgical Year*, trans. Dom Laurence Shepherd, OSB, vol. 10, bk. I (Westminster, MD: Newman, 1949) pp. 374–375.

[4] Cf. Sainte Thérèse de l'Enfant Jesus et de la Sainte Face, *Poésies*, vol. II (Paris: Cerf/DDB, 1979), pp. 46–47.

[5] Mother Agnes wrote, "I was not pleased that she had the idea to write poetry. It seemed to me–and I told her so–she would not be able to succeed at it. Only reluctantly did I give her the advice she asked for on this subject" *(Poésies*, vol. II, p. 28).

February 2, 1893   J.M.J.T.

The Divine Dew, or The Virginal Milk of Mary

1   My Sweet Jesus, You appear to me
     On your Mother's breast, all radiant with love.
     Love is the ineffable mystery
     That exiled you from your Heavenly Home...
     Ah! let me hide myself under the veil
     Concealing you from all mortal eyes,
     And near you, O Morning Star!
     I shall find a foretaste of Heaven.

2   From the moment a new dawn awakens,
     When we see the first lights of the sun,
     The young flower beginning to open
     Awaits a precious balm from on high.
     It is the good-giving morning dew,
     Which, producing an abundant sap,
     Makes the flower of the new bud open a little.

3   Jesus, you are that Flower just open.
     I gaze on you at your first awakening.
     Jesus, you are the ravishing Rose,
     The new bud, gracious and scarlet red.
     The ever-so-pure arms of your dear Mother
     Form for you a cradle, a royal throne.
     Your sweet sun is Mary's breast,
     And your Dew is Virginal Milk!...

4   My Beloved, my divine little Brother,
     In your gaze I see all the future.
     Soon, for me, you will leave your Mother.
     Already Love impels you to suffer,
     But on the cross, O Full-blossomed Flower!
     I recognize your morning fragrance.
     I recognize Mary's Dew.
     Your divine blood is Virginal Milk!...

5   This Dew hides in the sanctuary.
     The angels of Heaven, enraptured, contemplate it,
     Offering to God their sublime prayer.
     Like Saint John, they repeat: "Behold."
     Yes, behold, this Word made Host.
     Eternal Priest, sacerdotal Lamb,
     The Son of God is the Son of Mary.
     The bread of Angels is Virginal Milk.

6   The seraphim feeds on glory.
     In Paradise his joy is full.
     Weak child that I am, I only see in the ciborium
     The color and figure of Milk.
     But that is the Milk a child needs,
     And Jesus' Love is beyond compare.
     O tender Love! Unfathomable power,
     My white Host is Virginal Milk!...

                              (melody: "Minuit, chrétiens")

PN 2 – To Mother Marie de Gonzague for Her Sixtieth Birthday

(February 20, 1894)

This very minor poem, written for a special occasion, will certainly not contribute to Thérèse's literary glory!

The special occasion was the sixtieth birthday of Mother Marie de Gonzague, who was born in Caen on February 20, 1834. The coincidence not mentioned is that this was also the first anniversary of her appointment as Novice Mistress (February 20, 1893, the day Mother Agnes of Jesus replaced her as prioress).

The novitiate at that time consisted of:

• Sister Thérèse of the Child Jesus, age 20, who should have left the novitiate on September 8, 1893, if Mother Agnes had not given her to Mother Gonzague as senior companion to the other two sisters (cf. GCII, p. 725);

• Sister Martha of Jesus, 28, professed lay sister, whose time of formation would normally expire the following September 23;

• Sister Marie-Madeleine of the Blessed Sacrament, 24, lay sister, who would make her profession in November (cf. PN 10).

The theme of the rose (st. 5), or at least that of the flower (sts. 2 and 3), would have been suggested by the first name of the honoree: Rosalie. But even for all that, Thérèse was not inspired. It is true that Thérèse was not about to give spiritual advice to her Novice Mistress, though she would take advantage of similar occasions to do that with other sisters.

This little poem is presented as a prayer to Jesus (named four times). So it offers us a "Rosalie seen from above," or we would go so far as to say: Mother Marie de Gonzague as Jesus sees her and wants her to be. Here we are far from the sort of flattery that distorts so many compliments.

Thérèse's inexperience, at the beginning of her poetic activity, is obvious: "Let us sing, let us sing," or that "harvest" in which she becomes entangled—it is with flowers that they want to crown Mother Marie de Gonzague, and not with the harvest (st. 4).

However, we do notice some of Thérèse's favorite words or themes:

• the valley (3, 3), place of sweetness and beauty, the privileged place of the Flower *par excellence*, the "Lily of the valley" (Song of Songs 2:1), who is Jesus;

• the conquering quality of this Flower's perfume (Song of Songs 1:2) that "captivates" (SS, p. 254) and "draws" (*ibid.* and GCII, p. 761), virtue in which "sweet-smelling flowers"—especially lilies (consecrated souls)—share in its perfume: They "win hearts" (cf. st. 3 and PN 3);

• the "harvest," a summarizing term, a term of abundance dear to Thérèse. But this is a harvest of flowers, and undoubtedly of lilies, like the one Jesus is gathering on a holy card she loved (cf. GCII, p. 1129).

So in these awkward verses, for which the author could hardly have put herself to much trouble, we nevertheless see sketched out some poetic images that she will soon display luxuriantly (cf. RP 2 at Christmas, 1894) before gathering them together in the last year of her life into one very dense, dynamic insight: "Draw me, we shall run after you" in *Story of a Soul* (p. 254).

To Our Mistress and Dear Mother for her Sixtieth Birthday

1   Oh! what a happy birthday
We are celebrating on this beautiful day!
To our good and loving Mother
Let us sing, let us sing all our love.

2   For sixty years now on earth,
Divine Jesus, you have gazed on
A flower very dear to you.
You water it with your graces.

3   Jesus, your sweet-smelling flower
Has gained many hearts for you.
In this valley she has gathered
A beautiful harvest of flowers.

4   Divine Jesus, in our Heavenly Homeland
You will know how to reward her.
We will see you crown her
With the harvest she has gathered.

5   Jesus, your Rose is the Mother
Who directs our childlike hearts.
Deign to listen to their prayer:
May they celebrate her eightieth birthday!

The three little novices
Sr. Thérèse of the Child Jesus
Sr. Martha of Jesus
Sr. Marie-Madeleine
February 20 in the year of our Lord 1894

PN 3 Saint Cecilia (April 28, 1894)

This is Thérèse's first *long* poem (originally 120 verses) as well as her first *personal* one. It would have been as important to her as a first symphony to a musician. The vast composition, with its overlapping themes, a certain noble style, and her (later) arrangement of it into great irregular stanzas all confirm this impression of a great symphony.

The poem is dedicated to Céline on the occasion of her twenty-fifth birthday. Each year Thérèse would write her a "beautiful letter" for her birthday. Her only wish was that Céline would attain "the purpose for which Jesus had created her" (GCII, p. 786). From one stage of her life to another, Thérèse helped her discern her "mission" (cf. GCII, p. 747, p. 783, p. 850). What message did Thérèse give Céline in 1894 in her predicament of waiting?

Céline was alone, with an old father who was almost comatose. One after the other, her four sisters had left her for the cloister. In her circle of family and friends, happy marriages were multiplying. Although she had already consecrated herself to God by a private vow, Céline keenly felt the pull of human love. Several times she had to confront hard renunciations in this regard (cf. GCII, p. 731 and p. 821).

From Carmel, Thérèse could perceive Céline's struggles. She was too close to her sister—her "double" in a way—not to be interested in her great questionings in life. She herself cherished a dream:

> The most intimate of my desires, the greatest of them all, which I thought would never be realized, was my dear Céline's entrance into the same Carmel as ours. This *dream* appeared to be improbable: to live under the same roof, to share the joys and pains of the companion of my childhood; I had made my sacrifice complete by confiding to Jesus my dear sister's future.... The only thing I couldn't accept was her not being the spouse of Jesus, for since I loved her as much as I loved myself it was impossible for me to see her give her heart to a mortal being (SS, p. 176).

The side Thérèse took was clear: It was "impossible" that Céline would call into question the basic orientation of her life, which she had decided on several years before (cf. GCI, p. 435 and p. 448). In 1894, Thérèse's way of approaching her sister's personal problem was all intuitive. To try to express that, she instinctively resorted to *poetry*. This was an ambitious project for her, because her poetic craft was still weak. But she was supported by a great inspiration: Wasn't "the story of Cecilia" the prophetic parable of "the story of Céline"? Besides, Céline was used to taking her sister's hints. Thérèse sent a letter along with "The Melody of Saint Cecilia" to make her interpretation clear (cf. GCII, p. 850).[1]

In an *essentially poetic form* (music, flowers, perfumes, flight, land-scape, biblical images, colors, allegory, and symbols), Thérèse tried to "babble" (GCII, p. 850) the connections she felt between virginity, mar-riage, and martyrdom. The example of Cecilia and Valerian was likely to touch Céline because she had considered conjugal love "as the last word for two united hearts." [2] Thérèse did not discredit her sister's admiration for marriage; in a way she consecrated it. However, she oriented her to-ward an even greater spiritual fruitfulness: that of consecrated virginity, a "fruitful loss" of the highest degree (cf. PN 17, 13).

Although this poem was written for Céline, the song was nonethe-less Thérèse's personal song. Her sister's birthday only helped her ideas come into being after a long gestation.

This is a free song born of happy contemplation in which Thérèse expresses the "tenderness of a friend" for Cecilia, her "favorite Saint" (SS, p. 131). Everything thrilled her about this ideal figure of harmony and light, whom she had discovered in adolescence and had recently rediscov-ered in depth (cf. GCII, p. 827). In her are combined the privileges that Thérèse valued above all else: virginity, apostolic zeal, and martyrdom.

But above all, Cecilia is "the Saint of ABANDONMENT" (GCII, p. 850). And that is the highest expression of love, its "sweetest fruit" (PN 52). Abandonment alone can make one's life "a melodious song in the midst of the greatest trials" (SS, p. 132). Thérèse was soon to make it one of the main aspects of her "little way." And her last three years of life showed the seriousness of this choice—and the effectiveness of such radi-cal hope.

The importance Thérèse herself gave to this poem in her maturity stands out from the copies she made of it in 1896–1897, and from the re-touching she did to it. At the beginning of her illness she worked on a "sec-ond edition" with the thought that it might be distributed after her death. It is this last text, preserved in an authentic copy by Mother Agnes, that we are publishing here.

[1] [Readers who know French can refer to the detailed study of this poem in *Mes Armes—Sainte Cécile: Un choeur de musique dans un camp d'armée*, by Thérèse de Lisieux (Paris: Cerf/DDB, 1975) pp. 15–79—Trans.]
[2] *Ibid.*, p. 72.

Saint Cecilia

> While the instruments sounded
> Cecilia sang in her heart...
> (Office of the Church)

1   O beloved Saint, delighted, I contemplate
The luminous wake living on after you.
I still seem to hear your sweet melody.
Yes, your celestial song reaches even to me.
5   Listen to the prayer of my exiled soul.
Let me rest on your virginal heart,
That immaculate lily that shone on earth
With a marvelous luster, almost without equal.

O very chaste Dove, while going through life
10   You sought no other spouse but Jesus.
Having chosen your soul, He united Himself with it,
Finding it perfumed with all the virtues.
However, a mortal man, radiant with youth,
Breathed in your perfume, white and celestial flower!
15   In order to pluck you, to win your affection,
Valerian wanted to give you his whole heart.
Soon he prepared magnificent nuptials.
His palace resounded with melodious songs...
But your virginal heart repeated canticles
20   Whose truly divine echo rose right up to the Heavens!
What could you sing, so far from your Homeland
And seeing this fragile mortal so close to you?
Undoubtedly you wanted to surrender your life
And unite yourself forever to Jesus in Heaven...
25   But no... I hear your seraphic lyre sounding,
Your love's lyre with strains so sweet.
You sang this sublime canticle to the Lord:
"Keep my heart pure, Jesus, my tender Spouse!..."
Ineffable abandonment! Divine melody!
30   You disclose your love through your celestial song.
Love that fears not, that falls asleep and forgets itself
On the Heart of God, like a little child...

In the azure canopy appeared the white star
Coming with its timid fire to enlighten

35   The luminous night that lifted the veil for us
        On the virginal love of spouses in Heaven...

        Then Valerian dreamed of pleasure.
        Cecilia, your love was his only desire...
        He found happiness in your noble marriage.
40   You showed him life that never ends.
        "Young friend," you told him, "an angel of the Lord
        Always keeps vigil near me to keep my heart pure.
        He does not leave me, even when I sleep.
        He joyfully covers me with his azure wings.
45   At night, I see his lovable face shine.
        With a brightness so much sweeter than the morning light,
        His face seems the transparent image,
        The pure radiance of the divine face."
        Valerian replied: "Show me this fair Angel
50   That I may believe in your oath.
        Otherwise, begin fearing that my love change
        Into terrible fury, into hatred of you..."

        O Dove hidden in the cleft of the rock!
        You did not dread the hunter's snare.
55   The Face of Jesus revealed its light to you,
        The sacred Gospels rested on your heart...
        You replied at once with a sweet smile:
        "My Heavenly Guardian grants your desire,
        Soon you will see him, he will deign to tell you
60   That to fly to the skies, you must be a martyr.
        But before seeing him, baptism
        Must pour out a holy whiteness into your soul.
        The true God must dwell there alone.
        The Holy Spirit must be the life of your heart.
65   The Word, Son of God and Son of Mary,
        In his great love sacrifices himself on the altar.
        You must go sit at the Banquet of Life
        To receive Jesus, the Bread of Heaven.
        Then the Seraphim will call you his brother,
70   And seeing in your heart the throne of his God,
        He will have you leave earth's shores.
        You will see the dwelling of this spirit of fire."
        "I sense my heart burning with a new flame,"
        Cried the ardent patrician in his joy.

75   "I want the true God to dwell in my soul.
Cecilia, my love will be worthy of yours!..."

Clothed in the robe, the emblem of innocence,
Valerian was able to see the fair angel of Heaven.
Enraptured, he contemplated his sublime power.
80   He saw the sweet brightness of his radiant brow.
The brilliant seraphim held fresh roses
Mixed with beautiful lilies, dazzlingly white.
In the gardens of Heavens, these flowers had opened
Under the Creator Star's rays of Love.

85   "Spouses loved by Heaven, the roses of martyrdom
Shall crown your brows," says the angel of the Lord.
"There are no voices, there is no lyre
Able to sing of this great favor!
I lose myself in my God, I contemplate his charms,
90   But I cannot sacrifice myself and suffer for him.
I can give him neither my blood nor my tears.
Despite all my love, I cannot die...
The angel's purity is his brilliant lot.
His great joy will never end,
95   But you have the advantage over the Seraphim.
You can be pure, and you can suffer!...
....
You see the symbol of virginity
In these perfumed lilies the Lamb sends you.
You will be crowned with the white halo,
100   You shall always sing the new song.
Your chaste union will give birth to souls
Who will seek no other spouse than Jesus,
You shall see them shine like pure flames
Near the divine throne in the dwelling of the elect."

105   Cecilia, lend me your sweet melody.
I would like to convert so many hearts to Jesus!
Like you, I would like to sacrifice my life.
I would like to give him both my blood and my tears...
Obtain for me to taste perfect abandonment,
110   That sweet fruit of love, on this foreign shore.
O my dear Saint! soon, far from earth,
Obtain for me to fly beside you forever...
                                 April 28, 1894

PN 4 – Canticle to Obtain the Canonization of the Venerable Joan of Arc

(May 8, 1894)

This is patriotic and religious poetry, in which the expression is almost always trite and rather commonplace.

Naturally, Thérèse emphasizes the deep Christian values of her heroine. She is less concerned with praising "the illustrious warrior" than with honoring "the martyr" and the saint, for Joan's "true glories" were "her virtues, her love." Thérèse will again emphasize this aspect in her play of January 1895 ("Joan of Arc Accomplishing Her Mission," RP 3), for which this canticle is the natural conclusion: "If I am honored in Heaven, it is not for having been an illustrious warrior, but because I united virginity with martyrdom!"

If Joan is honored, she must be prayed to even more: for the conversion of France and for its true liberation, in Thérèse's own day (st. 10 and refrain); for children whose faith is threatened (st. 11 and refrain); and for the Carmelite nuns, themselves "virgin warriors" in their own way (st. 12 and refrain). The last stanza of the poem calls for the Church's official recognition of "Saint Joan of France." (She was canonized in 1920.)

In passing, we need to mention the historical context of this composition.

On January 27, 1894, Leo XIII authorized the introduction of Joan of Arc's cause for beatification, in virtue of which she received the title "Venerable." From then on it was permitted to "honor her and pray to her" publicly, as the Lisieux newspaper *Le Normand* explained on January 30.

In the weeks that followed, Thérèse's uncle Isidore Guérin devoted several articles to this event. From the outset he showed his colors: "God raised her up to show through her weakness the greatness of his power and so to confound the pride of men" ("Joan of Arc," *Le Normand*, 2/3/1894).

A commission presided over by Henri Wallon soon drafted a bill to the National Assembly proposing that May 8 be celebrated annually as a national holiday of "patriotism" to honor Joan of Arc (*Le Normand*, 3/10/1894). Monsieur Guérin saw this chiefly as a scheme of the Freemasons to take this French heroine back into their camp and to "secularize" her (*ibid.*, 5/5/1894).

If joy at Joan's rising glory was great all across France, Lisieux shared in it in a special way. In effect, the town represented Joan's "blood money": "It was at Orléans that she carried off one of her most brilliant successes, it was at Rouen where she was burned, and Lisieux was the price paid for her life" (I. Guérin, *ibid.*). The allusion to Judas's betrayal of Jesus was clear. But here the traitor was the bishop, Pierre Cauchon, who was made bishop of Lisieux in 1432 in return for "services rendered" to the English! So on May 8, 1894, "a precious flag of the glorious Liberatrix" was placed in the chapel built by Cauchon in the apse of the cathedral of Saint Peter right where he was buried: This was the very chapel where Thérèse, as a girl, had attended daily Mass!

The pastor of Saint Peter's set up a committee of young women to make preparations for the celebration on May 8. Céline Martin was one of its most active members. With Marie Guérin and other friends, she sewed "twelve great white banners strewn with *fleurs de lis*... each one over 21 feet long!" (letter from Marie Guérin to Mme. La Néele, May 1894).

Le Normand wrote that the holiday, "as patriotic as religious, promises to be particularly touching. The church will be brilliantly lighted" (5/1/1894). Five thousand people jammed into the cathedral. The atmosphere was more like a joyful village fair than a religious ceremony. *Le Normand's* chronicler with the sharp pen was hard put to control his displeasure! ("The Festivities for Joan of Arc," 5/12/1894, article signed "I.G." [Isidore Guérin])

We find varied nuances of this enthusiasm—with its ambivalent causes and effects—to a different degree in the titles Thérèse used for the original copy of her canticle: "A French Soldier, defender of the Church, admirer of Joan of Arc." Thérèse dedicated her poem to her sister, the "Gallant Knight C. Martin."

(Melody: "Pitié, mon Dieu")

Canticle to Obtain the Canonization of the Venerable Joan of Arc

1   God of hosts, the whole Church
       Soon wishes to honor at the Altar
       A Martyr, a warrior Virgin
       Whose sweet name resounds in Heaven.

Refr. 1   Refrain

       By your Power,
       O King of Heaven,
       Give to Joan of France
       The Halo and the Altar   }   repeat

2   A conqueror for guilty France,
           No, that is not the object of her desire.
           Joan alone is capable of saving it.
           All heros weigh less than a martyr!

3   Lord, Joan is your splendid work.
           A heart of fire, a warrior's soul:
           You gave them to the timid virgin
           Whom you wished to crown with laurels.

4   In her humble meadow Joan heard
           Voices from Heaven calling her into combat.
           She left to save her country.
           The sweet Child commanded the army.

5   She won over the souls of proud warriors.
           The divine luster of Heaven's messenger,
           Her pure gaze, her fiery words
           Were able to make bold brows give way....

6   By a prodigy unique in history,
           People then saw a trembling monarch
           Regain his crown and his glory
           By means of a child's weak arm.

7   It is not Joan's victories
           We wish to celebrate this day.
           My God, we know her true glories
           Are her virtues, her love.

8   By fighting, Joan saved France.
           But her great virtues
           Had to be marked with the seal of suffering,
           With the divine seal of Jesus her Spouse!

9   Sacrificing her life at the stake,
           Joan heard the voice of the Blessed.
           She left this exile for her Homeland.
           The Savior Angel reascended into Heaven!...

10   Joan, you are our only hope.
           From high in the Heavens, deign to hear our voices.
           Come down to us, come convert France.
           Come save her a second time.

Refr. 2   Refrain

By the power
Of the Victorious God
Save, save France,
Angel Liberator !...   } repeat

11   Chasing the English out of all France,
Daughter of God, how beautiful were your steps!
But remember that in the days of your childhood
You only tended weak lambs...

Refr. 3   Refrain

Take up the defense
Of the powerless.
Preserve innocence
In the souls of children.   } repeat

12   Sweet Martyr, our monasteries are yours.
You know well that virgins are your sisters,
And like you the object of their prayers
Is to see God reign in every heart.

Refr. 4   To save souls
Is their desire.
Ah! give them your fire
Of Apostle and Martyr!   } repeat

13   Fear will be banished from every heart
When we shall see the Church crown
The pure brow of Joan our Saint,
And then we shall be able to sing:

Refr. 5   Our hope
Rests in you,
Saint Joan of France,
Pray, pray for us!   } repeat

PN 5 – My Song for Today
(June 1, 1894)

In the spring of 1894, taking advantage of a "free day" when the observance of silence was lifted, Marie of the Sacred Heart and Thérèse had a conversation "as always about the things of the other life" (SS, p. 47) and about the brevity of life. They agreed that Thérèse would put their shared thoughts into a poem as a gift for Marie's feastday on the Feast of the Sacred Heart, June 1. From their conversation was born one of our Carmelite's best poems, and unquestionably one of her most famous.

Those who read French will note the charm of this poem even in its rhyme. The "ui" sound recurs in every other verse—with each stanza ending in "aujourd'h*ui*." This sound, gentle as a breeze, alternates with feminine rhyme and harmonizes well with the constant swaying back and forth of the meter. Even each verse, in Alexandrine meter, is almost always divided into two equal parts. The first two verses of the poem set this swaying in motion: "an instant... a passing hour... just a day... that escapes and flies away," like a bird on a branch. The whole poem is already contained in the first stanza.

Thérèse develops images and attitudes harmoniously, without forcing them, all through the poem. She is speaking of a weak soul who can neither promise anything nor ask for anything for tomorrow. She is unsure of herself, but she is completely given over to God and trusts in his grace. "My grace is sufficient for you," Jesus said to Saint Paul (2 Cor 12:9). In this sense we admire the fourth stanza, in which she accepts trials and suffering "just for today."

Thérèse's style is very simple here, with images she is at home with: "the eternal shore," "hide me in your Face," "to rest under your veil," "cover me with your wing."

Little by little her enthusiasm grows, yet at the same time it remains unassuming, thanks to the return of the same little refrain, "Just for today."

We note her two marvelous images of the cluster of grapes (sts. 9 and 10) and her solid interpretation of the allegory of the Vine that those images convey. The True Vine (Jesus) only bears fruit through its "weak" branches (us). This fruit is eminently *apostolic*, as is proper for the Risen Lord. This is a "cluster of love, whose seeds are souls" (the Church), and not virtues, as we might expect. Thérèse first wrote "*crimson* cluster," but Mother Agnes changed that later to "golden": Thérèse meant redemption by the blood of Christ.

The last stanza is very much Thérèse. With its powerful, once-and-for-all flight up to God, it concludes in the dazzling sun of eternity, "The Eternal Today," in which the little refrain of the preceding stanzas merges and reaches its fulfillment.

The Lamartinian tone of this poem is undeniable. There is nothing astonishing about that, since Marie, the most susceptible of the Martin sisters to that poet's listlessness and revery, helped to think it out. But to Lamartine's negative statement, "And we only have this day," (Cf. in "L'Homme") Thérèse responds positively: "What counts for us is today," this "today" of God, who gives us his grace. Thus, the main theme of the poem is less the flight of time than "the relation of *eternal life* with this furtive and pathetic shudder we call *time*" (Jean Guitton, "Le génie de Sainte Thérèse de l'Enfant Jésus", in *Vie Thérésienne* 18 [1965]: p. 36).

We need to emphasize how consistent "My Song for Today" is with all the writings and especially the life of Thérèse. Here are a few examples: "Let us see only each moment!... a moment is a treasure" (GCI, p. 558). "Each moment is an eternity, an eternity of joy for heaven" (GCI, p. 587). "We have only the short moment of this life to give to God" (GCII, p. 882). "Ah! let us profit from the short moment of life..." (GCII, p. 1117). "I'm suffering only for an instant. It's because we think of the past and of the future that we become disappointed and fall into despair" (DE, p. 155, #10 and p. 241 [Aug. 20]).

For Thérèse, the urgency of "profiting from the exile of earth" (GCII, p. 853), from the "fleeting moment of life," was becoming all the more pressing: Little by little tuberculosis was beginning to consume her (cf. DE, p. 805).

(Melody: "Dieu de paix et d'amour")

My Song for Today

1   My life is but an instant, a passing hour.
           My life is but a day that escapes and flies away.
           O my God! You know that to love you on earth
                I only have today!...

2   Oh, I love you, Jesus! My soul yearns for you.
           For just one day remain my sweet support.
           Come reign in my heart, give me your smile
                Just for today!

3   Lord, what does it matter if the future is gloomy?
           To pray for tomorrow, oh no, I cannot!...
           Keep my heart pure, cover me with your shadow
                Just for today.

4   If I think about tomorrow, I fear my fickleness.
           I feel sadness and worry rising up in my heart.
           But I'm willing, my God, to accept trial and suffering
                Just for today.

5   O Divine Pilot! whose hand guides me,
           I'm soon to see you on the eternal shore.
           Guide my little boat over the stormy waves in peace
                Just for today.

6   Ah! Lord, let me hide in your Face.
           There I'll no longer hear the world's vain noise.
           Give me your love, keep me in your grace
                Just for today.

7   Near your divine Heart, I forget all passing things.
           I no longer dread the fears of the night.
           Ah! Jesus, give me a place in your Heart
                Just for today.

8   Living Bread, Bread of Heaven, divine Eucharist,
           O sacred Mystery! that Love has brought forth....
           Come live in my heart, Jesus, my white Host,
                Just for today.

9   Deign to unite me to you, Holy and sacred Vine,
           And my weak branch will give you its fruit,
           And I'll be able to offer you a cluster of golden grapes
                Lord, from today on.

10   I've just this fleeting day to form
           This cluster of love, whose seeds are souls.
           Ah! give me, Jesus, the fire of an Apostle
                Just for today.

11   O Immaculate Virgin! You are my Sweet Star
     Giving Jesus to me and uniting me to Him.
     O Mother! Let me rest under your veil
              Just for today.

12   My Holy Guardian Angel, cover me with your wing.
     With your fire light the road that I'm taking.
     Come direct my steps... help me, I call upon you
              Just for today.

13   Lord, I want to see you without veils, without clouds,
     But still exiled, far from you, I languish.
     May your lovable face not be hidden from me
              Just for today.

14   Soon I'll fly away to speak your praises
     When the day without sunset will dawn on my soul.
     Then I'll sing on the Angels' lyre
              The Eternal Today!....

PN 6 – The Portrait of a Soul I Love
(June 1, 1894)

There is no lack of "portraits" of Marie Martin. Between the first quick sketches penned by her mother and Marie's thin autobiographical notebook of 1909—where she gladly exaggerates her own shortcomings—we could name the testimonies by Fr. Pichon (her spiritual father), Marie of the Angels (her novice mistress), or her uncle [Isidore] Guérin.[1] Here is what her uncle said about her:

> You are my oldest daughter [aînée], my incorrigible child [enfant terrible], whose heart I've known for forty years.... It's very nice to return a little affection to such a heart that expands so easily, that explodes like a bomb to be divided into little particles so as to be lavished on everyone. You are truly the perfect model of devotion and affection.... You have your whims, your outbursts, but we don't love you any less for it because we know that you love. (6/21/1900)

Graphological studies of Marie Martin's handwriting confirm these traits.

With "My Song for Today," this acrostic completes Thérèse's bouquet of poetry for her oldest sister on the feast of the Sacred Heart (June 1 in 1894). This poem was a very private gift and was not shown to others, unlike "My Song for Today."

In the spring of 1894, Thérèse seems to have been inspired by the ample rhythm of the Alexandrine (PN 3, 5, 6). This is not a great poem, but there is much harmony and freshness in it. The acrostic form is obviously awkward for her. The adjectives she uses are rather banal: "sublime, ardent, great and generous, bright star, pure flame." And the word "jouissance" ["delight" in English], which mars several of her poems, reappears here too.[2] If the first five verses are a little trite, her expression becomes stronger afterward. From verse 8 on, we have a real interior portrait, with the right movement from nature to grace to transcend the banality of her style. This is the portrait "of a soul," and the word itself recurs five times.

The impression of greatness of soul that comes from this portrait conveys well Marie's influence on her little sister and goddaughter, who became her "little girl" after Pauline entered Carmel (cf. GCI, p. 427, p. 501, p. 661; GCII, p. 1001, note 9).

We wonder why Mother Agnes of Jesus felt she had to make so many corrections on the manuscript, even in her old age after the death of Sr. Marie of the Sacred Heart.[3] No doubt the idealization of her memories made her be finicky over and over again with her older sister's portrait. But there is more truth in Thérèse's awkward attempt.

[1] For Mme. Martin, see the letters from 1863 to 1877 in *Family Correspondence*. For Fr. Pichon, see especially the letters written in 1882 in *Vie Thérésienne*, April 1976, n° 62. The "portrait" by Sister Marie of the Angels, from 1893, is published in CGII, p. 1176.
[2] ["Jouissance" can also have a sexual connotation in French.—Trans.]
[3] There have been so many erasures and corrections on the autograph of this poem that in many places the paper is worn through. All the changes are in Mother Agnes's handwriting, and some are as late as 1940–1950.

Feast of the Sacred Heart
June 1, 1894

The Portrait of a Soul I Love

Marie of the Sacred Heart

M	I know a very loving heart, a soul
A	Gifted from Heaven with a sublime Faith.
R	Nothing here below can delight this ardent soul:
I	There is only Jesus whom she calls her King.
E	In short, this beautiful soul is great and generous,
D	Both sweet and lively, always humble of heart.
U	A far-off horizon... a bright star
S	Are often enough to unite her to the Lord.
A	I used to see her loving her independence,
C	Looking for pure joy and true freedom....
R	Spreading good deeds was her delight,
É	And forgetting herself, her only wish!....
C	It was the divine Heart that captivated this soul,
Œ	The work of his love, worthy of the Creator.
U	One day I shall see her, like a pure flame,
R	Shining in Heaven close to the Sacred Heart.

The heart of a grateful child

PN 7 – Song of Gratitude to
Our Lady of Mount Carmel

(July 16, 1894)

Here are a few easy verses that flow nicely, without any one idea or word really holding our attention. The interest of these verses is more historical than poetic. They bring out Thérèse's affection for Sister Martha, and they give us information on the personality of the novice rather than on the Marian life of the author.

Sister Martha was born on July 16 (in 1865). The coincidence with the feast of Our Lady of Mount Carmel is what dictates the theme of this canticle. On the same date in 1893, 1895, and 1897, Thérèse offered her companion a prayer written especially for her.

Four stanzas encompass Sister Martha's life: her childhood, her Carmelite vocation, her present life in Carmel, and her future life in Heaven. Here are a few words of explanation for each one.

Childhood (st. 1): Florence Cauvin lost her mother when she was six years old and was entrusted to the Sisters of Saint Vincent de Paul. Her father, a shepherd in the Eure region of France, died two years later. So she grew up "in the shade of a holy cloister" (v. 8), first in Paris, then in Bernay until she entered Carmel in 1887.

"To take in her arms," "to protect," "to preserve," "soft nest," "to watch over": This is all part of Mary's maternal role, which this orphan doubly needed.

Vocation (st. 2): We do not know the circumstances surrounding "Jesus' call" to Martha. This stanza suggests the Blessed Virgin's intervention in her choice of an Order. Note the conception of Carmel that appears here: "Come sacrifice yourself for your Savior." Of the nineteen uses of the verb "to sacrifice oneself" [*s'immoler*] in Thérèse's writings, eleven deal with the Carmelite nun: Thérèse herself or other sisters.

In Carmel (st. 3): "Jesus alone." To reach that point, Martha would have had to agree to the great detachment from Mother Marie de Gonzague that Thérèse instigated on December 8, 1892 (SS, p. 235).

The second part of this stanza reflects Sister Martha's temperament. "Sadness" and "fear" were tendencies that Thérèse was trying to free her companion from (GCII, p. 1117 and p. 1138[1]). Trust and love had the last word, as Sister Martha's death notice testified: At the hour of death, she confided, "It's incredible the peace I feel. I can't get over it! God is all sweetness. Never would I have thought I'd find him so sweet. My confidence in him has no bounds" (p. 3). And she kept repeating her gratitude to be dying "in this Carmel of the way of love" (*ibid.*).

In heaven (st. 4): The finale of the poem is weak, even though "to fly away" and "exile" give it a very Theresian touch.

This *song* was surely written to be sung to a tune that Sister Martha knew well. No information has come down to us about this. The meter and rhyme [in the French] would adapt well to a song that was very popular then, "Par les chants les plus magnifiques," which Thérèse used for five of her poems.

¹ [This letter is incorrectly identified in the ICS English translation: GCII, p. 1138. It was written to Sister *Martha* of Jesus, not to Sister Marie of Jesus.—Trans.]

Song of Gratitude to Our Lady of Mount Carmel

1
From the first moments of my life,
You took me in your arms.
Ever since that day, dear Mother,
You've protected me here below.
To preserve my innocence,
You placed me in a soft nest.
You watched over my childhood
In the shade of a holy cloister.

2
Later, in the days of my youth,
I heard Jesus' call!...
In your ineffable tenderness,
You showed Carmel to me.
"Come, my child, be generous,"
You sweetly said to me.
"Near me, you'll be happy,
Come sacrifice yourself for your Savior."

....

3
Close to you, O my loving Mother!
I've found rest for my heart.
I want nothing more on earth.
Jesus alone is all my happiness.
If sometimes I feel sadness
And fear coming to assail me,
Always supporting me in my weakness,
Mother, you deign to bless me.

4   Grant that I may be faithful
           To my divine Spouse Jesus.
           One day may his sweet voice call me
           To fly away among the elect.
           Then, no more exile, no more suffering.
           In Heaven I'll keep repeating
           The song of my gratitude,
           Lovable Queen of Carmel!

PN 8 – Prayer of a Child of a Saint
(August 1894)

This is an important poem—the first one Thérèse wrote for herself. On the morning of July 29, 1894, her father died peacefully at the Guérin's château, "La Musse." For him it was the end of a "*death* of five years" (GCII, p. 882), during which mental illness had diminished his faculties.

Thérèse lived this deep shock in silence (cf. GCII, pp. 874-875). During the weeks that followed, many memories peacefully resurfaced for her. Her grief became blurred, and nothing remained except the sweetness of "remembering." In this "prayer" charged with emotion, Thérèse perfects her relationship with her father on the other side of death, a relationship painfully interrupted almost from the time she entered Carmel (1888): "I am finding him once more after an absence of six years, I feel him around *me*, looking at me and protecting me..." (GCII, p. 884, 8/20/1894).

Then, like a "little girl" still on earth and truly an orphan, she "makes a sign" to him to turn through the family memory album with her. She knows he is alive and blessed, "a Saint" (with a capital "S"), and undoubtedly she uses the word in its strong sense, as she does later in letter 261 (GCII, p. 1165). Near him she opens her heart in a meditation full of sweetness: "Remember!" This is an important word in Thérèse's vocabulary—the expression of a temperament quick to record everything once and for all.

This is historical or biographical poetry, a little "votive offering" in the family sanctuary. One stanza is dedicated to the Martin parents and then one to each of the four girls: Marie, "the dearest to your heart"; Pauline, "your fine bright pearl"; Léonie, "like her sisters" at last; and Céline, her father's "angel" during his trial. After the stanzas about Thérèse herself, the song concludes with Monsieur Martin's passion and glorification.

This "history" is not just a simple recollection of facts. It already contains an *interpretation,* just as in *Story of a Soul,* for which this poem forms a kind of prologue. This process is obvious in stanza 9. Thérèse's father's trial suggests some very beautiful images to her (5, 3–4 and 9, 3–4): sweet and majestic, they ennoble his humiliating ordeal.

Thérèse's portrait of each of her sisters is wrought with great precision of tone. The "baby of the family" has now been able to step back from her older sisters. She situates them very well in relation to their father.

In the stanzas so full of compassion that refer to Thérèse (6–8), her affection overflows. The images are more tender and radiant, almost in the tone of a letter the "little queen" or "the orphan of Bérésina" would sign.

Stanza 7 in particular, in the Belvedere, is a complex little tableau in a very few verses: the place, her father's lap; the prayer that rocks her with its "sweet refrain"; Thérèse, looking at her father whose face reflects "time and Eternity," where his "look was immersed"....

In these stanzas, she does not pray to her "papa" for herself, as she does for her sisters. Her meditation is based on the contemplation of the Face-to-face vision that her father now devotes himself to.

It is worth mentioning that Thérèse uses the same melody (a poem by Alfred de Musset put to music by Georges Rupès) for her great contemplative poem, "Jesus, My Beloved, Remember!" (PN 24).

The structure of this model by Rupès determined in part the poetic "then-now" structure of Thérèse's "Prayer." It is also worth noting that there is a break between the very constant rhythm of sts. 1–5 and that of sts. 6–9, which evoke Thérèse's own history with her father until she entered Carmel.

[In the French] the grammatical mistake that Thérèse made all her life unfortunately mars several verses.[1] On the other hand, in spite of the abundant "Ohs!" and "Ahs!," well-suited to the lyricism of this meditation, there is little filler in this flowing poem.

At the time Thérèse wrote this poem (summer 1894), she was experiencing a fruitful period in thought and style. Reread her admirable letter of July 7 on "the Word" and the Trinity (GCII, pp. 861–863); her intense letter, even in the handwriting, of July 18 (GCII, pp. 870–873); her insistent defense of a life given to Jesus of August 19 (GCII, pp. 881–883). Thérèse is becoming her own person, perhaps because of these circumstances:

- her "maternity" for Marie of the Trinity, her first "daughter," who entered Carmel on July 16;
- the death of Monsieur Martin on July 29;
- her strong stand in favor of Céline's vocation, even against that of Fr. Pichon, in July and August.

Moreover, this "fruitfulness" coincides (as it will in the summer of 1896) with a new attack of tuberculosis. From the doctor's superficial examination on July 1 (GCII, p. 1260) to her very impaired voice in October (GCII, pp. 892–893), her illness had worsened. Thérèse did not have much longer to be "the orphan of Bérésina." In three years, she would truly "find" her father again.

---

[1] [Thérèse often used "se rappeler *de*" instead of the correct "se rappeler"—Trans.]

✚

August 1894

Prayer of a Child of a Saint

1   Remember that formerly on earth
Your only happiness used to be to love us dearly.
Grant your children's prayer.
Protect us, deign to bless us still.
Up there you have again found our dear Mother,
Who had gone before you to our Holy Homeland.
Now in Heaven
You both reign.
Watch over us!.....

2   Remember your beloved Marie,
Your eldest daughter, the dearest to your heart.
Remember that she filled your life
With her love, charm, and happiness...
For God you gave up her sweet presence,
And you blessed the hand that offered suffering to you...
O! your Diamond
Always more sparkling
Remember!.....

3   Remember your fine bright pearl,
Whom you knew as a weak and timid lamb.
See her filled with divine strength
And leading Carmel's flock.
She has become the Mother of your other children.
O Papa! Come guide her who is so dear to you!...
And without leaving Heaven
Your little Carmel
Remember!...

4   Remember the ardent prayer
You made for your third child.
God granted it, for on earth she is
Like her sisters, a very brilliant beautiful Lily.
The Visitation hides her from the eyes of the world,
But she loves Jesus, she is flooded with his peace.
Her ardent desires
And all her sighs
Remember!...

5   Remember your dear Céline,
         Who was like an angel from Heaven for you
         When a glance from the Divine Face
         Came to test you by a glorious choice.....
   You reign in Heaven..... her task is complete.
   Now she gives her life to Jesus.....
                  Protect your child
                  Who repeats so often
                       Remember!...

6   Remember your little queen,
         The orphan of Bérésina.
         Remember her uncertain steps.
         It was always your hand that guided her.
   O Papa! remember that in the days of her childhood
   You wanted to keep her innocence for God alone!...
                  And her blonde hair
                  That delighted your eyes
                       Remember!...

7   Remember that in the belvedere
         You always sat her on your lap,
         And then whispering a prayer,
         You rocked her with your sweet refrain.
   She saw a reflection of Heaven on your face
   When your profound look was immersed in space,
                  And you sang the beauty
                  Of Eternity
                       Remember!...

8   Remember the radiant Sunday
         When you pressed her to your paternal heart.
         You gave her a white little flower,
         Allowing her to fly to Carmel.
   O Papa! remember that in her great trials
   You gave her proofs of the most sincere love.
                  In Rome and in Bayeux
                  You showed her Heaven
                       Remember!...

9   Remember that at the Vatican
        The Holy Father's hand rested on your brow,
        But you could not understand the mystery
        Of the Divine seal imprinted on you.....
Now your children pray to you.
They bless your Cross and your bitter suffering!...
        On your glorious brow
        Nine Lilies in bloom
          Shine in Heaven!!!...

             The Orphan of Bérésina

PN 9 – Prayer of an Exiled Child

(September 11, 1894)

There is no information in the documents from Thérèse's time on the circumstances surrounding this composition, which Sister Marie of the Sacred Heart had requested for the feastday of Father Almire Pichon, her spiritual director. Sister Marie, not Thérèse, is the "exiled child."

Rough draft 1, which Thérèse gave up on, described Fr. Pichon's role since 1882 with regard to Marie. That retrospective point of view was eliminated in the final version, which became this "Prayer."

Relations between the Carmel of Lisieux and the Jesuit who was then in Canada (since 1888) were a little strained at this time (August 1894) because of Céline's vocation (cf. GCII, p. 856). Thérèse herself was "heavy at heart!!!..." (GCII, p. 878). But she "did not hold it against him," since "he was only the docile instrument of Jesus" (*ibid.*).

The composition of this acrostic (which was laborious, judging from the rough draft) proves Thérèse did not hold a grudge—and that perhaps she lacked inspiration!

Fr. Pichon thanked her in a few words: "Thank you for your feastday wishes, your delightful poetry. Everything coming from the little lamb does my heart good" (GCII, p. 900).

Fr. Pichon came back to France for a few months in 1900, and for good in 1907.

Prayer of an Exiled Child

A   Near you, my God, I remember a Father,
L   The beloved apostle of your Sacred Heart.
M   But he is exiled on a foreign shore...
I   It's time; bring back my Pastor at last!
R   Give your children back their guide and their light.
E   Call your apostle home to France, Lord.

September 11, 1894

PN 10 – Story of a Shepherdess
Who Became a Queen
(November 20, 1894)

This fine poem is both lively and profound, different as night and day from the one Thérèse wrote for Sister Martha four months earlier (PN 7). Here it is really Thérèse who is speaking and who is herself enchanted with her little fairy tale.

"The shepherdess who became a queen" is as classic a theme as there ever was, from folklore the world over, in the style of a romance novel. Thérèse could have come to know it from fairy tales she heard as a child, but also perhaps from the Bible: we think of Ezekiel 16, which she later used in her autobiography (SS, p. 101) and again in PN 26. Thérèse would have naturally liked this image—sensitive as she was to the marriage of the littlest and the greatest—of the "less than nothing" and the eternal. It was a must here, since Marie-Madeleine (formerly Mélanie) really had been a shepherdess. Mother Agnes of Jesus also used this theme for her exhortation to the newly professed at the profession ceremony.

So with Sr. Marie-Madeleine, let's listen to the "charming story" that Thérèse sang, not in her place but close to her, to make her happy and to win her over.

Religious profession is a bond of love, a "marvelous, sweet chain" (st. 1). The whole poem expresses the *sweetness* of the great King (six times the word "sweet," one time "sweetness") who spares nothing to charm the shepherdess.

In order to "speak to her heart" (st. 3)—we are reminded of Hosea 2:16—Jesus leads his chosen one into solitude, not a desert, but a rustic setting full of charm: "lambs, little flowers, birds, deep forests, beautiful blue sky...." The image of Joan of Arc at Domrémy comes spontaneously to mind here, but this beautiful nature also evokes Thérèse's solitary afternoons as a child while her father was fishing (SS, p. 37). Nature is the "language" and the "image" that "reveals God" to her.

The King's Mother, the "Sweet Queen" of Carmel, is entrusted with taking the first steps, full of respect, toward the shepherdess: "Do you wish?" Then Jesus intervenes (st. 4). "I will espouse you to myself forever," Yahweh had already said to his people (Hos 2:19).

After the shepherdess' "yes," she begins her ascent up Carmel, and Mary becomes her guide and support. The first part of st. 5 brings about an imperceptible change in the tone of the poem: a musical transition discreetly announcing the demands that the following stanzas will relate in detail. The second part suddenly brings us back to present-day reality: the "shepherdess who became a queen" is not a myth. She is here, now, before our eyes: "It is you"—Marie-Madeleine, who made her profession on this November 20, 1894—"near Jesus, her love."

The hidden life of a Carmelite lay sister, serving and poor (refr. 1), is not unworthy of such royalty (st. 6), since "to serve God is to reign" (St. Augustine).

This is Carmelite life in its fullness: to be Martha *and* Mary (st. 7). With a deep understanding of the unity in this vocation—"love in the heart of the Church," she will say (SS, p. 194)—Thérèse does not dwell on the class distinctions in religious life that were so obvious in her day. "To pray, to serve" is every Carmelite nun's concern—and "true happiness" for her.

And also "to suffer for God" (st. 8). But with Thérèse, we learn to "turn bitter suffering into joy." Everything is born in joy ("delight," "sweetness," "tenderness"), and even leads to "flight."

Even the angels envy this destiny (st. 9): an idea dear to Thérèse. The triumphant emphasis of this stanza announces the tone of "The Responses of Saint Agnes" (PN 26). If Sister Marie-Madeleine will reign "soon," her dignity as royal spouse has value "even in this life." In the 1898 version of *Story of a Soul*, in which this poem was first published, Mother Agnes was uneasy with such daring, and so the stanza was changed, rendering it insipid.

Only Thérèse could have written such a free, sparkling poem for a novice so "tied up in knots": Mother Agnes wrote two years later, "I can't even begin to tell you how distant Sr. Marie-Madeleine is from Sr. Thérèse of the Child Jesus" (GCII, p. 1031). If things were not yet to that point in 1894, everything seemed to anticipate that Thérèse's love and devotion for her companion would never be repaid.

The eighth of eleven children, a "little shepherdess" at age five, apprenticed as a servant at fourteen, illiterate though intelligent, sullen and uncommunicative, Marie-Madeleine had been traumatized by some horrible memory from her adolescence (cf. Death Notice). Faced with Thérèse's perspicacity, she built a wall around herself. And yet deep down she loved her: When Thérèse was seriously ill, twice she made "some soup just for her." [1] Her testimony at the Beatification Process is one of the most beautiful portraits of Thérèse that we have.

On her side, Thérèse never lost patience. She always loved Marie-Madeleine with an unselfish love. This poem is especially enlightening on this point: There is not a shadow of reserve or anything leading us to guess some possible irritation or strain. This poem is merry as a lark, and yet at the same time it demands a great deal from a sister who was so touchy and withdrawn.

Here we enter into a beautiful mystery of love: that of the great King for a poor shepherdess—and of Thérèse for her neighbor, whom she loved as Jesus loved his neighbor. This is love stronger than death. Years later Marie-Madeleine admitted, "I was not then in a state to profit from her advice, but since her entry into heaven, I've surrendered the care of my soul to her, and how she has changed me! It's incredible! I'm so peaceful and trusting. I don't recognize myself any more" (Death Notice, p. 3). "She died a very holy death," Mother Agnes confided on January 13, 1916 (letter to Léonie two days later).

One last note: it is obvious that Thérèse's enthusiasm in this poem surpasses simply evoking Marie-Madeleine's happy future. She is singing of herself and her own nuptials. Soon she will begin the first part of her autobiography. Here she already takes the tone of someone who is "singing eternally the Mercies of the Lord" (SS, p. 13).

[1] Christopher O'Mahony, ed. and trans., *St. Thérèse of Lisieux by those who knew her: Testimonies from the process of beatification* (Dublin: Veritas, 1975), p. 263.

(Melody: "Tombé du nid")   November 20, 1894

Story of a Shepherdess Who Became a Queen

To my Sister Marie-Madeleine on the day of her
Profession, made in the hands of Mother Agnes of Jesus.

1   On this beautiful day, O Madeleine!
       We come close to you to sing
       Of the marvelous, sweet chain
       That unites you to your Spouse.
       Listen to the charming story
       Of the shepherdess whom a great King
       One day wished to overwhelm with glory
       And who responded to his voice.

Refrain

       Let us sing of the Shepherdess,
       Poor on this earth,
       Whom the King of Heaven
Weds this day in Carmel.

2   A little shepherd girl
        Used to tend her lambs while spinning.
        She admired every tiny flower.
        She listened to the bird songs,
        Understanding well the sweet language
        Of the deep forests and the beautiful blue Sky.
        For her everything was an image
        Revealing God to her.

3   She loved Jesus and Mary
        With a truly great ardor.
        They also loved Mélanie
        And came to speak to her heart.
        "Do you wish," said the Sweet Queen,
        "Do you wish to become Madeleine,
        Close to me, on Mount Carmel,
        And from then on win nothing less than Heaven?

4   "Child, leave this countryside.
        Don't long for your flock.
        There, on my holy mountain,
        Jesus will be your only Lamb."
        "O come! your soul has charmed me,"
        Jesus repeated in turn,
        "I take you as my fiancée.
        You shall be mine forever."

5   The humble shepherdess happily
        Responded to that sweet call.
        Upheld by Mary, her Mother,
        She reached the summit of Carmel.
        ....
        It is you, O Marie-Madeleine!
        Whom we honor on this great day.
        The Shepherdess has become a Queen
        Close to King Jesus, her love!...

6   You know, very dear Sister,
To serve our God is to reign.
During his life the Sweet Savior
Never ceased teaching this to us:
"If in the Heavenly Homeland
You want to be the first,
All your life you'll have to
Hide yourself... To be the last."

7   Blessed are you, Madeleine,
Praying to Jesus on Carmel.
Would there be any sorrow for you,
Being so near Heaven?
You imitate Martha and Mary.
To pray, to serve the sweet Savior
Is the goal of your life.
It gives you true happiness.

8   If sometimes bitter suffering
Should come to visit your heart,
Make it your joy:
To suffer for God... what sweetness!...
Then Divine tenderness
Will make you soon forget
That you walk on thorns.
Rather you will believe that you are flying...

9   Today the angels envy you.
They would like to enjoy the happiness
That you possess, O Marie!
As the Lord's spouse.
Yes, even in this life you are
The spouse of the King of the elect.
One day in our holy Homeland
You shall reign close to Jesus.

Last Refrain

Soon the Shepherdess,
Poor on this earth,
Flying away to Heaven,
Will reign close to the Eternal One.

To our Venerable Mothers

10   It is you, good and loving Mothers,
      It is to your care and your prayers
      That Madeleine our Sister
      Owes her peace and her happiness.
      She will be truly grateful
      For your tender and maternal love,
      Asking her Divine Master
      To overwhelm you with Heaven's riches.

Refrain

      And in your crowns,
      O very good Mothers,
      Will shine the flower
      You offer to God our Savior.

PN 11 – The Time of Tears Has Passed at Last
PN 12 – It's Close to You, Virgin Mary

(For Marie of the Trinity's Reception of the Habit)
(December 18, 1894)

One month after Sister Marie-Madeleine's profession, a postulant received the habit: Sister Marie Agnes of the Holy Face. (In the spring of 1896, she changed her name to Marie of the Trinity.) It was a very private ceremony, for this was the second time this young sister had received the habit. She had first been clothed in a Parisian Carmel [then located on the Avenue de Messine], but had had to leave in 1893 for health reasons. This new attempt still left room for doubt. Such circumstances called for a more modest poem.

Meant to be sung at evening recreation, this poem is made up of two parts: the soloist's song (PN 11), by the novice herself to a melody she knew well, and the choir's response (PN 12), sung by the entire community. The second part takes up the themes and even the same expressions as the first. Both are addressed to the Blessed Virgin Mary, whose "Expectation" (PN 12, 2) was being celebrated on that December 18, one week before the birth of Jesus.

Thérèse avoids the usual commonplace verses for a clothing ceremony by evoking concrete facts from the heroine's life: her exile "so long, so far from the holy ark" (PN 11, 1), her precocious, "bitter trial" (11, 2), her decided attraction to the Holy Face, "the adorable Face" (11, 3), her very obvious "faults," to be sure, but also her "good will," her "courage" (11, 4) and even her rather pale complexion that sometimes worried the Sisters (12, 6). The name Agnes itself calls to mind the image of the lamb: but a lamb by no means delightful—she even has "unattractive ways" (GCII, p. 872)—but she is still a "poor lamb" (11, Refr. 1, and 12, 9) and a "humble lamb" (12, 8). She sings in a begging voice so as to make the Virgin Mary feel sorry for her. She won't be able to do anything but "hide under her mantle" (11, Ref. 1, and 12, 9). She also wants to move the community, who until then had been rather reticent about this young woman who had come from another "flock"....

So this is how Thérèse fulfills her role as "angel" for Marie-Agnes of the Holy Face. With delicacy for her protégée and modesty toward her senior sisters, she makes herself a mediator. This discreet involvement in Sr. Marie's vocation blossomed two years later into a youthful, deep friendship. The six other poems Thérèse wrote for her (PN 20, 29, 30, 31, 49, 53) let us appreciate their closeness.

Also we already see sketched out Thérèse's influence as Marie's spiritual guide. At this stage in discovering her "little way," it was fortunate that

Thérèse had, listening in at her side, a disciple who was so vivacious and generous. Together, they were going to experience that "always remaining little" (11, 3) leads "very quickly" to "holiness" (PN 11, draft 2). For now, they were still in the babbling stage of the "cradle" (12, 8).

So the historical interest of these unpretentious verses makes up for their poetic weakness.

Thérèse's model for this poem, "Nina la Glaneuse" ["Nina the Gleaner"], has only one point in common with Sr. Marie: her enthusiasm at work. The model reads, "The poor village girl... Discreetly went to work" and "Night and day... she worked fervently." We have no information as to what melody was sung for the community's part.

[PN 11]

[For the Clothing of Marie-Agnes of the Holy Face]

1

Virgin Mary, in spite of my weakness,
On the evening of this beautiful day I want to sing
A canticle of gratitude   .
And my hope of being God's for ever.
Ah! for such a long time, so far from the holy ark,
My poor heart longed for Carmel.
I have found it, now no more fear.
Here I am tasting the first-fruits of Heaven!...

Refrain

The time of tears has passed at last. .
I have put back on the fleece of the flock.
A new horizon is opening for me.
Divine Mother, on this day so full of charms,
Oh! truly hide your little lamb
Under your mantle.

2

I am very young, and already suffering
And bitter trials have visited my heart.
Virgin Mary, my only hope,
You give happiness back to your lamb.
You give Carmel to me for family.
I am also the Sister of your children.
Dear Mother, I am becoming your daughter,
The fiancée of Jesus, my Savior.

3

Your Son's ineffable glance
Has deigned to lower itself to my poor soul.
I have searched for his adorable Face,
And in Him I want to hide myself.
I will always have to stay little
To be worthy of his glances,
But I'll grow quickly in virtue
Under the brightness of this star of Heaven.

4

Sweet Mary, I'm not afraid of work.
You know my good will.
I have faults, but courage too,
And my sisters' charity is great.
While awaiting the beautiful day of my nuptials,
I will imitate their sublime virtues;
For I sense that you give me the strength
To become the spouse of Jesus.

Last Refrain

Deign to bless the Venerable Mothers
Whose goodness gave Carmel back to me.
Virgin Mary, may I see them seated
Near you on an immortal throne,
And may your maternal heart
Crown them in Heaven.

[PN 12]

J.M.J.T.

December 18, 1894

1   It's close to you, Virgin Mary,
That we have come to sing tonight,
Praying to you for this dear child
Whose only hope you are.

2   On the blessed feast of your expectation
You make her heart truly happy.
She is pitching her tent on Carmel
And is only awaiting her Holy Vows.

3   O tender Mother, this beautiful day
Brings back sweet memories for her.
On another day in her life
You came to cover her with your mantle.

4   At last the rough serge is given back to her.
Twice she has received your habit.
Mother, may she receive
A double portion of your spirit.

5   She sang, "I have courage!..."
"That's true," we've said among ourselves.
She sang, "I like to work!"
Work won't be lacking here!...

6   But strength is a very good thing.
So that she may work wholeheartedly,
Mother, put on her cheeks
The brilliant color of a rose!...

7   For her the waiting is over.
Her heart knows the peace of Heaven.
This Christmas Jesus wants to see her
In her Fiancée's habit.

8   Tender Mother, may He deign
       To hide your humble lamb in his Face.
       That is where she craves a place,
       Not wanting any other cradle.

9   O Mary, deign to grant
       The wishes of your poor lamb.
       During the night of this life,
       Hide her under your mantle.

10   Listen to all her prayers,
       And may your maternal heart
       Keep safe for a long, long time the Mothers
       Who give her back her dear Carmel!...

PN 13 – The Queen of Heaven to Her Beloved Child
(December 25, 1894)

This poem has the freshness of a Christmas carol, but it is also structured and meticulous, with precisely chosen wording, despite the ease and apparent freedom of the style.

Céline, for whom this poem was written, wrote several times on the circumstances surrounding its composition.[1] Assigned as assistant in the habit office after she entered Carmel (9/14/1894), Céline soon saw her talents as a painter put to good use as well. Before Mother Agnes of Jesus' feast (1/21/1895), the sisters kept coming to her to bring all sorts of objects to decorate. But those "silly things" got on her nerves, for she had never painted anything but large canvases. Besides, the work on the habits was affected. The sister in charge of that office, Marie of the Angels, who was usually "good to a fault," occasionally complained, "Sister Marie of the Holy Face isn't doing anything at all. I can't count on her to help me" (Remembrances, p. 236). The postulant was wounded to the core, for she was well aware of her talents, which had been so appreciated in the family before she entered. To help Céline get over this "big heartbreak," Thérèse wrote the poem we are about to read. She put it in her sister's shoe on Christmas morning. It was a complete success (cf. CSG, p. 151). Stanzas 15 and 16 especially were often consoling for Céline afterward.

Thérèse was really aiming much higher. As with Sister Marie of the Trinity, Thérèse was leading Céline in the way of childhood she herself was in the process of discovering. By affirming the primacy of "Love," she was headed toward her decisive Offering to Merciful Love of June 1895.

The language of this poem is simpler than in the preceding ones. Many stanzas have the grace of a lullaby. [In the French version] this rocking can be seen in the back-and-forth movement of the octosyllabic meter in alternating rhyme. Or sometimes there is a back-and-forth movement from one stanza to another. For example, st. 10 is the tender response to st. 9, which is veiled with sadness.

This pretty Christmas song is just as much a song of Nazareth and hidden childhood. Mary's presence is of prime importance for an introduction to the "simplicity" and the "silence" of "love" and to "resembling" (1, 1) the "only Lamb," the Word made Child.

---

[1] She wrote up to six times between 1908 and 1952: in CMG I, pp. 141 ff.; NPPO 1908, p. 21; Personal Remembrances from 1909, p. 236; CMG IV, pp. 273, 352; CSG, pp. 50 and 151; Collection of artistic works by Sister Geneviève, I, p. 25. Here we summarize these accounts that repeat themselves and often complement one other.

J.M.J.T.

The Queen of Heaven to Her Beloved Child
Marie of the Holy Face

1   I'm looking for a little girl who resembles
Jesus, my only lamb,
So I can keep them both
Together in the same cradle.

2   An Angel from the Holy Homeland
Would be jealous of such happiness!...
But I give it to you, Marie.
The Child God will be your Spouse!...

3   It is you I have chosen
To be Jesus' sister.
Do you wish to keep Him company?...
You will rest on my heart....

4   I will hide you under the veil
Where the King of Heaven takes refuge.
From now on my Son will be the only star
That shines for you.

5   But to shelter you always
Under my veil beside Jesus,
You must stay little,
Adorned with childlike virtues.

6   I want sweetness and purity
To shine on your brow,
But the virtue that I give you
Above all is Simplicity.

7   God, Unique in three persons,
Whom the angels, trembling, adore,
The Eternal One wants you to give Him
The simple name of Flower of the fields.

8   Like a white daisy
Always looking up to Heaven,
May you also be the simple little flower
Of the little Christmas Child!...

9   The world does not recognize the charms
       Of the King who is exiled from Heaven.
       Very often you will see tears
       Glistening in his sweet little eyes.

10   Forgetting your troubles
       To gladden that Lovable Child,
       You must bless your sweet chains
       And sing softly!....

11   The all-powerful God
       Who calms the roaring sea,
       Borrowing the features of childhood,
       Wants to become weak and little.

12   The uncreated Word of the Father
       Who exiles himself for you here below,
       My sweet Lamb, your little Brother,
       Won't speak to you, Marie!...

13   This silence is the first pledge
       Of his inexpressible love.
       Understanding this silent language,
       You will imitate him each day.

14   And if sometimes Jesus sleeps,
       You will rest beside Him.
       His Divine Heart that always keeps vigil
       Will serve as your sweet support.

15   Don't worry, Marie,
       About each day's duties,
       For your task in this life
       Must only be: "Love!"

16   But if someone comes to find fault
       That your works cannot be seen,
       You can say, "I love much,
       That is my wealth here below!..."

17 Jesus will weave your crown
If you only desire his love,
If your heart abandons itself in Him,
He will have you reign forever.

18 Invited by His sweet Glance
After the night of this life,
Your enraptured soul will fly
To Heaven without any delay!...

Christmas night 1894

(Melody of the canticle: "Sur le grand mât d'une corvette")

PN 14 – To Our Father Saint Joseph
(1894)

We know nothing about the circumstances concerning this "Canticle," as it was entitled in the original draft. According to the official "Copy of the Writings" [for the diocesan "Ordinary" Process (1910)] from the beatification process, it was written at the request of Sister Marie of the Incarnation (Josephine Lecouturier). We can safely date it in the year 1894, without being able to provide more precise details. All things considered, it is a mediocre poem.

The main themes are contemplation and service of Jesus and Mary, in poverty and solitude: These characteristics of Saint Joseph's hidden life correspond well to the life of Carmelite nuns. When they lovingly invoke the Protector of the universal Church and of Carmel in particular, they are only following the example and advice of their Mother Teresa of Avila (*Life*, chap. VI).

To Our Father Saint Joseph

1

Joseph, your admirable life
Took place in poverty,
But you contemplated the beauty
Of Jesus and Mary.

Refrain

Joseph, O tender Father,
Protect Carmel.
May your children on earth
Always savor the peace of Heaven! } repeat

2

The Son of God, in his childhood,
Often happily
Submitted to your authority
And rested on your heart.

3

Like you, we serve Mary and Jesus
In solitude.
Pleasing them is our only aim.
We desire nothing more...

4

Saint Teresa our Mother
Invoked you with love.
She confirms that you
Always granted her prayer.

5

After this life's exile,
We have the sweet hope
That we shall go to see you, Saint Joseph,
With our dear Mother.[1]

Last Refrain

Bless, tender Father,
Our little Carmel.
After this earthly exile,
Reunite us all in Heaven!   } repeat

---

[1] Here Thérèse is not referring to Saint Teresa, whom she calls elsewhere in her writings "our Holy Mother" or "our seraphic Mother," but rather to the Blessed Virgin Mary. See *Poésies*, vol. II, p. 96.

PN 15 – The Atom of the Sacred Heart
(1894)

For Thérèse, the Sacred Heart is the very Person of Jesus (cf. PN 23). It is truly his whole Person—his "smile" (3, 4), his "glance" (4, 1), his "voice" (5, 2), his "heart" (5, 3), and his "hand" (6, 1)—that these short quatrains evoke.

We seek his presence in the Eucharist, which was a special devotion of Sister Saint Vincent de Paul: She calls herself an "atom" that remains "at the door" (1, 1) or inside the "tabernacle" (8, 3) and even in the "ciborium" as in "a nest" (2, 3)—an image of questionable taste!

Despite the liveliness of these little stanzas—at times nicely done—and despite a few tender expressions ("My only love," "O my sweet Friend!") which, coming from Thérèse, have a real ring of truth to them, this composition is still weak.

Sister Saint Vincent de Paul asked Thérèse for a second poem on the theme of the atom (PN 19).

[The Atom of the Sacred Heart]

Refrain
Divine Heart, your atom
Gives her life to You.
Her peace, her happiness
Is to delight you, Lord.

1
I'm at your door
Night and day.
Your grace upholds me.
Long live your love!...

2
O hide your glory!
Make me a soft nest
In the holy Ciborium
Day and night.

3
How marvelous! Your wing
Shelters me.

When I awake,
Jesus, you smile...

4

Your glance inflames me.
My only love,
Consume my soul,
Jesus, forever.

5

Filled with tenderness,
Your voice charms me,
And your heart moves me,
O my sweet Friend!...

6

Your hand comforts me
And serves as my support.
You give courage
To the moaning heart.

7

Console my heart
From all fatigue,
And be the Good Shepherd
For the Prodigal.

8

Oh! the sweet sight,
Prodigy of love,
In the tabernacle
I always stay.

9

Set free from the world
And without any support,
Your grace overwhelms me,
My only friend!...

10

Oh! what a sweet martrydom.
I burn with love.
To you I sigh,
Jesus, each day!...

PN 16 – Song of Gratitude of Jesus' Fiancée
(February 5, 1895)

This poem seems to inaugurate a second phase in Thérèse's poetic work (cf. General Introduction). A certain majesty of tone—the ten-syllable meter [in French] is perhaps the reason—ushers in Thérèse's great poems, although the last stanzas of this one are weaker than the first. If Jesus' reply in sts. 5 and 6 is, on the whole, mediocre, Thérèse's hopes and experience are strong. And the road Céline is taking (for it is she who is supposed to be expressing herself here) is lightened and ennobled because of it.

On February 5, 1895, less than five months after she entered Carmel, Céline received the habit. For the address on that occasion, Thérèse suggested to Abbé Ducellier, a friend of the family, a Biblical theme: "The winter is past, the rains are over and gone, arise, my beloved, and come" (Song 2:10–11). She even proposed this rough sketch to the orator: Before being able to answer the divine call heard long before, Céline, "like the Spouse of the Song of Songs," had to "go through winter, the winter of suffering." That winter was, above all, the humiliating ordeal of Monsieur Martin. "He had offered himself in sacrifice. God judged the victim worthy of Himself." And the congregation was invited to review in the light of faith the events of recent years (1889–1894), which were well-known to Monsieur Martin's friends. Céline had remained at her "post of devotion, for entire years, night and day, until his last sigh." In this way, she prepared herself for the "life of devotion and sacrifice of the daughters of Saint Teresa." But today, the long-desired time had finally come to surrender to the voice of her Beloved.

That is essentially what Thérèse's poem celebrates: gratitude for "the inexpressible grace of having suffered," for "the new season" that was beginning, and for the "immense joy" of having been chosen by love.

For Thérèse even more than for her sister, "a new horizon" was being revealed. A little before, she had begun to write down her childhood memories, which would become *Story of a Soul*. She had stated: "I find myself at a period in my life when I can cast a glance upon the past; my soul has matured in the crucible of exterior and interior trials. And now, like a flower strengthened by the storm, I can raise my head.... It is with great happiness, then, that I come to sing the mercies of the Lord with you, dear Mother" (SS, p. 15).

Two weeks before Céline's clothing, Thérèse—in the role of Joan of Arc dying at the stake—heard the voice of Our Lord:

> O my beloved Sister! Your sweet voice calls me
> And I break the bonds that chain you to this place.

Ah! fly to me, my very beautiful dove.
Come, the winter has passed... Come reign in Heaven.
(RP 3, 1/21/1895)

This call resonated deeply in Thérèse's heart. After groping along in the darkness during 1894 (GCII, p. 857), "at last day is going to take the place of night," the great day of Love. "Living on Love," written three weeks later, was like the glorious sunrise that reached its zenith in the blazing feast of the Trinity (June 9, 1895), when she made her offering to Merciful Love.

And perhaps that "day," for Thérèse, would soon be the day of eternity. She had been ill for a year now. She knew she was "very close to Heaven"....

This is a very serious song, in the shadow of the cross (sts. 1, 2, 3), but transfigured by hope (sts. 4, 5, 6). This is a song of spring.

Song of Gratitude of Jesus' Fiancée

(melody: "Oh! saint Autel")

1   You have hidden me forever in your Face!...
Divine Jesus, deign to hear my voice.
I have come to sing the inexpressible grace
Of having suffered... of having born the Cross...

2   For a long time I have drunk from the chalice of tears.
I have shared your cup of sorrows,
And I have understood that suffering has its charms,
That by the Cross we save sinners.

3   It is by the Cross that my ennobled soul
Has seen a new horizon revealed.
Under the rays of your Blessed Face,
My weak heart has been raised up very high.

4   My Beloved, your sweet voice calls me:
"Come," you said to me, "already the winter has fled.
A new season is beginning for you.
At last day is taking the place of night.

5   Raise your eyes to your Holy Homeland,
       And on thrones of honor you will see
       A beloved Father... a dear Mother
       To whom you owe your immense happiness!...

6   Your life will pass like an instant.
       On Carmel we are very near Heaven.
       My beloved, my love has chosen you.
       I have reserved a glorious throne for you!...."

PN 17 – Living on Love!

(February 26, 1895)

We cannot help but be struck by the solemn fervor of this love poem—rich, profound, and great. This is no literary trifle, no "madrigal" to God, but rather a declaration that takes in the whole breadth of the love of God, just as one considers all the consequences of an act before making a serious decision. "Living on love — Dying of love" is at the heart of this great meditation, written just when Thérèse was really certain of her approaching death. This is also the period when she had begun her autobiography, a very special vantage point for the past, the present, and the future. That Thérèse should write such a poem *spontaneously* is significant.

She speaks "without parable" in at least ten of the fifteen stanzas. There are fewer symbolic images than in other poems. Her ideas and insights get the better of the poetry now and then, or at least the theological thought is so strong that it is embodied with more difficulty in poetic form. In this case, Thérèse forces it or does without it.

Her way of beginning each stanza is perhaps monotonous: "Living on Love *is*" weighs down the poem. (Twelve of the fifteen stanzas begin with "is" or "is not.") No doubt Thérèse had to sacrifice to the style of her day, when romances would use and abuse a leitmotif. She is also bound by her objective: a "catechism" of love, which multiplies definitions and descriptions. We find this enumerative method in other poems (PN 32 and PN 45, for example). Key words stay in our minds and characterize most of the stanzas. The beautiful ways she invokes Jesus (for example, 2, 2 and 7; 3, 2; 6, 5; 8, 3; 11, 3, etc.) also testify to Thérèse's lyric emotions at the time she composed the poem. This can be felt in the beat of these concentrated, burning verses. Moreover, her lyric state of mind is confirmed in a letter she wrote the same week: During the Lent that was beginning, she wrote, "I shall content myself with following Jesus on his painful way, I shall hang up my harp on the willows of the shores of the rivers of Babylon," etc. (GCII, p. 899, 2/24/1895).

Thérèse's opening line, "On the evening of Love," has a great and daring beauty, like an opening stroke of a cello. With it, without any explanation, we break through time and space. This is truly "*the* great evening of Love." And that gives all the more power to "speaking without parable." Already in just one verse, we are face to face with Love.

The boldness of st. 2 is no less startling: In eight verses, beginning with the "uncreated Word," Thérèse takes the Trinity prisoner! This boldness of thought is strengthened in st. 3, where Jesus and Thérèse exchange the language of "lovers."

But such daring is not presumptuous or frivolous, as st. 4 shows, when the blazing image of Tabor sobers down in the image of Calvary. This is a beautiful poetic transposition of the Transfiguration, where Jesus's glory suddenly disappears and he announces his passion.

This is the first turning point in the poem: After the vision of victorious glory and utter happiness in the first twenty-four verses, the shift from Tabor to Calvary reveals the suffering, struggling side of this vision. But Thérèse does not dwell on sorrow: The Cross is a treasure, and exile and suffering are inherent to the human condition of living on love.

This total offering of self makes her burdens light: "I run," she says, like Saint Paul or the Bride in the Song of Songs. Love casts out all fear and consumes every fault (st. 6). Weakness is blessed, for it brings down grace (st. 7). Love radiates all around—with that curious image of the boat, unexpected here, but preparing us for st. 9. Perhaps this eighth stanza brings the second turning point of the poem, when images come in to refresh the dryness of the preceding "catechism."

Strong in faith, hope, and love, in st. 9 our daring Thérèse now completely turns around the Gospel story of the calming of the stormy sea. No, she will not wake up Jesus, as hard as the storm may blow. And in the future she will never go back on her word (cf. PN 24, 32, 42).

This life of love urges her to pray for priests and the Church (st. 10)—one of the great missions of the Carmelite nun—and for sinners (sts. 11), in whose repentance she shares, like Mary Magdalene (beginning of st. 12).

The broken jar (herself, cf. 7, 2) symbolizes her death of love and directly introduces sts. 13 and 14. Here we have a strong structure of images, with the image of perfume wafting all through st. 13: This stanza is about the "folly" of love, which calls for a total gift of self, with dying of love as its logical conclusion...

As *sweet* as it may be, the "martyrdom" of love is no less a martyrdom. Thérèse knows that this is the indispensable condition on the road to God (cf. PN 3)—for her, just as for Christ (cf. PN 31). While waiting to be thus consumed, she who was so light just a moment ago (st. 5) once again finds the "burden" of life "so heavy" (14, 6).

In the last stanza, between "dying of love" and "living on love," Thérèse gathers together her whole poem as in a bouquet—the glory and the suffering.

"Living on Love" sprang from just one flow of inspiration during Thérèse's long adoration in choir before the Blessed Sacrament, which was exposed for the three days of the Forty Hours services (Sunday, Monday, and Tuesday before Ash Wednesday, 1895). The atmosphere of those fervent hours was very much like that of a vigil on Holy Thursday. We also know from a secret Thérèse shared when she was in the infirmary that during those three days the image of the Holy Face was very much present to her heart and brought tears of love to her eyes (HLC, p. 134, #7). It was only during the evening of Tuesday, February 26 (Mardi Gras) that she wrote down from memory the fourteen stanzas she had composed without any "rough draft" during the day. (Stanza 4 was added later at Sister Geneviève's request.[1])

One night two and a half years later when she was in the infirmary and could not sleep (a few days before July 16, 1897), she "very easily" wrote a sixteenth stanza: "You who know my extreme littleness" (PS 8). The Sisters sang it, along with part of "Living on Love," for Thérèse as she received Communion on the feast of Our Lady of Mount Carmel (GCII, p. 1146).

This literary sketch of the poem is only the groundwork for a real spiritual commentary, but such a study would go beyond the scope of our work. Besides, each generation of Thérèse's disciples has been devoted to this poem and has deepened its meaning. It would take many more generations still to exhaust the vitality of this poem, which Sister Geneviève thought would always be the "king" among her sister's compositions.[2]

---

[1] Sister Geneviève said many times that she was responsible for st. 4: "When Thérèse had written her Canticle 'Living on Love,' she brought it to me. 'It is beautiful,' I said, 'but it is incomplete. You should add a stanza on this subject: *Living on Love is not setting up one's tent at the top of Tabor...*'" (Letter to Fr. Piat, 6/24/1949) in *Poésies*, vol. II, p. 109.

[2] CGII, p. 1160.

(Melody of the cant. - "Il est à moi")

Living on Love!...

1   On the evening of Love, speaking without parable,
Jesus said: "If anyone wishes to love me
All his life, let him keep my Word.
My Father and I will come to visit him.
And we will make his heart our dwelling.
Coming to him, we shall love him always.
We want him to remain, filled with peace,
    In our Love!...."

2   Living on Love is holding You Yourself.
Uncreated Word, Word of my God,
Ah! Divine Jesus, you know I love you.
The Spirit of Love sets me aflame with his fire.

In loving you I attract the Father.
My weak heart holds him forever.
O Trinity! You are Prisoner
          Of my Love!...

3   Living on Love is living on your life,
Glorious King, delight of the elect.
You live for me, hidden in a host.
I want to hide myself for you, O Jesus!
Lovers must have solitude,
A heart-to-heart lasting night and day.
Just one glance of yours makes my beatitude.
          I live on Love!...

4   Living on Love is not setting up one's tent
At the top of Tabor.
It's climbing Calvary with Jesus,
It's looking at the Cross as a treasure!...
In Heaven I'm to live on joy.
Then trials will have fled forever,
But in exile, in suffering I want
          To live on Love.

5   Living on Love is giving without limit
Without claiming any wages here below.
Ah! I give without counting, truly sure
That when one loves, one does not keep count!...
Overflowing with tenderness, I have given everything,
To his Divine Heart.... lightly I run.
I have nothing left but my only wealth:
          Living on Love.

6   Living on Love is banishing every fear,
Every memory of past faults.
I see no imprint of my sins.
In a moment love has burned everything.....
Divine Flame, O very sweet Blaze!
I make my home in your hearth.
In your fire I gladly sing:
          "I live on Love!..."

7   Living on Love is keeping within oneself
    A great treasure in an earthen vase.
    My Beloved, my weakness is extreme.
    Ah, I'm far from being an angel from heaven!...
    But if I fall with each passing hour,
    You come to my aid, lifting me up.
    At each moment you give me your grace:
            I live on Love.

8   Living on Love is sailing unceasingly,
    Sowing peace and joy in every heart.
    Beloved Pilot, Charity impels me,
    For I see you in my sister souls.
    Charity is my only star.
    In its brightness I sail straight ahead.
    I've my motto written on my sail:
            "Living on Love."

9   Living on Love, when Jesus is sleeping,
    Is rest on stormy seas.
    Oh! Lord, don't fear that I'll wake you.
    I'm waiting in peace for Heaven's shore....
    Faith will soon tear its veil.
    My hope is to see you one day.
    Charity swells and pushes my sail:
            I live on Love!...

10 Living on Love, O my Divine Master,
    Is begging you to spread your Fire
    In the holy, sacred soul of your Priest.
    May he be purer than a seraphim in Heaven!...
    Ah! glorify your Immortal Church!
    Jesus, do not be deaf to my sighs.
    I, her child, sacrifice myself for her,
            I live on Love.

11 Living on Love is wiping your Face,
    It's obtaining the pardon of sinners.
    O God of Love! may they return to your grace,
    And may they forever bless your Name.....
    Even in my heart the blasphemy resounds.

To efface it, I always want to sing:
"I adore and love your Sacred Name.
            I live on Love!..."

12   Living on Love is imitating Mary,
Bathing your divine feet that she kisses, transported.
With tears, with precious perfume,
She dries them with her long hair...
Then standing up, she shatters the vase,
And in turn she anoints your Sweet Face.
As for me, the perfume with which I anoint your Face
            Is my Love!....

13   "Living on Love, what strange folly!"
The world says to me, "Ah! stop your singing,
Don't waste your perfumes, your life.
Learn to use them well..."
Loving you, Jesus, is such a fruitful loss!...
All my perfumes are yours forever.
I want to sing on leaving this world:
            "I'm dying of Love!"

14   Dying of Love is a truly sweet martyrdom,
And that is the one I wish to suffer.
O Cherubim! Tune your lyre,
For I sense my exile is about to end!...
Flame of Love, consume me unceasingly.
Life of an instant, your burden is so heavy to me!
Divine Jesus, make my dream come true:
            To die of Love!...

15   Dying of Love is what I hope for.
When I shall see my bonds broken,
My God will be my Great Reward.
I don't desire to possess other goods.
I want to be set on fire with his Love.
I want to see Him, to unite myself to Him forever.
That is my Heaven... that is my destiny:
            Living on Love!!!.....

1. Sr. Thérèse of the Child Jesus (Thérèse Martin) 2. Sr. Marie of the Sacred Heart (Marie Martin) 3. Mother Agnes of Jesus (Pauline Martin)
4. Sr. Geneviève of the Holy Face (Céline Martin) 6. Mother Marie de Gonzague 7. Sr. St. Stanislaus of the Sacred Hearts 8. Mother Hermance of the Heart of Jesus 9. Sr. Marie of the Angels and of the Sacred Heart
11. Sr. St. John the Baptist of the Heart of Jesus 13. Sr. Teresa of Jesus of the Heart of Mary 14. Sr. Marguerite Marie of the Sacred Heart of Jesus
15. Sr. Teresa of St. Augustine 17. Sr. Marie Emmanuel 18. Sr. Marie of St. Joseph 19. Sr. Marie of Jesus 20. Sr. Marie Philomena of Jesus
21. Sr. Marie of the Trinity 22. Sr. Anne of the Sacred Heart
23. Sr. Marie of the Incarnation 24. Sr. St. Vincent de Paul 25. Sr. Martha of Jesus 26. Sr. Marie-Madeleine of the Blessed Sacrament

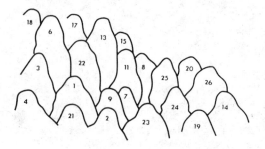

1. Sr. Thérèse of the Child Jesus (Thérèse Martin) 2. Sr. Marie of the Sacred Heart (Marie Martin) 3. Mother Agnes of Jesus (Pauline Martin)
4. Sr. Geneviève of the Holy Face (Céline Martin) 6. Mother Marie de Gonzague 7. Sr. St. Stanislaus of the Sacred Hearts 8. Mother Hermance of the Heart of Jesus 9. Sr. Marie of the Angels and of the Sacred Heart
11. Sr. St. John the Baptist of the Heart of Jesus 13. Sr. Teresa of Jesus of the Heart of Mary 14. Sr. Marguerite Marie of the Sacred Heart of Jesus
15. Sr. Teresa of St. Augustine 17. Sr. Marie Emmanuel 18. Sr. Marie of St. Joseph 19. Sr. Marie of Jesus
21. Sr. Marie of the Trinity
22. Sr. Anne of the Sacred Heart
23. Sr. Marie of the Incarnation
24. Sr. St. Vincent de Paul
25. Sr. Martha of Jesus
26. Sr. Marie-Madeleine
of the Blessed Sacrament

PN 18 – The Canticle of Céline

("What I Loved" April 28, 1895)

This is Thérèse's "canticle of creatures" even more than Céline's. Like the canticle of the three young Hebrew men in the fiery furnace or the one St. Francis of Assisi composed in his hut, the song of this voluntary "prisoner" of Carmel (st. 32) is the song of someone set free by Love.

After rising to the heights in the beautiful preceding poem, here we come back down to the meadows of Normandy. In the freshness of childhood rediscovered, Thérèse joyfully makes an inventory of the many riches of creation that enchanted her early years. She freely gave them up, without any disdain. Now she finds them all again, transformed, in her Beloved.

This symphony of flowers, perfumes, greenery, and birds was written to orchestrate two verses that Céline wrote one Sunday in March 1895. That day, as she was getting ready to pick one of the first snowdrop flowers in the cloister garden, Thérèse stopped her: "You must ask for permission!" Subjugation pushed to that degree grieved the novice. Back in her cell, Céline tried to find consolation by reminding Jesus in a poem of all that she had given up for Him. But the muse, who was never favorable to her, disappointed her this time too. Only these words broke through her sadness:

> The flower that I pick, O my King,
> Is You!

Learning that Céline had been disappointed twice over, Thérèse came to her aid. With the sure instinct of a spiritual mother, she made sure that nothing was overshadowed by joys from the past. Sister Geneviève said, "While she was writing this poem, she often came to me to ask my advice about what I wanted, if we had left anything out, if it was really complete" (CMG IV, p. 356). Thérèse's concern to satisfy Céline led her to stretch out her poem unnecessarily. It is the longest in her repertoire—in terms of the number of stanzas (fifty-five). What was important for her was that *everything* be vigorously taken into account so that no hint of nostalgia would remain.

"He who has Jesus has everything." Thérèse's personal certitude of this is akin to the mystical experience sung by Saint John of the Cross in *The Spiritual Canticle* (sts. 13–14).[1]

> My Beloved, the mountains,
> and lonely wooded valleys,
> strange islands,

and resounding rivers,
the whistling of love-stirring breezes,
the tranquil night
at the time of the rising dawn,
silent music,
sounding solitude,
the supper that refreshes and deepens love.

Although John of the Cross interprets these familiar words allegorically, Thérèse generally stays close to their literal meaning. These are really her and Céline's common memories of childhood and adolescence that she is referring to here.

This poem—about love, family, and especially nature—is divided into two main parts: before entering Carmel (sts. 1–31) and "now" (sts. 32–55). The first part in turn takes in several segments of time: in Alençon (1–9), at Les Buissonnets (10–18), and the years Céline devoted to her father (19–31). The second half, dealing with life in Carmel, details all that one discovers or rediscovers in Jesus about the charms of nature, but now purified. Then it focuses our attention on his Person, which we find even here on earth in love (st. 50, admirable for its images, strength, movement—perhaps the most beautiful stanza in the poem—and st. 51) and will contemplate "soon" in Heaven (52–55).

We can see a possibility of sisterly emulation in Thérèse's evoking so many memories at the very time when she was writing the first pages of *Story of a Soul.* It is interesting to observe on the two very crossed-out rough drafts for this poem in what order the images of the past come back to her.

Sister Geneviève testified to the spontaneity of this poem and the precarious way it unfolded: "While she was writing 'The Canticle of Céline' ('What I Loved'), one day while we were working in the laundry, she composed some verses on 'the Knight.' She hummed them for me, but since we didn't have anything to write them down on and since it was work time, and since I was wondering if that was too personal to be in this Canticle, we left them out. I really regret that now."[2]

A revised draft of the poem was completed for Céline's twenty-sixth birthday on April 28, 1895. In March of 1897, Thérèse chose ten stanzas from it to present to Abbé Bellière (cf. PN 18a). In May of 1897 she made a few more corrections and revised the order of several stanzas, indicating the importance she attached to this poem. The text with her final corrections is the one we present here.

The melody Thérèse chose to accompany the poem, "Combien j'ai douce souvenance!" ["How I've sweet recollections"] was a favorite of Monsieur Martin. His daughters never forgot the feeling he put into the verses, "Ah! who will bring back my Hélène to me?" He had never gotten over the loss of his little girl by that name, who had died at five and a half [on 2/22/1870]. Unfortunately, Thérèse had to use a few "acrobatics" to adapt her poem to this melody—especially the third line of each stanza!

Using the same tune, Sister Agnes of Jesus had written a canticle "To the Holy Face" in 1891. In spite of some similarities of style, the aim of the two compositions is clearly different.

Bringing back the authentic text (which the first version of *Story of a Soul* had cut down from 55 stanzas to 51 and retouched in about 30 places) will promote the investigation of a theme that has already attracted many writers: Thérèse's relationship with creation.

¹ Saint John of the Cross, *The Collected Works of St. John of the Cross,* trans. Kieran Kavanaugh, O.C.D., and Otílio Rodriguez, O.C.D. (Washington: Institute of Carmelite Studies, 1991), p. 46.
² Letter to Mother Agnes of Jesus, 3/17/1936, quoted in *Vie Thérésienne,* no. 62, 155.

The Canticle of Céline

1   Oh! how I love the memory of
The blessed days of my childhood....
To protect the flower of my innocence
The Lord always surrounded me
With love!....

2   Also, despite my littleness
I was truly filled with tenderness,
And the promise slipped from my heart
To wed the King of the elect,
Jesus!...

3   In the springtime of my life I loved
Saint Joseph, the Virgin Mary.
Already my soul was immersed, enthralled,
When the Heavens were reflected
In my eyes!...

4   I loved the wheat fields, the plains.
I loved the distant hills.
Oh! in my joy I could scarcely breathe
As I gathered flowers
With my sisters.

5   I loved to pick the short grass,
             Corn-flowers... all the little flowers.
        I found the smell of violets,
             And especially the cowslips,
                  So sweet...

6   I loved the white daisy,
             The walks on Sundays,
        The little birds singing on the branches,
             And the ever-radiant blue
                  Of the Heavens.

7   Each year I loved to put
             My shoe in the chimney.
        Rushing down as soon as I was awake
             I would sing of the feast of Heaven,
                  Christmas!...

8   I loved Mama's smile.
             Her deep gaze seemed to say:
        "Eternity overwhelms me and attracts me.
             I'm going to go up in the blue Sky
                  To see God!

9   "In our Homeland I'll find
             My Angels... the Virgin Mary.
        I shall offer the tears, the hearts
             Of my children whom I leave on earth
                  To Jesus!..."

10   Oh! how I loved Jesus in the Host,
             Who came to betroth himself to my enchanted soul
        In the morning of my life.
             Oh! how I opened my heart
                  With happiness!....

11   Later I loved the creature
             Who seemed pure to me.
        Seeking the God of nature everywhere,
             In *Him* I found peace
                  Forever!...

12   Oh! in the belvedere
             Flooded with joy and light,

How I loved receiving my Father's caresses,
   Gazing upon his hair,
     White and snowy...

13   Sitting on his lap
     With Thérèse in the evening,
I remember being rocked for a long time.
    I still hear the echo
     Of his sweet song.

14   O memory! You give me rest.
     You remind me of so many things....
Supper in the evening... the smell of roses!...
    Les Buissonnets full of glee
     In the summer!.....

15   I used to love being able to blend
     My soul with Thérèse's.
The moment the sun was going down,
    I was just one heart
     With my sister...

16   Then our voices blended,
     Our hands intertwined.
Together we sang of Sacred Nuptials.
    Already we were dreaming of Carmel....
     Of Heaven!....

17   The blue skies, the golden fruit
     In Switzerland and Italy delighted me.
I especially loved the lively way
    The Holy Old Pontiff-King
     Looked at me....

18   Holy ground of the Coliseum,
     I kissed you with love!...
The sacred vaults of the catacombs
    Very sweetly echoed
     My song.

19   After joy came tears!...
     So great was my alarm...
I put on the weapons of my Spouse,
    And his Cross became my support,
     My wealth.....

20   Ah! for a long time I was exiled,
            Deprived of my beloved family.
    Poor wounded doe, I only had
            The flowering eglantine
                    For refuge!.......

21   But one evening my tender soul
            Saw Mary's smile,
    And one blessed drop of her blood
            Changed (what a favor!) into milk
                    For me!....

22   Then I loved, while fleeing the world,
            To hear the faraway echo answer me!...
    In the solitary, fertile valley,
            I gathered flowers
                    Through my tears!...

23   I loved to hear the faint bell
            Of the faraway church.
    I loved to sit in the fields
            To hear the sighs of the breeze
                    In the evening.

24   I loved the swallows' flight,
            The plaintive song of the turtledoves.
    I listened to the sound of the insects' wings,
            Loving the song
                    Of their buzzing.

25   I loved the morning dew
            And the graceful cicada.
    I loved to see the virginal bee
            Making honey
                    As soon as she awoke.

26   I loved to pick the heather
            Running on the thin moss.
    I caught butterflies fluttering on the ferns
            With pure reflection
                    Of blue.

27   I loved the fire-fly glittering in the shadow.
            I loved the stars beyond counting.

Above all I loved the moon beam
With its bright silver disk
Shining in the dark blue sky.

28   I loved to overwhelm with affection
My little Father in his old age.
He was everything to me... happiness... child... wealth!
Ah! I often kissed him
Tenderly.

29   We loved the soft sound of the waves.
Hearing the roaring storm
In the evening in deep solitude,
The voice of the nightingale
Deep in the woods!

30   But one morning his fair face
Searched for the image of the Crucifix.
He left me the pledge of his love,
Giving me his Last Look....
"My share!......."

31   And Jesus' divine hand
Took Céline's only treasure,
And taking it ever so far from the hill,
Placed it near the Eternal One
In Heaven!...

32   Now I am a prisoner.
I have fled the groves of earth.
I have seen that all is passing there.
I have seen my happiness fade
And die!..............

33   Beneath my steps the grass has been crushed.
The flower in my hands has withered.
Jesus, I want to run in your meadow
My steps won't leave a trace
On it.....

34   As a stag in its ardent thirst
Longs for running springs,
O Jesus! I run, faltering, to you.
To calm my fervor I must have
Your tears!...

35   It's your love alone that transports me.
            I leave my flock on the plain.[1]
      I don't take the trouble to tend it.
            I only want to please my one
                  New Lamb.

36   Jesus, you are the Lamb I love.
            You are all I need, O supreme good!
      In you I have everything, the earth and even Heaven.
            The Flower that I pick, O my King,
                  Is You!...

37   Jesus, fair lily of the valley,
            Your sweet perfume has captivated me.
      Bouquet of myrrh, O sweet-smelling corolla!
            I want to keep you on my heart
                  To love you...

38   Your love always goes with me.
            In you, I've the forests, the countryside.
      I've the reeds, the meadows, the mountains,
            The rain and the snowflakes
                  From Heaven.

39   In you, Jesus, I have everything.
            I've the wheat, the half-closed flowers,
      Forget-me-nots, buttercups, beautiful roses.
            I've the freshness, the smell
                  Of the white lily of the valley.

40   I've the melodious lyre,
            Sounding solitude,
      Rivers, rocks, gracious waterfalls,
            Nimble deer, gazelle, squirrel,
                  Roe-deer.

41   I've the rainbow, pure snow,
            The vast horizon, greenery,
      Distant islands... The ripe harvest,
            Butterflies, the bright springtime,
                  The fields.

42   In your love I further find
            The sun-gilded palm trees,

Night like the sunrise,
    The sweet babbling of the brook,
      The bird.

43   I've delicious grapes,
      Graceful dragonflies,
The virgin forest with its mysterious flowers,
    I've all the little blond children,
      Their songs.

44   In you, I've springs and hills,
      Liana vines, periwinkles, hawthorn,
Fresh water lilies, honeysuckle, eglantine,
    The slight rustling of the light
      Poplar.

45   I've the trembling wild oats,
      The solemn, powerful voice of the winds,
The gossamer, the ardent flame,
    The gentle breeze, bushes in bloom,
      Bird nests.

46   I've the beautiful lake, I've the valley,
      Lonely and all-wooded.
I've the ocean's silvery wave,
    Golden fish, diverse treasures
      Of the seas.

47   I've the ship slipping away from the beach,
      The golden wake and the shore,
I've the lights of the sun decorating the cloud
    As it disappears
      From the sky.

48   In you, I've the pure dove.
      In you, under my coarse habit
I find ring, necklaces, and jewelry,
    Gems, pearls and brilliant
      Diamonds.

49   In you I've the brilliant star,
      Often your love is unveiled;
And when the day is drawing to a close,
    I perceive your hand
      As through a veil.

50   You whose hand upholds the spheres,
            Who plant the deep forests,
      You who at a mere glance make them fertile,
            You always watch over me
                  With a look of love.

51   I've your Heart, your adored Face,
            Your sweet look that has wounded me.
      I've the kiss of your sacred mouth.
            I love you and want nothing more,
                  Jesus.

52   With the angels I'll go to sing
            The praises of sacred love.
      Make me fly soon in their processions.
            O Jesus! may I die one day
                  Of love!....

53   Drawn to the gentle flame,
            The moth flies and catches on fire.
      So your love draws my soul.
            In it I want to fly,
                  To burn!....

54   My God, I already hear
            Your eternal feast being prepared.......
      Taking my silent harp from the willows,
            I'm going to sit on your lap
                  To see You!...

55   Close by You, I'm going to see Mary....
            The Saints.... my dear family!...
      After this life's exile I'll go
            To see my Father's house again
                  In Heaven!.......

[1] [In French, the word "troupeau" can mean "herd" or "flock." In the Kavanaugh/
Rodriguez English translation of "The Spiritual Canticle," the word used is "herd."
But in the context of Thérèse's poem, we can only translate "troupeau" as "flock"–
Trans.]

PN 18A – He Who Has Jesus Has Everything
(March 1897)

After copying seventeen of her poems for Abbé Bellière in March of 1897, Thérèse came to page twenty-four in her notebook. She had half a page left over: just enough to copy, in two columns, ten stanzas of "The Canticle of Céline."[1] This is an excellent, very concentrated synthesis that keeps just the essential and often the best part of the original. This "fragment"—as the official "Copy of the Writings" at the Beatification Process called it[2]—really becomes another poem. And it is Thérèse's last version. So we publish it as an independent piece.

Thérèse's choice of stanzas is a testimony to her delicate sense of the seminarian's spiritual needs at this time.

The first verse (a rewriting of 32, 1) seems to have a negative meaning, like Ecclesiastes: "Vanity of vanities..." But Thérèse had noticed in her brother's letters that he was still susceptible to the seductions of the world. She had to help him, by the power of her example, to break those attachments.

Her choice of the fifth stanza (= 41) must have been inspired by the missionary resonance verse 3 could suggest: "distant islands... ripe harvest."

In copying the sixth stanza (= 47), Thérèse remembered that Maurice Bellière lived on the beach at Langrune [in Normandy]. Soon he would set sail for Africa [to enter the novitiate of the White Fathers in Algiers].

She will refer to the "look of love" of the seventh stanza (= 50) in a future letter, deliberately underlining the phrase (GCII, p. 1133).

The stanza about the moth (= 53) was only too well-suited to a fickle young man who was inclined to let his wings be burned by false lights before "returning to the real and gentle light of Love" (SS, p. 83).

But Thérèse could not suspect how much she would touch sensitive feelings when she represented "the eternal feast" of heaven as a family reunion. Maurice missed his "father's house" all his life.

All through the notebook Thérèse made for her first missionary brother, we find a remarkable illustration of her desire to "do good for souls" through her poetry (SS, p. 175).

[1] Sts. 32, 33, 35, 36, 41, 47, 50, 53, 54, 55. Note the variants in sts. 32, 41, and 54.
[2] For the diocesan "Ordinary" Process (1910). The sixth stanza was omitted from this text.

Several thoughts are taken from the
spiritual cant. of St. J. of the +

(Melody: "Combien j'ai douce souvenance")

He Who Has Jesus Has Everything

1
        Scorning earthly joys,
        I've become a prisoner.
  I've seen that all pleasures are passing.
        You are my only joy,
            Lord!...

2
        Beneath my feet the grass has been crushed.
        The flower in my hand has withered!...
 Jesus, I want to run in your meadow.
        My steps won't leave a trace
            On it!...

3
        It's your love alone that transports me.
        I leave my flock on the plain.
 I don't take the trouble to tend it.
        I just want to please my one
            New Lamb.

4
        Jesus, you are the Lamb I love.
        You are all I need, O supreme good!
 In you I have everything, the earth and even Heaven.
        The Flower that I pick, O my King!
            Is You!...

5
        In you, I've the beauty of nature.
        I've the rainbow, pure snow,
 Distant islands, the ripe harvest,
        Butterflies, the bright springtime,
            The fields.

6
        I've the ship slipping away from the beach,
        The golden wake and the shore,
 I've the sun decorating the cloud
        As it disappears
            From the sky.

7   You whose hand upholds the spheres,
            Who plant the deep forests,
      You who at a mere glance make them fertile,
            You always watch over me
                  With a look of Love!....

8   Drawn to the gentle flame,
            The moth flies and catches on fire.
      So your love draws my soul.
            In it I want to fly,
                  To burn!...

9   My God, I already hear
            Your eternal feast being prepared.
      Taking my silent harp from the willows,
            I'm going to sit down near you,
                  To see You.

10   With You, I'll see Mary,
            The Saints, my dear family...
      After this life's exile I'll go
            To see my Father's house again
                  In Heaven!...

N.B. PN 23, "To the Sacred Heart of Jesus," could be read
here if it was dated June 21, 1895.

PN 19 – The Atom of Jesus-Host

(summer 1895?)

"Who of us doesn't remember our good Sister Saint Vincent de Paul prostrate at the Communion grille during the whole hour of silence in the evening?" (Death Notice, p. 4). In that particularly dark corner of the choir, but as close as possible to the tabernacle in the chapel, the "atom" whom we have already met (PN 15) loved to "hide in the shadows." Love of the Eucharist was one of the major themes of the four poems that Sister Saint Vincent de Paul requested of Thérèse (PN 15, 19, 25, 32).

We are not sure that Thérèse really felt at ease with the "thoughts" of this "client." Of course people then did not know about the energy concealed in the atom—this discovery would have fascinated Thérèse, who was so dynamic. The "speck of dust," synonymous with the atom in Sister Saint Vincent de Paul's mind, would have hardly fostered poetic inspiration! For Thérèse, dust was too associated with fragility and death.

The date we have proposed for this poem is approximate.

In any case, this is second-rate poetry that we will quickly pass over.

The Atom of Jesus-Host

(Thoughts of Sr. St. Vincent de Paul put into verse at her request.)

1   I am just a speck of dust,
But I want to make my dwelling
In the shadow of the sanctuary
With the Prisoner of Love.
Ah! my soul longs for the host.
I love him and want nothing more.
It is the hidden God who attracts me.
I am the atom of Jesus.....

2   I want to stay not knowing,
In forgetfulness of all created things,
And by my silence console
The Host of the sacred ciborium.
Oh! I would like to save souls,
And make elect from sinners.
Give the flames of an apostle
To your atom, sweet Jesus!....

3   If I am despised by the world,
     If it considers me as nothing,
     A divine peace floods me.
     For I have the host as my support.
     When I draw near the ciborium,
     All my sighs are heard...
     To be nothing is my glory.
     I am the atom of Jesus....

4   Sometimes when Heaven is overcast
     And this atom cannot take flight,
     It loves to hide in the shadow
     And attach itself to the golden door.
     Then the Divine light,
     Which makes all the elect rejoice,
     Comes to earth to warm up
     This poor atom of Jesus...

5   Under the warm rays of grace,
     The atom sparkles.
     When the light breeze passes by,
     It gently sways...
     Oh! what ineffable delight!
     What favors has it not received?...
     Right next to the host slips
     The poor atom of Jesus.....

6   Pining away near the host
     In the tabernacle of love,
     Thus my life will be spent
     While waiting for the last day.
     When our trials will be over,
     Flying to the dwelling of the elect,
     The atom of the Eucharist
     Will shine near her Jesus!...

Melody: "Par les chants les plus magnifiques"

PN 20 – My Heaven on Earth
(Canticle to the Holy Face, August 12, 1895)

In the radiance of Mount Tabor the day after the feast of the Trans-figuration, this poem presents an outpouring of emotions from someone seduced by the Face of God. As on the holy mountain in the Gospels, here the "sorrows" of the Passion are evoked, but only to be immediately "embellished" and bathed in *sweetness*. In the middle of the summer of 1895, this poem is like an anticipation of the *Face to face* that Thérèse invoked a few weeks earlier in her Act of Oblation to Merciful Love (SS, p. 276). The title expresses this in no uncertain terms: "My Heaven on Earth." And this beautiful verse says it again:

> Your Face is my only Homeland.

This is already "the peace of Heaven."

The recipient of this poem, Marie Agnes of the Holy Face (soon to be Marie of the Trinity) testified: "Sr. Thérèse of the Child Jesus had a very special devotion to the adorable Face of Jesus, and she saw in It a mirror of the humiliations and sufferings of Jesus in his Passion. The sight of this divine Face kindled in her soul a passionate desire to resemble Him, as she put it to me" [See *Procès de Béatification et Canonisation II* (Procès Apostolique), p. 468]. Elsewhere Sr. Marie emphasized Thérèse's need, arising from the contemplation of his Face, to imitate and *resemble* Jesus (rather than to make reparation, as was the case for Sr. Marie of Saint Peter of the Carmel of Tours [see PN 1, note 2]). That is what the prayer expressed that Thérèse wrote a short time later and that she wore day and night over her heart: "Make me resemble you, Jesus!"

But we should not expect to find the entire wealth of this theme for Thérèse in this one composition, titled "Canticle to the Holy Face" in the 1898 edition of *Story of a Soul*. Other writings of hers complement it (such as RP 2, "The Angels at the Crib of Jesus," which centers entirely on the joyous, sorrowful and glorious characteristics of the Face of Jesus). *Her Last Conversations* also offers important information (for example, p. 135, #9).

Poetically, this very tender song is not particularly original, though it does have a few evocative images and some very beautiful Christian antitheses that Thérèse was fond of. Yet this poem remains a secondary one, in spite of the real beauty of sts. 3 and 4 or the harmony of st. 5. No doubt it offers us a summary of numerous Theresian themes, but they are not really that inspiring here. In this composition Thérèse's writing remains one-dimensional, and her poetic craft is less developed than in certain earlier ones.

Offered to Marie of the Trinity for her twenty-first birthday, this poem is not especially personalized: There is no allusion to the concrete events that led this young sister to place herself under the sign of the Holy Face from her childhood. Thérèse wanted it to be more universal, a love song from every heart fascinated by the Face of light.

J.M.J.T.

(Melody: "Mignon sur la rive étrangère")

My Heaven on Earth!...

1   Jesus, your ineffable image
     Is the star that guides my steps.
     Ah! you know, your sweet Face
     Is for me Heaven on earth.
     My love discovers the charms
     Of your Face adorned with tears.
     I smile through my own tears
     When I contemplate your sorrows....

2   Oh! To console you I want
     To live unknown on earth!....
     Your beauty, which you know how to veil,
     Discloses for me all its mystery.
     I would like to fly away to you!....

3   Your Face is my only Homeland.
     It's my Kingdom of love.
     It's my cheerful Meadow,
     Each day, my sweet Sun.
     It's the Lily of the Valley
     Whose mysterious perfume
     Consoles my exiled soul,
     Making it taste the peace of Heaven.

4   It's my Rest, my Sweetness
     And my melodious Lyre....
     Your Face, O my sweet Savior,
     Is the Divine bouquet of Myrrh
     I want to keep on my heart!...

5   Your Face is my only wealth.
    I ask for nothing more.
    Hiding myself in it unceasingly,
    I will resemble you, Jesus....
    Leave in me the Divine impress
    Of your Features filled with sweetness,
    And soon I'll become holy.
    I shall draw hearts to you.

6   So that I may gather
    A beautiful golden harvest,
    Deign to set me aflame with your fire.
    With your adored Mouth,
    Give me soon the eternal Kiss!...

PN 21 – Canticle of a Soul
Having Found the Place of Its Rest
(August 15, 1895)

Thérèse composed three poems for her cousin Marie Guérin: The one we are going to read here was written for her entrance into Carmel, on the same day as her feast (August 15, 1895). "Jesus Alone" (PN 36) was written—once again for her feastday—in 1896, and "My Weapons" (PN 48) for her profession on March 25, 1897. There is a quite a distance between entering into the rest that the first canticle extols and the militant strength asserted in "My Weapons." This evolution can no doubt be explained by the progress Marie of the Eucharist made in fathoming the spirit of Teresa of Avila, who was so opposed to a life of rest. Even more, it lets us measure the distance our author herself traveled in nineteen months, for it is Thérèse's own itinerary that is reflected in these three compositions.

It was the custom for a new postulant to "sing something" for the community on the evening of her entrance. The choice of this simple piece was a good test for Marie in every respect: She was gifted with a beautiful soprano voice. Thérèse wanted to show it off to its advantage by choosing a romance she had adapted for the occasion. And this song expressed a spiritual plan of action for the new arrival. As always in such cases, Thérèse knew how to put herself in the place of those she was writing for so as to emphasize their own ideas and awaken their sensitivity. Nevertheless, the poems remain her own.

Although it was uncommon for Thérèse, this poem copied its model, the romance "Mignon," very closely, at least for the refrain. But Thérèse skillfully made the transposition from human love to mystical love.

Despite the title, supposedly about rest, a deep burst of feeling runs through this poem. When one drops anchor in Carmel, it is only a temporary port of call. It is impossible to forget the true goal of the crossing: "You have broken my bonds," "if I have left," "in this oasis," "I want to follow you," "soon I must follow you to the eternal shore." From one departure to the next, following Jesus only reaches its goal in the fullness of life that lasts "forever."

The common denominator between life in Carmel and life in Heaven is "love." And so on that same day Marie entered the monastery, Thérèse privately gave her cousin the poem "Living on Love" (PN 17) as a guide. She put a copy of it, surrounded by flowers, on Marie's bed. Marie died in the same little cell less than 10 years later saying, "Oh! how I would like to die of love!... of love for God.... My JESUS, I LOVE YOU!" (her last words, Death Notice, p. 18).

J.M.J.T.

(Melody: "Connais-tu le pays")

Canticle of a Soul Having Found the Place of Its Rest!...

1 O Jesus! on this day you have broken my bonds...
In the blessed Order of the Virgin Mary
I shall be able to find true wealth.
Lord, if I have left my dear family,
You will know how to heap heavenly favors on them,
And to me, you will give the pardon of sinners....

2   Jesus, in Carmel I want to live,
Since to this oasis your love has called me.
  It's there (repeat) that I want to follow you
  To love you, to love you and to die.
  It's there that I want to follow you
  There, yes, there!......

3 O Jesus! on this day, you have fulfilled all my desires.
From now on, near the Eucharist, I shall be able
To sacrifice myself in silence, to wait for Heaven in peace.
Keeping myself open to the rays of the Divine Host,
In this furnace of love, I shall be consumed,
And like a seraphim, Lord, I shall love you.

4   Jesus, soon I must follow you
To the eternal shore when my days will come to an end.
  Always (repeat) I shall live in Heaven
  To love you and never to die again....
  Always in Heaven I shall live,
  Always, yes, always!.....

PN 22 – To My Dear Mother, The Fair Angel of My Childhood

(September 7, 1895)

This is a little "compliment" to Mother Agnes of Jesus for her thirty-fourth birthday.

Its style has much in common with the poetry Pauline herself used to write for Thérèse to recite for their father at Les Buissonnets on the feast of Saint Louis (cf. GCI, pp. 230–234), so this looking back to the past is not accidental.

By now Thérèse was very far along in writing Manuscript A of what would be *Story of a Soul,* which she had begun in January 1895. For months she had been conversing on paper with her "little Mother" and going over her childhood memories with her. Thus she could measure the extent of Pauline's providential role in her life: the very same role the Lord assigns to each person's guardian angel—and especially to those of little ones.

Both Thérèse's recognition of this mission of love and her gratitude for it inspired her to write this poem, so full of tenderness. We can understand it as the epilogue in verse to what many pages of Manuscript A of *Story of a Soul* had just emphasized in prose: what Pauline was and still is for Thérèse.

We note a circular movement in this poem, and this gives it its charm. This is the very same movement as the main thought and goal expressed by the image "Love gives wings." Thérèse has come down from her heavenly homeland into exile. But she is not alone, for an angel (Pauline) came before her. The poem speaks of their homeland (above) and the flower (below). Thérèse would like to fly with this angel up to heaven. But, "alas," the fair angel flies away to Carmel. Thérèse joins her there. Her love gives her wings. She is going to fly away to Heaven. But she will come back down from there "without leaving the heavenly court" as Pauline's angel. Then both will fly off to their homeland once and for all "on the other side of the blue sky."

This concern with angels corresponds with an "old" stage of development in Thérèse's way of thinking. When she was a little girl, she thought people went up to heaven and came back down again on their own, without any difficulty. People were angels. There was no reason for the resurrection.... One year after this poem (in September 1896), Thérèse had to admit that love does *not* give wings in the way she saw it in 1895: "The little bird wills to *fly* toward the bright Sun... but to fly is not within its *little* power" (SS, p. 198). The little bird must remain "without strength and without wings" (*ibid.,* p. 200). Thérèse had to go through a long passion before she could write: "nothing could prevent me from flying away, for I no longer have any great desires except that of loving to the point of dying of love" (SS, p. 214, June 9, 1897). If flight was her hope, who could not see the distance she traveled in the next two years? We might dare say she went from the ascension to the assumption—by means of the "elevator" of the arms of Jesus (cf. SS, p. 208).

So this poem, written in the manner of a child, might be the starting point for a study of the ways Thérèse views her departure for heaven over the years. It also offers other themes, such as the song that Pauline's presence awakens in her soul. Thérèse felt this right up to the end of her life: "For me you're a lyre, a song" (HLC, p. 187, #2).

More so than any other tokens of affection, this poem took its place among the "little consolations" that Mother Agnes liked to copy over and reread at the end of her life.

J.M.J.T.

September 7, 1895

To My Dear Mother, the Fair Angel of My Childhood

1   Though so far from beautiful Heaven, my Homeland,
I'm not alone on earth,
For in this life's exile
A fair Angel guides my steps.

2   This fair Angel, O dear Mother!
Sang by my cradle,
And the sound of her melody
Still seems so new.

3   She sang of the charms of Jesus,
She sang of the joy of a pure heart.
Drying my tears with her wing,
She sang of beautiful blue Heaven.

4   She sang of the All-Powerful
Who made the golden star and the flower.
She sang of the God of childhood
Who preserves the lilies' whiteness.

5   She sang of the Virgin Mary
And the sky-blue of her vast mantle
And of the hills and meadows
Where the virgins follow the Lamb.

6   O deep mystery! this fair Angel
       Called me her baby sister.....
       She had a Mother's features,
       And I would rest on her heart!......

7   In the shadow of her white wings,
       I soon grew up.
       Already the eternal shore
       Delighted my childlike eyes.

8   Leaving the earth with my Angel,
       I would have liked to fly to Heaven
       To see divine Light
       Surrounding us both.

9   But alas! instead of taking me to Heaven,
       One day the fair Angel,
       Seeking the Virgins' procession,
       Took her flight toward Carmel!....

10   Ah! how I wanted to follow her
       To contemplate her virtues up close.
       Like her, I wanted to live,
       And like her, to unite myself to Jesus.

11   Oh! pure happiness!
       Jesus granted my desires.
       Near my fair Angel in Carmel
       I look forward to nothing but Heaven!...

12   And now I can hear
       Her sweet song every day.
       At her voice, my delighted soul
       Is set aflame with the fire of Love.

13   Mother, Love gives wings....
       Soon I'll be able to fly away
       To the Everlasting Hills
       Where Jesus deigns to call me...

14   But without leaving the Heavenly Court,
       I'll come down to this foreign shore,
       Close by my Mother,
       To take my turn as her angel.

15   Heaven would be without charms for me
       If I could not console you.
       Changing your tears into smiles....
       Telling you all my secrets!....

16   Without you I couldn't enjoy
       Those deep, heavenly joys.
       Oh! I couldn't bear
       To leave you long in this world!...

17   We shall fly to our Homeland
       On the other side of the blue Sky.
       O my dear Mother! Together
       We shall always see God!!!....

PN 23 – To the Sacred Heart of Jesus

(June or October 1895)

"You know, I don't see the Sacred Heart like everybody else!" (GCII, p. 709.) The beautiful, profound poem we will read now gives full meaning to this 1890 statement of Thérèse that seems at first just a witty remark. Written at the request of Marie of the Sacred Heart, who, she assures us, had had "all these thoughts" during her retreat [Sr. Geneviève's Notebook, November 1936, p. 194], this poem, like a finale, has a great many similarities with the Act of Oblation to Merciful Love (6/9/1895) and could very well have been written about the same time.[1]

Thérèse does not linger over the *symbol* of Christ's Heart wounded by the lance, which was so popular in her day. She goes straight to the *reality:* the loving Person of Jesus, his deep feelings, and the love that fills his Heart. For her, the most special revelation of that love was not at Gethsemane (in the spirit of the "Holy Hour" widespread in her day and at the Carmel of Lisieux) or in contemplating Jesus pierced on Calvary. It was rather in Jesus' response to the passionate pursuit of Mary Magdalene on the morning of the Resurrection: in the "whisper of her name." (It is significant that Thérèse makes no allusion to "Do not touch me," which in the Gospel is closely connected to the calling of the name: "Mary!")

Fortified by Jesus' answer assuring her that "the Heart of her Bridegroom is hers alone, just as hers is His alone" (cf. GCII, p. 709), her confidence as spouse knows no bounds. She will go farther and farther in her daring until she enters "straightaway" into the Heart of her God. It is this extraordinary dynamism that gives the poem its unity.

So in the first two stanzas, we join Mary Magdalene at the Tomb. Like the Spouse in the Song of Songs, she lingers, weeping, looking for the One she loves. Thérèse's way of evoking this has movement and a kind of passionate life ("*her* Jesus... she wanted... *to take him in her arms*, to carry him far away"). The consolations of the sympathetic angels leave Mary Magdalene indifferent. Then the God whom we cannot "vanquish in love" (one more discovery by this passionate soul) reveals himself in "just one word springing from his heart": the name "Mary!"

Suddenly in the third stanza the poem's tone is renewed by the unexpected (and very romantic) apostrophe to nature, creating an effect of surprise. Calling nature a "tomb" in this beautiful way is a little emphatic, and of course makes us think of the "tomb of Christ," with just the right consistency of images: Here nature speaks of God, but is He still *alive*?

Then Thérèse begins her quest, which is as passionate and absolute as Mary Magdelene's (st. 4). She is vigorously demanding: "burning... forever... night and day... always... never...." She even becomes insistent: "I *need* a heart... I *must* have a God." And He must love *everything* about her, "even her *weakness.*" What human being could ever meet such requirements? Thérèse "must" have nothing less than a God who makes himself like her in everything, a "Brother." Similarly, she expresses an analogous "law" concerning Mary, her Mother: Mary "has to be"... "human and suffering like me" (PN 52, 4). And her cry is heard.... Then the tone becomes tender (st. 5). Her astonishment and gratitude for this was perhaps more obvious in the first version of the poem, where she used an antithesis that is so typical of the great lover she was: "Creator of the world/For my love alone you became man." And in that same version there is the beautiful image of "your blood, the fruitful dew" (cf. vol II, p. 146).

Thérèse would have been just as affected as Mary Magdalene by "the brilliance of the Face" of Jesus and by "his sweet voice." Yet it is in her power to "live by his grace," to "rest on his Heart," not just allegorically, but as an experienced reality.

The sixth stanza is more relaxed. Here Thérèse delights in the "tenderness" that Jesus and she have for one another. Then the last two verses of that stanza ("It's in your ever-infinite goodness/That I want to lose myself, O Heart of Jesus!") give another burst of momentum to the poem. This continues on to the end.

Thérèse's desire to lose herself in Jesus comes true as her daring and enthusiasm grow (sts. 7 and 8). She does not tremble either before her own helplessness ("righteousness... sacrifices without *any* value") or before the power of the God of Sinai, who "gives his law in the midst of lightning": She "casts" her works into Jesus' Heart. She "hides herself" in it and throws as a challenge: "My Virtue... is You," changing the usual word order [in French] with magnificent daring and triumph.

Finally, if we have to "pass through fire to contemplate God's glory," she chooses to do her purgatory—with sovereignty and as a true spouse—in the burning Heart of Christ! Then one last daring leap takes her "straightaway" into that furnace of Love.

So this poem is a powerful tableau in which Thérèse expresses the most intense human and supernatural love. Here we are as far from the charming, intimate family sharing we saw in "The Canticle of Céline" as a Fra Angelico fresco is from a watercolor by Dufy.

Thérèse used an astonishing poetic form to express these original thoughts: [In the French] we note a very unusual decasyllabic rhythm broken in two equal hemistiches (two uneven measures of 5 + 5) to blend evenness and unevenness. This creates a mounting intensity, more and more vibrant right to the end.

[1] In this case, the poem would have been a feastday gift to Marie in 1895 (Sacred Heart: June 21), just as PN 5 and PN 33 were, respectively, in 1894 and 1896.

(Melody: "Quand viendra Noël")

To the Sacred Heart of Jesus

1   At the holy sepulchre, Mary Magdalene,
Searching for her Jesus, stooped down in tears.
The angels wanted to console her sorrow,
But nothing could calm her grief.
Bright angels, it was not you
Whom this fervent soul came searching for.
She wanted to see the Lord of the Angels,
To take him in her arms, to carry him far away.

2   Close by the tomb, the last one to stay,
She had come well before dawn.
Her God also came, veiling his light.
Mary could not vanquish him in love!
Showing her at first his Blessed Face,
Soon just one word sprang from his Heart.
Whispering the sweet name of: Mary,
Jesus gave back her peace, her happiness.

....

3   O my God, one day, like Mary Magdalene,
I wanted to see you and come close to you.
I looked down over the immense plain
Where I sought the Master and King,
And I cried, seeing the pure wave,
The starry azure, the flower, and the bird:
"Bright nature, if I do not see God,
You are nothing to me but a vast tomb.

4   "I need a heart burning with tenderness,
Who will be my support forever,
Who loves everything in me, even my weakness...
And who never leaves me day or night."
I could find no creature
Who could always love me and never die.
I must have a God who takes on my nature
And becomes my brother and is able to suffer!

5   Your heard me, only Friend whom I love.
    To ravish my heart, you became man.
    You shed your blood, what a supreme mystery!...
    And you still live for me on the Altar.
     If I cannot see the brilliance of your Face
    Or hear your sweet voice,
    O my God, I can live by your grace,
    I can rest on your Sacred Heart!

6   O Heart of Jesus, treasure of tenderness,
    You Yourself are my happiness, my only hope.
    You who knew how to charm my tender youth,
    Stay near me till the last night.
    Lord, to you alone I've given my life,
    And all my desires are well-known to you.
    It's in your ever-infinite goodness
    That I want to lose myself, O Heart of Jesus!

7   Ah! I know well, all our righteousness
    Is worthless in your sight.
    To give value to my sacrifices,
    I want to cast them into your Divine Heart.
    You did not find your angels without blemish.
    In the midst of lightning you gave your law!...
    I hide myself in your Sacred Heart, Jesus.
    I do not fear, my virtue is You!...

8   To be able to gaze on your glory,
    I know we have to pass through fire.
    So I, for my purgatory,
    Choose your burning love, O heart of my God!
    On leaving this life, my exiled soul
    Would like to make an act of pure love,
    And then, flying away to Heaven, its Homeland,
    Enter straightaway into your Heart.

PN 24 – Jesus, My Beloved, Remember!...

(October 21, 1895)

Sister Geneviève had been in the novitiate since February 5, 1895. She was generous enough for Thérèse to suggest that she offer herself totally to Love on June 9. She was struggling enough to feel the need to encourage herself by counting her past merits. For that she called on Thérèse's poetic talents. She later recounted,

> I asked Thérèse to write a long poem for me that would remind Jesus of all that I had given up for Him. And each stanza would end with a word from a song we liked, 'Remember.' In my mind, Jesus was very indebted to me for the great sacrifices I had made for Him!! and I thought, yet without really realizing it, that I would find in such a poem a list of all my merits.
>
> Even though I had explained all this well to Thérèse, what was my astonishment when she handed me the poem entitled, 'My Beloved, Remember!' It was exactly the opposite of what I had wanted, since she did not mention the sacrifices I had made for Jesus, but rather Jesus's sacrifices for me.... All the glory, all the merit was Jesus's, nothing was mine. What I had done was probably not worth the trouble of talking about! I didn't say anything to her about it then, and it was only later that I understood how right my little sister was" [Sr. Geneviève, unedited Recollections, 1909, pp. 263 ff].

"Exactly the opposite": Thérèse really did reverse the perspective in her poem. But she did not do this out of contrariness, much less to "teach a little lesson" to her novice (CSG, p. 73) with whom she made herself very little. Her inspiration took her in a quite a different direction. More than ever, her life was motivated by a very strong sense of Jesus' *prevenient*, gratuitous love for his creature. Since her offering to Merciful Love in June, this love for her had been overflowing in "waves of tenderness" (SS, p. 277), "penetrating and surrounding" her at each moment (*ibid.*, p. 181).

So this poem goes far beyond her sister's situation. In a fresco of thirty-three stanzas (was this a coincidental number or was it intentional to remember the thirty-three years of Christ?), Thérèse unfolds a "life of Jesus" based on the Gospels. As a matter of fact, it was "especially the Gospels" that were nourishing Thérèse in this period of illuminating contemplation she was savoring. She wrote, "I am constantly discovering in them new lights, hidden and mysterious meanings" (SS, p. 179).

As the epigraph—added later—conveys, Thérèse seeks out those words of Jesus "that most exude love," those words "from his sweet heart" that reveal more of the Heart of God. She gathers them in this poem as in a "reliquary."

Thérèse does not speak *of* Jesus, in the third person. (Besides, the melody she chose kept her from it.) She addresses him in the second person singular, as she usually did when she prayed (CSG, p. 82). In each stanza, except for rare exceptions (such as 1,5,7), the familiar You ["Tu"] and I are joined in a delicate, reciprocal tenderness. The reader might be surprised that she "corners" her Lord in this way. But she is only taking St. Paul's words as her own: "He loved *me* and gave himself *for me*" (Gal 2, 20).

Not by chance does the word "heart" reappear eighteen times in this poem in which affectivity plays such a large part. But her meditation cannot be reduced to some sentimental outpouring. Thérèse intervenes in and commits herself completely to the love story of the Incarnation.

To the Wayfarer who does "not even have a stone" on which to rest his head, she offers rest on her heart (st. 8). In st. 14, she borrows the "love songs" of Jesus praying at night so she herself may keep watch in prayer (st. 14). To the Sower of the eschatological harvest, she offers the help of her own life sacrificed to hasten the harvest (st. 15). We know these are not just empty words. She accepts being consumed—even as a holocaust— by the Fire Jesus comes to light on the earth (st. 17). She offers herself to him agonizing in Gethsemane as the living, loving proof of the fruitfulness of his annihilation (st. 21). She affirms her faith in the Son of God at the very time his glory is veiled, before the Sanhedrin, for example (st. 23).

There is no verbal inflation in all this. Thérèse's real experience is embodied in each episode she evokes.

At the time when she wrote this, Thérèse was "bathing in light." Her faith was alive and clear. Here she shows her understanding of faith in the very personal way she reads and rereads Gospel themes.

There is a rather astonishing structure to this very contemplative meditation. It is obvious that no one ever taught her the secrets of poetic symmetry or complex rhyming or word and phrase inclusion. [In the French] we see that she nevertheless uses them with a virtuosity that even the author of the Letter to the Hebrews would not disdain. She is quite at ease with alternating rhythm (10-12-6-4). Verses 5 and 6 of most of the stanzas are written in Alexandrine meter, and are usually successful.

The poem calls for a detailed analysis, but this brief introduction is not the place for it. After all this, it is easier to accept Thérèse's incorrect grammatical use of "se rappeler de" that we have already pointed out in "Prayer of the Child of a Saint" (PN 8). Unfortunately [in the French] this mars the beauty of twelve stanzas.

Along with her last poem, "Why I Love You, O Mary!" (PN 54), this poem offers a special vantage point for studying Scripture in Thérèse's writings. *La Bible avec Thérèse de Lisieux* [1] helps us go deeper into this subject and undoubtably stands as the best commentary on "Remember."

---

[1] *La Bible avec Thérèse de Lisieux*, ed. Sr. Cécile, O.C.D., and Sr. Geneviève, O.P., (Paris: Cerf/DDB, 1979). [An indispensable tool for studying Scripture in the writings of St. Thérèse—Trans.]

(Melody: "Rappelle-toi")

Jesus, My Beloved, Remember!...

"My daughter, seek those words of mine which most exude love. Write them down, and then, keeping them preciously like relics, take care to reread them often. When a friend wishes to reawaken the original vigor of his affection in the heart of his friend, he tells him: 'Remember what you felt in your heart when I said such and such a word,' or 'Do you remember your feelings at such a time, on such a day, in such a place?'... Be assured then that the most precious relics of mine on earth are my words of love, the words which have come from my most sweet Heart."

(Words of Our Lord to Saint Gertrude) [1]

1   Remember the Father's glory,
        Remember the divine splendor
        You left in exiling yourself on earth
        To redeem all the poor sinners.
   O Jesus! Humbling yourself to the Virgin Mary,
   You veiled your infinite greatness and glory.
            Ah! Your mother's breast
            Was your second heaven,
            Remember.

2   Remember that on the day of your birth,
        The Angels, leaving Heaven, sang:
        "Glory, honor, and power to our God
        And peace in hearts of good will."
   You have kept your promise for nineteen hundred years.
   Lord, peace is the wealth of your children.
            To enjoy forever
            Your ineffable peace,
            I come to you.

3   I come to you, hide me in your swaddling clothes.
        I want to stay in your cradle always.
        There, singing with the angels,
        I'll be able to remind you of the joys of your first days.
   O Jesus! remember the shepherds and the wise men
   Who joyfully offered you their hearts and homage.
            The innocent procession
            Which shed its blood for you,
            Remember.

[1] *The Life and Revelations of Saint Gertrude,* [ed.] (Westminster: Christian Classics, 1983), 460.

4   Remember that you preferred Mary's arms
         To your royal throne.
         Little Child, to sustain you in life
         You had nothing but virginal milk.
    Oh! Jesus, my little Brother, deign to invite me
    To that feast of love Your Mother gives you.
             Your little sister
             Made your heart pound,
                 Remember!...

5   Remember that you chose for your father
         The humble Joseph, who on order from Heaven
         Tore you away from a man's madness
         Without waking you on your mother's breast.
    ......Word-God, remember that strange mystery.
         You kept silent and made an angel speak!
                 Your far-off exile
                 On the banks of the Nile,
                 Remember.

6   Remember that on other shores
         The golden stars and silver moon
         On which I gaze in the cloudless sky
         Delighted and charmed your Infant eyes.
    With your little hand that caressed Mary
    You upheld the world and gave it life,
                 And you thought of me,
                 Jesus, my little King,
                 Remember...

7   Remember that you worked in solitude
         With your divine hands.
         To live forgotten was your sweetest task.
         You rejected human learning.
    O You who with just one word could charm the world,
    You took delight in hiding your profound wisdom.
                 You seemed unlearned,
                 O All-powerful Lord!
                 Remember.......

8 Remember that you wandered as a Stranger on earth.
You, The Eternal Word,
You had nothing... no, not even a stone,
Not a shelter, like the birds of heaven...
O Jesus! come within me, come rest your Head,
Come, my soul is truly ready to receive you.
  My Beloved Savior,
  Rest in my heart.
  It is Yours...

9 Remember the heavenly affection
You heaped on the littlest children.
I too want to receive your caresses.
Ah! give me your ravishing kisses.
To enjoy your sweet presence in Heaven,
I'll practice the virtues of childhood.
  Didn't you often say:
  "Heaven is for children..."?
  Remember.

10 Remember that alongside the fountain
A Traveler tired by the journey
Made waves of love from within his breast
Overflow on the Samaritan woman.
Ah! I know Him who asked for a drink.
He is the Gift of God, the source of glory.
  He is Water springing up.
  It's He who said to us,
  "Come to me."

11 "Come to me, poor burdened souls,
Your heavy loads will soon be lightened,
And, quenched forever,
From your breast waters shall spring up."
O my Jesus! I thirst for this water, I crave it.
Deign to flood my soul with its divine torrents.
  To make my dwelling
  In the Ocean of Love,
  I come to you.

12   Remember that as a child of light
        I often forget to serve my King well.
        Oh! Take pity on my great misery.
        In your love, Jesus, forgive me.
    Make me wise in the ways of Heaven.
    Show me the secrets hidden in the Gospel.
                Ah! that golden book
                Is my dearest treasure,
                Remember.

13   Remember that your divine Mother
        Has a marvelous power over your Heart.
        Remember how one day at her prayer
        You changed water into delightful wine.
    Deign also to transform my imperfect works.
    Make them perfect, Lord, at Mary's voice.
                That I am your child,
                O Jesus! Very often,
                Remember.

14   Remember that you would often climb
        The hills at sunset.
        Remember your divine prayers,
        Your love songs at the hour of sleep.
    O my God, I offer your prayer with delight.
    During my hours of prayer, and then at the Divine Office,
                There so close to your Heart
                I sing with joy:
                Remember!

15   Remember that on seeing the countryside,
        Your Divine Heart anticipated the harvests.
        Raising your eyes to the holy mountains,
        You whispered the names of your elect....
    So that your harvest may soon be gathered in,
    Each day, O my God, I sacrifice myself and I pray
                That my joys and my tears
                Are for your Harvesters,
                Remember.

16 Remember the Angels' feast,
  Remember Heaven's harmony
  And the joy of the sublime hosts
  When a sinner raises his eyes to you.
 Ah! I want to increase that great joy.
 Jesus, I want to pray unceasingly for sinners.
    That I came to Carmel
    To fill your beautiful Heaven,
    Remember.......

17 Remember the ever gentle Flame
  Which you wanted to enkindle in hearts.
  You put this Fire of Heaven in my soul.
  I also want to spread its intense heat.
 One weak spark, O mystery of life,
 Is enough to light a huge fire.
    That I want, O my God,
    To carry your Fire far and wide,
    Remember.

18 Remember the splendid banquet
  That you gave for your repentant son.
  Remember that you yourself nourish
  The pure soul at each moment.
 Jesus, you welcome the prodigal son with love.
 But no dikes separate me from the waves of your Heart.
    My Beloved, my King,
    All your wealth is mine,
    Remember.

19 Remember how you scorned glory.
  In lavishing your divine miracles,
  You cried out, "How can you believe,
  You who seek human esteem?...
 The works that I do seem surprising.
 My friends will do many more remarkable ones..."
    How humble and gentle you were.
    Jesus, my tender Spouse,
    Remember.

20   Remember that in a holy rapture
        The Virgin Apostle drew near your heart.
        He knew your tenderness at rest.
        He understood all your secrets, Lord...
    I am not at all jealous of your beloved disciple.
    I know your secrets, for I am your spouse.
            O my divine Savior,
            I fall asleep on your Heart.
                It is mine!...

21   Remember that on the night of your agony
        Your tears mingled with your blood.
        Dew of love, its infinite worth
        Made virginal flowers spring up.
    An angel, showing you this choice harvest,
    Made joy reappear on your blessed Face.
            Jesus, you saw me
            Among your lilies,
            Remember.

22   Remember that your fruitful Dew
        Made the flowers' corollas virginal
        And made them able even in this world
        To give birth to a great number of hearts.
    I am a virgin, O Jesus! yet what a mystery.
    When I unite myself to you, I am the mother of souls.
            The virginal flowers
            Who save sinners,
            Remember.

23   Remember that a Condemned Man,
        Overwhelmed with suffering, turning to Heaven,
        Cried out, "Soon You will see me
        Appear glorious in power."
    No one wanted to believe that He was the Son of God,
    For his ineffable glory was hidden...
            O Prince of Peace,
            As for me, I recognize you,
                I believe in you!...

24   Remember that your divine Face
         Was always unknown to your own people;
         But you left your sweet image for me,
         And, you know it well, I did recognize you......
    Yes, I know you, all veiled in tears.
    Face of the Eternal One, I discover your charms.
              Jesus, all the hearts
              Who gather your tears,
                 Remember.

25   Remember the loving moan
         That escaped from your Heart on the cross.
         Ah! Jesus, that moan is impressed in my heart,
         And I share your burning thirst.
    The more I feel myself burning with your divine flames,
    The more I thirst to give you souls.
              With love's thirst
              I burn night and day,
                 Remember.

26   Remember, Jesus, Word of Life,
         How you loved me and even died for me.
         I also want to love you to folly.
         I also want to live and die for You.
    You know, O my God! all that I desire
    Is to make you loved and one day be a martyr.
              I want to die of love.
              Lord, my desire,
                 Remember.

27   Remember that on the day of your victory
         You told us, "He who has not seen
         The Son of God all radiant with glory
         Is blessed if still he has believed!"
    In the shadow of Faith, I love you and adore you.
    O Jesus! I'm waiting in peace for the dawn to see you.
              I don't desire
              To see you here below,
                 Remember.....

28   Remember that in ascending to the Father
        You could not leave us orphans;
        And in making yourself a prisoner on earth,
        You knew to veil all your divine rays.
   But the shadow of your veil is luminous and pure.
   Living Bread of faith, Celestial Food,
                O mystery of love!
                My daily Bread,
                        Jesus, is You!....

29   Jesus, it is you who, despite the blasphemies
        Of the enemies of the Sacrament of love,
        It is you who want to show how much you love me,
        Since you make your dwelling in my heart.
   O Bread of the exiled! Holy and Divine Host,
   It is no longer I who live, but I live on your life.
                Jesus, the golden ciborium
                You prefer to all others
                        Is I!

30   Jesus, I am your living sanctuary
        That the wicked cannot profane.
        Stay in my heart; is it not a flower bed
        Where each flower wants to turn to you?
   But, O white Lily of the valley, if you withdrew,
   You know well, my flowers would quickly lose their petals.
                My Beloved Jesus,
                Sweet-smelling Lily, always
                        Blossom in me!.....

31   Remember that on earth I want
        To console you for the forgetfulness of sinners.
        My only Love, grant my prayer.
        Ah! give me a thousand hearts to love you.
   But that is still too little, Jesus, Beauty Supreme.
   Give me your divine Heart Itself to love you.
                Lord, my burning desire,
                At each moment,
                        Remember.

32 Remember that your holy will
   Is my rest, my only happiness.
   I abandon myself and I fall asleep without fear
   In your arms, O my divine Savior.
  If you also fall asleep when the storm rages,
  I always want to stay in deep peace.
     But, Jesus, while you are asleep,
     Prepare me
       For the awakening!.........

33 Remember how I often long
   For the day of your great coming.
   Send the angel to tell us soon:
   "Wake up, time is no more!..."
  Then I'll swiftly pass through space.
  Lord, right near you I'll take my place.
     In the Eternal Home
     You're to be my Heaven,
      Remember!...

PN 25 – My Desires Near Jesus Hidden in
His Prison of Love

(Autumn ? 1895)

In 1897, Thérèse wanted to express "everything she thought" about the Blessed Virgin Mary in a poem (cf. PN 54). We have nothing like that on the subject of the Eucharist, which nevertheless holds a central place in her spiritual life.

Thérèse's first poem, "The Divine Dew" (PN 1), is both eucharistic and Marian. At her sisters' request, three poems praise the Host more directly (PN 19, 25, 40). About twenty other stanzas scattered throughout this collection are also devoted to the Eucharist.[1] Nowhere, however, do we find a complete treatise of Thérèse's doctrine on this subject. And it would be useless and disappointing to look for one in this poem.

Following sound Christian tradition, Thérèse sees the Eucharist in two main ways:

(1) as the sacrament of transforming union. (The word *communion* is totally absent from her poems. The key words are "to transform" or "to change.") That is really the ultimate end of her desires.

(2) as a permanent Presence, which in turns calls for her loving presence and adoration, completely concerned with assimilating herself to the *hidden* life of Christ in this sacrament.

"The Atom of Jesus-Host" (PN 19) falls in this second category. "My Desires Near Jesus Hidden..." combines the two themes. From the "visit to the Blessed Sacrament" (sts. 1–2), evoked in a very nineteenth-century style, we move to the "Sacrifice" at the altar (sts. 3–6).

In this eucharistic and liturgical poem, Thérèse does not let her imagination take flight. This is a meditation in a very sober tone centered on objects of worship that are treated as words or images from Scripture. Only in the last stanza does she let her love and enthusiasm break through. And this abrupt movement—indicated by exclamation marks (in the first version) and the rhythm [in the French]—gives a special burst and brillance to the poem.

Unlike PN 19 and PN 32, we have no copy specifying that these are "the thoughts of Sister Saint Vincent de Paul," for whom this poem was written. So Thérèse was able to choose her own ideas and images. The rhythm and several expressions in "My Desires" are almost the same as those of an anonymous poem printed on a holy card with a lace border that she had. The originality of Thérèse's poem is seen in her exacting realism. She does not limit herself to the conditional tense, "I would like," as does the poem on the holy card. Her faith lets her discover here and now the way to realize her desires, "But I can...." She does not have to be jealous of the tabernacle key, sanctuary lamp, altar stone, sacred vessels, etc. She has, she *is* incomparably more than those inanimate objects. It is as a victim—even if she does not say the word—that the "spouse" shares in the sacrifice. She sings this with "delight": "O what a sweet miracle!... Oh! what happiness... Jesus fulfilling my hopes... Ah! what joy...."

We can date "My Desires" with certainty from the second half of 1895, perhaps in the fall.[2] When Thérèse copied this poem over in her red notebook for Fr. Roulland after Easter in 1896, she had truly already gone from the liturgical *sign* to the human, incarnate reality. Identifying herself with the offerings ("cluster of grapes," "wheat") that have to disappear to make way for Jesus, she is learning "under the wine press of suffering"— her trial of faith—at just what price we "lose our life" for Him.

[1] These poems deal at least in part with the Eucharist (the first number indicates the poem; the second, the stanza): PN 1, 5 & 6; PN 5, 8 (& 9?); PN 15, 1 & 2; PN 17, 3; PN 18, 10; PN 19, all; PN 21, 3; PN 24, 28–30; PN 25, all; PN 26, 8; PN 32, 3; PN 40, all; PN 46, 5; PN 52, 11, 12 & 18; PN 54, 5 & 23; PS 8.

[2] The original manuscript is not dated. But Thérèse's handwriting and the type of double sheet of paper she used are unquestionably very close to PN 20 and PN 24.

My Desires Near Jesus Hidden in His Prison of Love

1 Little Key, oh, I envy you!
 For each day you can open
 The prison of the Eucharist
 Where the God of Love resides.
 But, O what a sweet miracle!
 By just an effort of my faith
 I can also open the tabernacle
 To hide near the Divine King...

2 Being consumed near my God
 In the sanctuary, I would like
 To burn forever with mystery
 Like the Lamp of the Holy Place....
 Oh! what happiness... I have flames within me,
 And each day I can win
 A great number of souls for Jesus,
 Inflaming them with his love...

3   At each daybreak I envy you,
        O Sacred Altar Stone!
        As in the blessed stable,
        On you the Eternal One wants to be born...
        Ah! Deign to grant my prayer.
        Come into my soul, Sweet Savior...
        Far from being a cold stone,
        It is the sigh of your Heart!

4   O Corporal surrounded by angels!
        How enviable is your lot.
        On you, as in his humble swaddling clothes,
        I see Jesus, my only treasure.
        Virgin Mary, change my heart
        Into a pure, beautiful Corporal
        To receive the white host,
        Where your Sweet Lamb hides.

5   Holy Paten, I envy you.
        Upon you Jesus comes to rest.
        Oh! may his infinite grandeur
        Deign to humble itself even to me...
        Fulfilling my hope, Jesus
        Does not wait until the evening of my life.
        He comes within me; by his presence
        I am a living Monstrance!...

6   Oh! how I envy the happy chalice
        Where I adore the divine Blood....
        But at the Holy Sacrifice
        I can take it in each morning.
        To Jesus my soul is dearer
        Than precious vessels of gold.
        The Altar is a new Calvary
        Where his Blood still flows for me...

7   Jesus, holy and sacred Vine,
        O my Divine King, You know
        I am a cluster of golden grapes
        Which must disappear for you.

Under the wine press of suffering,
I shall prove my love for you.
I want no other joy
Than to sacrifice myself each day.

8   Ah! what joy, I am chosen
Among the grains of pure Wheat
Who lose their lives for Jesus...
My delight is truly great!...
I am your dear spouse,
My Beloved, come live in me,
Oh! come, your beauty has ravished me.
Deign to transform me into You!....

PN 26 – The Responses of Saint Agnes

(January 21, 1896)

Resplendent as a bride all adorned for her Husband: That is how Thérèse appears to us in this poem. With it concludes a year of peace, love, and light. That same January 21, 1896, she handed her first autobiographical notebook to Mother Agnes. In different styles, both Manuscript A of *Story of a Soul* and this poem sing the same "Magnificat."

This is a betrothal poem. Reading it, we instinctively think of the marvelous page in *Story of a Soul* where Thérèse recounts the prophesy of Ezekiel (16:8–13), a text she borrows from *The Spiritual Canticle* of Saint John of the Cross (cf. DE, p. 494): "Behold the time had come for me to be *loved*"—that was in 1887—"He made a covenant with me and I became *his*.... He spread his garment over me... he clothed me with garments, putting chains about my neck and priceless ornaments.... Yes, Jesus did all this for me" (cf. SS, pp. 101–102).

The year 1887 was still just the dawn of Thérèse's engagement. Her Beloved's visits at the great moments of her religious life (her clothing in 1889, her profession in 1890—where her letters again take up texts from the Office of Saint Agnes) revived the joys and enriched the ornaments of his fiancée. In 1896, after the fulfilling year then drawing to a close, Thérèse's spiritual betrothal was coming to pass in secret. Now she was ready for marriage. Soon the "first call" would be heard. It was to be a tragic call, to be sure, since we are talking about her first hemoptysis, but a joyous one nevertheless, "like a sweet and distant murmur announcing the Bridegroom's arrival" (SS, p. 211). This would leave Thérèse "flooded with joy" (*ibid.*, p. 210).

But, as on the evening before her profession, if "Jesus had already placed many jewels in the basket" of his fiancée, "there was one of incomparable beauty missing" (GCI, p. 683), and she had to be "very beautiful" (DE, p. 786). Jesus was going to give her "the most precious diamond" (*ibid.*) of all: her great trial of faith that would begin in ten weeks, at Easter 1896. Thérèse's nuptials would be consummated on the cross, in the night of faith.

Thérèse had no way of knowing this during the period of calm assurance when she wrote "Saint Agnes." For the time being, she just wanted to put the "Responses" from the Office of the young martyr Agnes into poetry for her Little Mother. She had first planned a prologue and a conclusion for this poem, which had Agnes herself singing a "hymn" from "earth's exile" (see *Poésies*, vol. II, pp. 177–178). But in fact these weakened the poem, giving a rather insipid picture of "the wise virgin, the spouse of the Savior, on the sad shore where she knew sorrow...." (But the tone did improve in stanzas C and especially D of the first version, which are beautiful [*ibid.*, p. 177]). So it was fortunate that she deleted those supplementary verses. As we have it now, the poem is true to life. It is *present reality*, and thus takes on a whole new strength.

This is really Thérèse's engagement poem. In it she speaks for herself, in the first person, even if she identifies herself with Saint Agnes.

Our Carmelite never cared about her spiritual progress according to the reference points proposed by Teresa of Avila or John of the Cross. But that does not stop her historians from looking, for example, in the Sanjuanist description of the spiritual betrothal—particularly in *The Spiritual Canticle*—to go deeper into this poem.

One more aspect of this poem holds our attention, especially if we compare it to its sources [*ibid.*, pp. 179–180]. We note so many identical ideas and images and such a desire for Thérèse to identify herself with the text of the Divine Office that every difference we do find is significant, spiritually and poetically. From this comparison, it is evident that *virginity*—in its extreme modesty—is the very foundation of this "Magnificat." Thérèse *possesses* nothing, but she receives everything as a free gift from her Spouse. The sixth stanza, so exquisitely human, like a Fra Angelico, offers us a remarkable example of this. Here virginity becomes *spiritual poverty:* Overwhelmed, streaming with light and jewels, and conscious of these riches, Thérèse does not attribute any of this to herself or take anything for herself either. The reader almost expects to hear Thérèse already whispering: "All that He has given me, Jesus can take it back" (PN 54, 16).

This liberty is accompanied by an exceptional poetic quality. It is interesting how Thérèse transforms words from her models in the Divine Office to her poem and how, in an admirable poetic organization, she makes honey from all the images scattered throughout the Latin text. Here we have a grand vision in an harmonious movement with a potential antithesis surfacing: that of the "Virgin"/"Spouse," of the "child"/"spouse of the All-Powerful God," and of "littleness" looked on and overwhelmed by "Mercy": "Then I was made exceedingly beautiful in his eyes, and He made me a powerful queen!" (SS, p. 102).

The Responses of Saint Agnes

(Melody: "Dieu de paix et d'amour")

1   Christ is my Love, He is my whole life.
         He is the Fiancé who alone delights my eyes.
         Thus I already hear the melodious sounds
              Of his sweet harmony.

2   He has adorned my hand with pearls beyond compare.
       He has adorned my neck with necklaces of great price.
       The rich diamonds that one sees on my ears
               Are a gift of Christ.

3   He has completely adorned me with precious stones.
       Already his engagement ring sparkles on my finger.
       He has deigned to cover my virginal mantle
               With luminous pearls.

4   I am the fiancée of Him whom the angels
       Will serve, trembling, for all eternity.
       The moon and the sun proclaim his praises,
               Admire his beauty.

5   His Empire is Heaven, his nature is divine.
       He chose the Immaculate Virgin for his Mother.
       His Father is the true God who has no origin.
               He is pure Spirit....

6   When I love Christ and when I touch him,
       My heart becomes purer, I am even more chaste.
       The kiss of his mouth has given me the treasure
               Of virginity.

7   He has already put his sign on my forehead
       So that no lover dare come near me.
       I feel sustained by the divine grace
               Of my Loving King.

8   My cheeks are colored with his precious blood.
       Already I feel I am tasting the delights of Heaven,
       For I can gather both milk and honey
               From his sacred lips.

9   So I fear nothing, neither sword nor flame.
       No, nothing can trouble my ineffable peace,
       And the fire of love which consumes my soul
               Shall never go out!....

PN 27 – Remembrance of February 24, 1896

(Sister Geneviève's Profession)

One would expect quite a different poem for Céline's profession, which was such a great joy for Thérèse. She wanted to write the customary verses for such an occasion. And Sister Geneviève even clearly stated that "it was her place to do so on account of her duties in the novitiate. But because of particularly painful events for the four of us,[1] she had to stay in the background... and Mother Marie de Gonzague had Sister Marie of the Angels write the canticle for the community."[2]

Céline had to be satisfied with a "little scrap"—she said—"written to a melody I liked and that she gave me privately."[3] That romance began in this way: "On earth, life is not all roses." Gentle irony, given the circumstances.... Thérèse gave her sister some other compositions in prose and various mementos besides: a long description of the "celebrations in Heaven" (GCII, pp. 925–930), an illuminated parchment of the "marriage contract of Jesus with Céline" (GCII, pp. 932–934), a relic of Mother Geneviève (GCII, p. 935), and, later, for her veiling, a holy card with calligraphy (GCII, pp. 935–936).

In the midst of such a profusion of gifts, this poem cuts a poor figure. Thérèse herself was disappointed with how it turned out: "She was not happy with it, and when she wrote 'My Weapons' to be sung to Sister Marie of the Eucharist on the night of her profession, she told me, 'That is the one I wanted to give to you. Consider it written for you.'" (CMG IV, p. 340) "As a matter of fact the canticle 'My Weapons' went well with the ideas of chivalry that I was enthusiastic about then" (letter of 3/17/1936).

Should we see a connection between the "painful events" alluded to earlier (cf. CGII, pp. 827 and 1182) and Thérèse's unusual underlining on the manuscript of the words, "Jealous" and "Jealousy"? If such an intention did exist, it is important to understand its full implication: Thérèse's concern to help her sister go beyond the secondary causes of this suffering, to see beyond human passions to the "Divine Jealousy" of Jesus Himself. Once before Thérèse had seen "the divinely jealous hand" of her Beloved in her bitter disappointment on September 23, 1890—the day before she herself received the black veil (cf. GCI, p. 683). In such a light of faith, nothing could diminish the "incomparable sweetness" of being "united to Jesus by the bonds of Love."

For Thérèse, she could now "reach the other shore" (her first hemoptysis occurred a few weeks later) since Céline was settled once and for all "in the same Carmel," "under the same roof" as her sisters (SS, p. 176).

---

[1] [Although Mother Agnes of Jesus was prioress at the time, Mother Marie de Gonzague tried to use her influence to pressure the community to postpone Sister Geneviève's profession until she herself could receive her vows. She was assuming

that she would win out over Mother Agnes in the community's upcoming elections.—Trans.]

[2] Letter from Sister Geneviève to Mother Agnes of Jesus, 3/17/1896; complete text in *Vie Thérésienne*, no. 62 (April 1976): p. 151ff.

[3] Note by Sister Geneviève on a loose sheet of paper.

J.M.J.T.

(Melody: "Sur terre tout n'est pas rose")

Remembrance of February 24, 1896

1st C.

O ineffable remembrance
Of that beautiful day of days.
I will keep forever
Your incomparable sweetness....

2nd C.

I am united to Jesus
By the bonds of Love,
And his infinite Grandeur
Makes his dwelling within me.

1st Refrain

Oh! what inexpressible intoxication
I feel palpitating within me:
The burning, tender heart
Of my Spouse, of my King.

3rd C.

I suffer this exile without difficulty,
Living with my Spouse...
The chain joining me to the *Jealous* God
Is so sweet!...

4th C.

O Divine *Jealousy*,
You have wounded my heart!...
You will be my rest and my happiness
All my life.

2nd Refrain
Deign to consume my whole being.
Jesus alone must live within me.
From now on I only want to be
The veil of my King!...

(Thérèse of the Child Jesus of the Holy Face
to her little Sister a thousand times loved.)

PN 28 – The Eternal Canticle Sung Even in Exile

(March 1, 1896)

The very Sunday after Sister Geneviève's profession, Thérèse began devoting her spare time to writing a few verses for the feastday of Sister Marie of Saint Joseph (March 19)—a "sick sister," as the Beatification Process simply put it. In this poem Thérèse does not dwell on the psychological problems of her companion. She "forgets her great misery," just as Jesus does. She only speaks of "love" for this willing disciple, whose "assistant" in the vestry she would soon become (CGII, pp. 884 ff.).

For this poem Thérèse chose the melody from "Mignon regrettant sa patrie: Votre Ciel est d'azur" ["Mignon missing her country: Your sky is blue"—Trans.]. The sky was also blue for Thérèse, who was already tasting "the joys of the other life" in a kind of fleeting Tabor (the mystery calling to mind the Gospel of the Transfiguration for the second Sunday of Lent).

But the complex rhythm of the model Thérèse chose, which was difficult to sing, gave "The Eternal Canticle" a very special structure. This is a weak poem, even if it is invaluable to know that Thérèse was *living to the letter* what she was singing in her companion's name.

J.M.J.T.

March 1, 1896

The Eternal Canticle Sung Even in Exile

1   Your exiled spouse, on the foreign shore,
     Can sing the eternal canticle of Love,
     Since, my Sweet Jesus, you deign on earth as in Heaven
     To set her aflame with the fire of your Love .

2   My Beloved, Beauty supreme,
     You give yourself to me,
          But in return,
          Jesus, I love you,
     And my life is but one act of love!

3   Forgetting my great misery,
     You come to dwell in my heart.
     My weak Love, ah, what a mystery!   } repeat
     Is enough to captivate you, Lord.

My Beloved, etc......

4   Love which sets me aflame,
    Pierce my soul.
    Come, I beg you,
    Come, consume me.

5   Your ardor impels me,
    And, Divine Furnace,
    I want to lose myself
    Unceasingly in you.

6   Lord, suffering
    Becomes delight
    When the soul leaps
    Toward you forever.

7   Heavenly Homeland,
    Joys of the other life,
    My enraptured soul
    Always delights in you.

8   Heavenly Homeland,
    Joys of the other life,
    You are nothing but Love!

PN 29 – "How Sweet It Is for Us..."

(Profession of Sister Marie of the Trinity, April 30, 1896)

This is a very simple poem for the profession of Sister Marie of the Trinity, with pretty images and a tone from which a deep friendship emanates.

As much as—if not more than—for Sister Geneviève, the "success" of this novice was to a great degree Thérèse's doing.

> It is really thanks to her that I managed to be a Carmelite. My lack of virtue and health and the lack of sympathy I found in the community because I came from another Carmel caused me a thousand almost insurmountable difficulties. In those painful times, only the Servant of God consoled and encouraged me. She would cleverly make the most of every opportunity to plead my cause with the Sisters who were against me. 'How I would willingly give my life for you to be a Carmelite!' she would tell me. On the day of my Profession, April 30, 1896, she confided that it was one of the most beautiful days of her life. Her joy seemed to equal mine" (CRM, pp. 42 ff).

Elsewhere, Marie of the Trinity wrote more about her profession: "That day was more heaven than earth.... Sr. Thérèse of the Child Jesus seemed as happy as I: She told me, 'I feel like Joan of Arc witnessing the coronation of Charles VII!'" (Autobiographical Remembrances, 1904).

As a matter of fact, we do note a sort of pride overflowing on Thérèse's face in the photo taken on April 30, 1896.[1] Between the child and the old woman, between the kneeling novice with the mischievous smile and the prioress, marked by the "irreparable outrage" of old age, Thérèse stands as a mediator—sweet and strong, serene and serious.

Nobility and fervor meet in this song about "the greatest love"—"life for life"—in response to Jesus' sacrifice for us. In the last two stanzas (13 and 14), Thérèse elevates even the most human ambitions to the dignity of true sacrifice.[2]

From then on, the newly professed sister's only task was to "be consumed each day" (11, 4). Saint John of the Cross would be her master, and Thérèse would translate his message.

This poem should be read together with the following one, her letters LT 187 and 188 (GCII, pp. 952 and 953) and the poem Thérèse wrote for Marie of the Trinity on May 31 (PN 31). They are all different expressions of the same deep love.

[1] See pp. 166–169 (poses 32, 32A, and 32B) in *The Photo Album of St. Thérèse of Lisieux* (Westminster: Christian Classics, 1990).

[2] [Before the community elections of March 1896, Mother Marie de Gonzague attempted to persuade Mother Agnes of Jesus, then prioress, that the professions of

Sister Geneviève and Sister Marie of the Trinity should be postponed until after the elections, because Mother Gonzague was convinced that she herself would be elected. An unfair compromise was reached: Mother Agnes would be allowed to remain in office for two more months—long enough to receive the vows of Sister Geneviève. But Sister Marie of the Trinity would have to wait until after the elections to make her profession—presumably in the hands of Mother Gonzague.— Trans.]

J.M.J.T.

Remembrance of April 30, 1896

To our dear little Sister
Marie of the Trinity and of the Holy Face.

1   O dear Sister! how sweet it is for us
     To sing on this radiant day,
     The most beautiful day of your life,
     When you are united to the King of Heaven.

2   This morning your exiled soul
     Was clothed in splendor,
     In immaculate attire,
     As you sacrificed yourself for the Lord.

3   Once the Blessed Trinity,
     Gazing upon your soul,
     Marked you with his Flame
     And revealed his beauty to you.

4   Contemplating the Divine Face,
     You felt the desire
     To scorn all passing things,
     Everything that must soon come to an end.

5   Fearing the world's flood,
     You called on Heaven.
     It helped you find refuge
     In the blessed ark of Carmel.

6   But alas! poor fugitive,
     You had to leave the ark.
     Like the doleful dove,
     For a long time you had to moan.

7   The green foliage of the olive tree
    Finally caught your eye.
    It pointed out the shade
    Of the little Carmel of Lisieux.

8   Immediately overcoming distance
    You came among us,
    Seeking the lowest place,
    Wanting to suffer, wanting to love!...

9   Jesus, in sacrificing Himself,
    Told us on his last day:
    "There is no greater love
    Than to give one's life for those one loves."

10 Your heart was all inflamed
    At this blessed word.
    You gave life for life
    To Jesus your Beloved.

11 Now, happy victim
    Who sacrifice yourself to Love,
    Taste the joy, the intimate peace
    Of sacrificing yourself each day.

12 Your soul longs for Love.
    That is your shining star.
    Love will be your martyrdom.
    Love will open the Heavens for you.

            (To our Mother)

13 O dear Mother, it is because of you
    That this morning we saw
    This white, new host
    Sacrifice herself to our Divine Lamb.

14 This host will be your glory.
    Jesus will make her shine
    In the mysterious ciborium
    That your heart knew how to fill.

Profession day of Sr. Marie of the Trinity, April 30, 1896 (see PN 29).
front, l.r.: Sr. Geneviève of the Holy Face (Céline Martin), Sr. Marie of the Trinity, Mother Marie de Gonzague
standing, l.r.: Sr. Martha of Jesus, Sr. Marie of the Sacred Heart (Marie Martin), Sr. Marie-Madeleine of the Blessed Sacrament, Sr. Marie of the Eucharist (Guérin), Sr. Thérèse

PN 30 – A Gloss on the Divine

(April 30, 1896)

No one has spoken like Marie of the Trinity about Thérèse's love for her Father John of the Cross. Long after Thérèse's death, the Carmelites of Lisieux could hear her novice of 1896 earnestly recite one of the two's favorite texts from back then. (And Sister Marie's face, half eaten away by lupus, showed that this was not just literature for her): "O souls who desire to walk in security and consolation, etc."[1]

Thérèse made these comments on this line: "To accept suffering well merits for us the grace of an even greater suffering, or rather of an even deeper purification in order to attain the perfect union of love. Ah! once I understood this, I received the strength to suffer everything."[2]

Thérèse had "understood this" even from the beginning of her novitiate, at the time of her great "exterior" trials, and during her father's humiliating illness in particular. The years passed. The time had now come for her to know "a deeper purification." She made her way toward it all during the last eighteen months of her life, "to the perfect union of love."

"For Love, I am willing," was her heroic response to the worst trials: in the past, in her great family sorrow ("to will all that Jesus wills," GCI, p. 553); now, as she was entering into the night, "without Light and in the Shadows"; and soon grappling with her last agony ("Yes, my God, everything that You will," HLC, p. 205). Such is the power of Love....

Putting this little poem—incidentally, very close to its model—in such a context gives it a moving authenticity and intensity. But at the time only Thérèse knew its full significance, for she was bearing her trial "in silence and hope."

When Thérèse gave this poem to Marie on the day of her profession, she only pointed out to her "the thought she liked best: Love makes use of everything—the good and *the bad* it finds in us."[3] This certainty was the powerful motor of their journey on the "little way." The faults of a young and still fragile Carmelite nun and the purifying trials of a saint on her way to fulfillment: everything can be included and even surpassed in an absolute trust in this "consuming and transforming Love" (GCII, p. 999).

[1] In a note dated 11/8/1942, Sister Marie of the Trinity wrote, "There was one passage especially from *The Living Flame of Love* that marvelously strengthened St. Thérèse during the time of her great trials: She said to me, 'It was so great and profound that while I was reading it I was infatuated, I had to catch my breath'" (cf. *Poésies*, vol. II, pp. 196–197). [See st. 2, 28–29 of "The Living Flame of Love" in *The Collected Works of St. John of the Cross*, trans. Kieran Kavanaugh, O.C.D., and Otilio Rodriguez, O.C.D., (Washington: ICS, 1991), pp. 668–669.—Trans.]

[2] From a note by Sister Marie of the Trinity on a loose sheet of paper, undated, but later than 1926.

[3] *Ibid.*

A Gloss on the Divine

Written by O[ur] F[ather] St. John of the Cross and put into verse
by the littlest of his daughters to celebrate the Profession
of her dear Sister Marie of the Trinity and of the Holy Face.

Without support yet with support,
Living without Light, in darkness,
I am wholly being consumed by Love....

1   I have said an eternal goodbye
     To the world (what extreme happiness)!......
     .... Lifted higher than myself,
     I have no other Support than my God.
     And now I proclaim:
     What I value near Him
     Is to see and feel my soul
     Supported without any support!....

2   Though I suffer without Light
     In this life which lasts but a day,
     At least on earth I possess
     The Heavenly life of Love....
     In the way I have to walk,
     Lies more than one danger,
     But for Love I am willing to live
     In exile's Shadows.

3   Love, I have experienced it,
     Knows how to use (what power!)
     The good and the bad it finds in me.
     It transforms my soul into itself.
     This Fire burning in my soul
     Penetrates my heart forever.
     Thus in its delightful flame
     I am being wholly consumed by Love!....

April 30, 1896. Thérèse of the Ch. Jesus, of the Holy Face
     rel. Carm. ind. [unworthy Carmelite religious]

PN 31 – The Canticle of Sister Marie of the Trinity

("I Thirst for Love," May 31, 1896)

Although this poem takes up numerous themes we have seen before, it has a strong tone in and of itself and opens a third phase in Thérèse's poetry (cf. General Introduction). This poem is a sort of mystical dialogue in which we can clearly distinguish Jesus' voice and Thérèse's response. It leaves the rather dramatic impression of a glowing furnace of love, which the title from the 1898 edition of *Story of a Soul* well expresses: "I thirst for Love." The tone of this poem is more sorrowful and less joyful than other poems, and it anticipates the author's last ones.

"It is nearly evening, the day is now far spent." For almost two months Thérèse has known that death is near, night is descending on her soul....

But Jesus "stays with her" on this dark road in her climb up the "hill" of Calvary. He repeats to her what he said to the pilgrims on the road to Emmaus, "Did not Christ have to suffer all this so as to enter into his glory?" And his "words of flame burn her heart." For her, there is no other way: love and death. So she "craves" suffering.

First, the suffering of "contempt": the humiliation that left its mark on the Holy Face, the hidden Face. Here her "little way" will bring about the "resemblance" with him. This outlook in st. 4 becomes a haven of peace, the only peaceful one in the poem.

She suffers from "thirst" too: the unquenchable "thirst for love" of the Crucified One, which implores like a death rattle and awakens a similar thirst in Thérèse's heart.

"The martyrdom of love," which the last stanza untiringly repeats, is both admirable and pathetic, like a prefiguration of Thérèse's own agony. We can read into that martyrdom both a most absolute love and an anguish, a passionate hope that borders on despair.

Thérèse's numerous retouches of the rough draft for this poem show that her great passion flowed with difficulty into the mold of poetry [see *Poésies*, vol. II, pp. 199–200]. But the end result does not show the effects of her labor. The pattern is clear, and strong verbs express well Thérèse's active, generous love in this summer of 1896.

Marie of the Trinity, honored here for the first time with this name so full of meaning for her, could see the best of her aspirations in this poem. That is why she wanted to have a holy card made with it so that she could keep it in a prayer book. More and more as they became closer, Marie was discovering the exceptional qualities of her companion and friend. For the second anniversary of her entrance into Carmel on June 16, she in turn dedicated a few verses to Thérèse [*ibid.*, p. 202]:

> "A burning furnace of love
> Is the heart of my dear sister..."

J.M.J.T.

The Canticle of Sister Marie of the Trinity and of the Holy Face

Written by her little Sr. Th. of the Ch. J.

1   In your love, exiling yourself on earth,
     Divine Jesus, you sacrificed yourself for me!
     My Beloved, take my life completely.
     I want to suffer, I want to die for you...

R.1   Lord, you yourself told us:
        "You can do nothing greater
        Than to die for those you love,"
            And my supreme Love
            Is you, Jesus!...

2   It is getting late, the day is now far spent.
     Come guide me, Lord, on the way.
     With your cross, I'm scaling the hill,
     Stay with me, Heavenly Pilgrim........

R.2   Your voice echoes in my soul.
        I want to resemble you, Lord.
        I crave suffering.
            Your fiery word
                Consumes my heart!....

3   The eternal victory is yours.
     The angels are delighted to sing it,
     But to enter into your sublime glory,
     Lord, it was necessary for you to suffer!...

R.3   What scorn did you not receive
        For me, on the foreign shore?...
        On earth I want to hide myself,
            To be the last in everything
                For you, Jesus!...

4 My Beloved, your example invites me
  To humble myself, to scorn honors.
  To delight you I want to stay little.
  In forgetting myself, I'll charm your Heart.

R.4 My peace is in solitude.
   I ask for nothing more...
   To please you is my only task
    And my beatitude
     Is you, Jesus!...

5 You, the Great God whom all Heaven adores,
  You live in me, my Prisoner night and day.
  Constantly your sweet voice implores me.
  You repeat: "I thirst... I thirst for Love!..."

R.5 I am also your prisoner,
   And I want in turn to repeat
   Your tender, divine prayer:
    "My Beloved, my Brother,
     I thirst for Love!..."

6 I thirst for Love, fulfill my hope.
  Lord, make your Divine Fire grow within me.
  I thirst for Love, so great is my suffering.
  Ah! I would like to fly away to you, my God!...

R.6 Your Love is my only martyrdom.
   The more I feel it burning within me,
   The more my soul desires you...
    Jesus, make me die
     Of Love for You!!!...

              May 31, 1896

PN 32 – Heaven for Me

(June 7, 1896)

This is a sweeter poem than the preceding one—a little melancholic, but brightened by a smile and full of trust, to answer a request of Sister Saint Vincent de Paul. Here, at the beginning and end of the poem, Thérèse discreetly evokes her "trial of faith" and calls it by name. But she tries to minimize her trial in her expression of it. She is trying to allude to it courageously, by "singing what she wants to believe" (SS, p. 214).

In good, solid, often well-rounded Alexandrines [in the French], she sings one after another of Jesus' "gaze full of love," of her "heart to heart" with Him in prayer that becomes intercession for the Church, of "the union of love" in the transforming Eucharist, of her filial "resemblance" to him, of her "total surrender" on the Father's Heart, of the indwelling of the "Blessed Trinity" in the heart that loves.

She expresses all this in the present tense: "Jesus *smiles* at me," "I *can* obtain everything," "My Sweet Savior *listens* to me," "the Blessed Trinity ... *dwells* in my heart." Here her doctrine does not waver and neither does her faith, but to grow stronger her certitude has to triumph over "the trial" and "the storm." The finale of the poem ("to suffer while waiting for Him to look at me again") suggests, *mezza voce*, the real-life context in which it is written. Her many reworkings of the rough draft of the first stanza—going back again and again to the "look" and the "smile" of Jesus who is hiding himself—make this more explicit.

To find consolation in the darkness for her love, our Carmelite has two powerful aids at her disposal: her apostolic zeal (the rough draft speaks of drawing down on souls "the gazes of Jesus") and the total surrender of "the child." On this last point, she is living out her own advice to one of her sisters, who is grappling with the "chimeras of the night" (GCII, p. 1033).

To keep on "smiling" no matter what at God who is hiding from her, "to double her tenderness" (PN 45, 4), to pay him "all sorts of compliments" (HLC, p, 75, #3): this was Thérèse's response right up to her last evening on earth, with that inimitable delicacy of hers.

In spite of her concern to make herself "very little" (her signature to this poem) toward her demanding client, Thérèse was not very well paid for the trouble she went to for her! Just a few weeks before the Saint's death, Sister Saint Vincent de Paul still had a dismissive opinion of her: "She's a sweet little Sister, but what will we be able to say about her after her death? She didn't do anything..." (From a note by Sr. Geneviève).

J.M.J.T.

Feast of Corpus Christi. June 7, 1896
(Melody: "Dieu de paix et d'amour")

Heaven for Me!...

1   To bear the exile of this valley of tears
    I need the glance of my Divine Savior.
    This glance full of love has revealed its charms to me.
    It has made me sense the happiness of Heaven.
    My Jesus smiles at me when I sigh to Him.
    Then I no longer feel my trial of faith.
    My God's Glance, his ravishing Smile,
        That is Heaven for me!...

2   Heaven for me is to be able to draw down on souls,
    On the Church my mother and on all my sisters
    Jesus' graces and his Divine flames
    That can enkindle and rejoice hearts.
    I can obtain everything when mysteriously
    I speak heart to heart with my Divine King.
    That sweet prayer so near the Sanctuary,
        That is Heaven for me!...

3   Heaven for me is hidden in a little Host
    Where Jesus, my Spouse, is veiled for love.
    I go to that Divine Furnace to draw out life,
    And there my Sweet Savior listens to me night and day.
    "Oh! what a happy moment when in your tenderness
    You come, my Beloved, to transform me into yourself.
    That union of love, that ineffable intoxication,
        That is Heaven for me!"...

4   Heaven for me is feeling within myself the resemblance
    Of the God who created me with his Powerful Breath.
    Heaven for me is remaining always in his presence,
    Calling him my Father and being his child.
    In his Divine arms, I don't fear the storm.
    Total abandonment is my only law.
    Sleeping on his Heart, right next to his Face,
        That is Heaven for me!...

5   I've found my Heaven in the Blessed Trinity
That dwells in my heart, my prisoner of love.
There, contemplating my God, I fearlessly tell him
That I want to serve him and love him forever.
Heaven for me is smiling at this God whom I adore
When He wants to hide to try my faith.
To suffer while waiting for him to look at me again
     That is Heaven for me!...

    (Thoughts of Sister Saint Vincent de Paul put into verse
      by her very little sister Thérèse of the Child Jesus.)

PN 33 – What I'll Soon See for the First Time
(June 12, 1896)

"Soon, to fly, to see, to love": That is Thérèse's passionate desire in June of 1896—what her love demands and what she "wants."

One month before, she asked this burning question of Ven. Mother Anne of Jesus, who had come to her in a dream, "'I beg you, tell me whether God will leave me for a long time on earth. Will He come soon to get me?' Smiling tenderly, the saint whispered, '*Yes, soon, soon... I promise you*'" (SS, p. 191).

"A ray of grace in the midst of the darkest storm" (*ibid.*, p. 190): that dream echoes in the present poem. This is a poem full of fervor, lively, straining upward to the next world, with a certain underlying anguish or melancholy. The "soon, soon" that Thérèse joyfully repeats stirs up her longing to rend the veil. "Soon" it will no longer be the wings of the dove that she will ask for—like the psalmist—"to fly away and rest" (cf. st. 2), but "the Divine Eagle's own wings" (SS, p. 200).

"Soon" she "will see!" For a long time, for her whole life long, she has "dreamed of the joys of the other life." Here she says this to Marie of the Sacred Heart for her feastday in almost the same words Marie herself had used before Thérèse's profession in September of 1890:

> There are two weddings for His spouses, the spiritual wedding of this exile and the wedding of the homeland.... And it is for the homeland that all the joys are kept. On earth, Jesus is not generous with His joys, these would harm celestial goods, and He who only dreams of giving deprives us of them now in order to enrich us later. Ah! if only His little fiancée were to see His smile, if she were only to hear the sound of His voice! she would no longer live, she would die of love.... That is why He *hides Himself*, that is why He is *silent*. But He hides *for A SHORT time*, He is silent for AN HOUR AT MOST! After the *dream* of this life, He will speak unceasingly to His little spouse, He will give her nothing but caresses, her heaven will be the *eternal smile* of her Spouse! (GCI, p. 657)

As in her canticle "To the Sacred Heart" (PN 23), which has the same addressee, Thérèse expresses a love that is both human and supernatural: she writes of the "smile," the "Heart," and the "Face" of the Beloved (st. 3).

This love is also the source of "martyrdom," and no doubt we need to give full force to this word that springs up spontaneously (st. 4). Like an impatient fiancée, Thérèse is suffering martyrdom because of her love for Jesus that cannot yet blossom in his presence.

But Thérèse only sighs all the more ardently for this heaven where she will be able "to love without limit and without law." (What a powerful expression!) Neither does she fear the wear and tear of time, since eternity is genesis in perpetual becoming. That will be the "instant," that will be exalting newness, the "ineffable joy" of that "First time," that Thérèse lovingly decorated in the title with a capital letter.

Is it possible that, submerged in the night of faith, she really felt "no joy" (SS, p. 214) while singing of such great hope?

J.M.J.T.

Feast of the Sacred Heart of Jesus
June 12, 1896

What I'll Soon See for the First Time!...

1   I am still on the other shore,
But sensing eternal happiness,
Oh! I would already like to leave this earth
And gaze on the wonders of Heaven....
When I dream of the joys of the other life,
I no longer feel the weight of my exile,
Since soon toward my only Homeland
I'll fly for the first time!.......

2   Ah! Jesus, give me white wings
That I may take flight to you.
I want to fly to the eternal Shores.
I want to see you, O my Divine Treasure!
I want to fly into the arms of Mary
To rest on that choice throne
And receive from my dear Mother
A sweet Kiss for the first time!....

3   My Beloved, let me soon catch a glimpse
Of the sweetness of your first smile,
And let me, in my divine delirium,
Ah! let me hide in your Heart!...
Oh! what a moment! what ineffable happiness
When I'll hear the sweet sound of your voice,
When I'll see the divine brilliance
Of your Adorable Face for the first time!...

4   You know well, Sacred Heart of Jesus,
My only martyrdom is your love.
If my soul sighs for your beautiful Heaven,
It's to love you, to love you more and more!...
In Heaven, always intoxicated with tenderness,
I'll love you without limit and without law,
And my happiness will unceasingly seem
As new as the first time!!!...

The little sister of the Child Jesus

PN 34 – Strewing Flowers

(June 28, 1896)

Every night during June of 1896, Thérèse and the five young sisters in the novitiate would meet after Compline—about eight o'clock—at the granite cross in the courtyard. They would gather the petals shed beneath the twenty or so rose bushes there and throw them at the Crucifix. Thérèse would say, "Let's see whose will go highest and touch the Face of our good Jesus!" (Sister Marie of the Eucharist, 6/24/1896). Thérèse herself would carefully choose her petals "so as only to strew very fresh ones" (Sister Geneviève, PO, p. 309).

Naturally Mother Agnes of Jesus liked this symbolic rite. For her feastday (June 29, Saints Peter and Paul), Thérèse composed—we do not know whether of her own accord or by request—a canticle on this theme.

In spite of some nice ideas (Refr. 1, 2–3) and some beautiful verses (2, 1), this text makes no great poetic pretentions. Its Virgilian grace and sweet tone, its tender style, and its charming images (not always developed very coherently) diminish somewhat the strength of this powerful symbol (cf. GCI, pp. 182–183). Perhaps too our sensitivity is a little irritated by the stereotyped image associated with Thérèse (strewing flowers, the unpetalled rose, saccharine statues, little angels) for which this poem is a special medium.

Nevertheless, it would be a shame for all that to make us neglect this essential poem in Thérèse's repertory. The symbol of the unpetalled rose has deep roots in her childhood: "How I loved the *feasts!*... I especially loved the processions in honor of the Blessed Sacrament. What a joy it was for me to throw flowers beneath the feet of God!... I was never so happy as when I saw my roses *touch* the sacred Monstrance..." (SS, p. 41).

In 1896, Thérèse's childhood gesture took on a new expressive power. Those flowers strewn on the Christ in the courtyard signify her whole life of love as a Carmelite. Three months later, she made this explicit in a text that is even more powerful and beautiful, even richer and more triumphant: pages 196–197 of Manuscript B of her autobiography. In that passage sacrificial love and giving to others are inseparable, in accord with her Carmelite vocation.

She sings the ultimate stage in this giving of self in "The Unpetalled Rose" (PN 51). In that poem it is no longer a matter of *acts* of love, but *her very life* that she is lavishing. This is the harsh reality of the sacrifice that, right up to the end, she wants to give meaning to this elegant symbol. Flowers also illumine *Her Last Conversations* with their "smile"[1] (HLC, p. 319).

That vivid image of Thérèse's mission after death, "a shower of roses"

(HLC, p. 62) unveils—or rather should not veil—her only ambition in heaven as on earth: to love Jesus and make Him loved.

[1] "The flower is the smile of God," she wrote at Christmas of 1894 (RP 2).

(Melody: "Oui, je le crois")

Strewing Flowers

1 Jesus, my only Love, how I love to strew Flowers
Each evening at the foot of your Crucifix!...
In unpetalling the springtime rose for you,
    I would like to dry your tears......

R.1 Strewing Flowers is offering you as first fruits
My slightest sighs, my greatest sufferings.
My sorrows and my joys, my little sacrifices,
    Those are my flowers!.....

2 Lord, my soul is in love with your beauty.
I want to squander my perfumes and my flowers on you.
In strewing them for you on the wings of the breeze,
    I would like to inflame hearts!....

R.2 Strewing flowers, Jesus, is my weapon
When I want to fight to save sinners.
The victory is mine.... I always disarm you
    With my flowers!!!...

3 The flower petals, caressing your Face,
Tell you that my heart is yours forever.
You understand the language of my unpetalled rose,
    And you smile at my love.

R.3 Strewing Flowers, repeating your praise,
That is my only delight in this valley of tears.
Soon I shall go to Heaven with the little angels
    To strew Flowers!...

PN 35 – To Our Lady of Victories
(July 16, 1896)

[In the original French] this is rhymed prose rather than true poetry. However, it represents an important aspect of Thérèse's vocation: her apostolic goal. This page is a step toward the opening out of her vision to the entire universe, which unfolds in Manuscript B of *Story of a Soul.*

Receiving her first spiritual brother (Maurice Bellière) in October 1895 struck "musical strings" for the very first time in Thérèse's soul (SS, p. 251). She felt nothing like that when she accepted a second spiritual brother (Adolphe Roulland) in May 1896. Naturally she was delighted, but she was also hesitant (SS, p. 253), yet the repercussions were just as deep.

In 1895 Thérèse expressed her feelings in an intimate prayer for the first seminarian she had "adopted." [1] In 1896, she wrote this spontaneous, personal poem to render her "song of love and gratitude" for Fr. Roulland. In it her apostolic zeal becomes more passionate. Better still than the previous year, she sings of victory: "Now my desire will come true" (Pri 8), and this would take place "through him" (Fr. Roulland), two words she repeats insistently. [2]

Thérèse's spiritual companionship with Abbé Bellière took longer to mature. With Fr. Roulland, everything took place very quickly, in one burst. Entrusted to our Carmelite on May 30, 1896, this young priest of the Foreign Missions of Paris celebrated a first Mass at the Carmel of Lisieux on July 3. He spoke with his Sister in the parlor and talked of his future mission in Eastern Szechuan. [3] He left her a book to help her locate *their* mission field. Thérèse soon had herself photographed with this book beside her. For that photo, she held in her hand a scroll of paper with this thought by St. Teresa of Avila: "I would give a thousand lives to save just one soul!..." (GCII, pp. 974–975). Fr. Roulland set sail for China on August 2. In the meantime, his sister copied about ten of her best poems for him. She ended the collection with the canticle "To Our Lady of Victories." Before he set sail, Fr. Roulland had "already read and reread it" (GCII, p. 981). He added, "I would like to be able to respond to it, but God wills me to be prosaic: I do enjoy, however, the beauties of poetry that comes from the heart" (*ibid.*).

These events powerfully reactivated the missionary flame in Thérèse. Her relationship with Fr. Roulland brought a temporary relief to her great desires for apostolic fruitfulness. "Through him" she will be an "apostle"— and "what hope!"—"a martyr"—and better yet, through that "communion of saints" that was being revealed more and more to her.

All this added fuel to the fire. Soon Thérèse's desires were causing her "a veritable martyrdom" (SS, p. 193). The poem "To Our Lady of Victories" (whose title was given careful consideration) [4] and the incandescent letter of September 8, 1896 (that forms Manuscript B of *Story of a Soul)* should be read one after the other to measure the progress of this fire of love. It will no longer be enough for Thérèse to be associated with "the works of *one* missionary." To satisfy her "desires greater than the universe," she had to take on "the deeds of all the Saints" and "embrace all times and places." There was only one solution: "to be Love... in the heart of the Church" (SS, p. 194) even to the point of being a total holocaust.

Truly, what "giant steps" Thérèse was taking in these three summer months of 1896!

[1] cf. *Vie Thérésienne*, no. 66, p. 158.

[2] [It is interesting that Thérèse capitalized "Him" (referring to Fr. Roulland) throughout most of this poem—Trans.]

[3] [Written "Su-tchuen" in French and often in English as well—Trans.]

[4] [The reader might wonder why Thérèse did not dedicate this poem "to Our Lady of Mount Carmel," since it was written on July 16. The Parisian sanctuary of Notre-Dame des Victoires, visited by Thérèse herself in 1887, was the site where several important missionary congregations in the nineteenth century came to pray to Our Lady for their apostolates. In keeping with the custom of the Foreign Missions of Paris, Fr. Roulland celebrated one of his first Masses at Notre-Dame des Victoires after his ordination on June 29—Trans.]

July 16, 1896

To Our Lady of Victories
Queen of Virgins, Apostles, and Martyrs

1   You who fulfill my hope,
O Mother, hear the humble song
Of love and gratitude
That comes from the heart of your child.....

2   You have united me forever
With the works of a Missionary,
By the bonds of prayer,
Suffering, and love.

3   He will cross the earth
To preach the name of Jesus.
I will practice humble virtues
In the background and in mystery.

4   I crave suffering.
I love and desire the Cross....
To help save one soul,
I would die a thousand times!........

5   Ah! for the Conqueror of souls
      I want to sacrifice myself in Carmel,
      And through Him to spread the fire
      That Jesus brought down from Heaven.

6   Through Him, what a ravishing mystery,
      Even as far as East Szechuan
      I shall be able to make loved
      The virginal name of my tender Mother!...

7   In my deep solitude,
      Mary... I want to win hearts.
      Through your Apostle, I shall convert sinners
      As far as the ends of the earth.

8   Through Him, the holy waters of Baptism
      Will make of the tiny little newborn babe
      The temple where God Himself
      Deigns to dwell in his love.

9   I want to fill with little angels
      The brilliant eternal abode...
      Through Him, hosts of children
      Will take flight to heaven!...

10   Through Him, I'll be able to gather
      The palm for which my soul yearns.
      Oh what hope! Dear Mother,
      I shall be the sister of a Martyr!!!
      ....

11   After this life's exile,
      On the evening of the glorious fight,
      We shall enjoy the fruits of our apostolate
      In our Homeland.

12   For Him, Victory's honor
      Before the army of the Blessed.
      For me... the reflection of His Glory
      For all eternity in the Heavens!....

                              The little sister of a Missionary

Taken March 17, 1896. Thérèse holds a book given her by her "missionary brother," Fr. Adolphe Roulland, along with a scroll containing the words of St. Teresa of Avila, "I would give a thousand lives to save just one soul!" (see PN 35).

PN 36 – Jesus Alone
(August 15, 1896)

Thérèse excelled at putting herself in someone else's place and yet fully expressing herself at the same time. From that, as we have already shown in these pages, comes the possibility of a double interpretation for a number of her poems: in terms of the recipient and of the author as well.

"Jesus Alone" is a characteristic, even subtle, example of this, with intertwinings that are difficult to disintangle. In this love song, it is certainly easy to recognize Thérèse, the great passionate lover of Jesus in the summer of 1896. But we can just as well read in it a spiritual biography of Marie of the Eucharist. To lift the ambiguity of a "double grille," we thought it best to present here a Theresian interpretation of the poem.[1]

In July and August of 1896, Thérèse was experiencing weeks of exceptional spiritual intensity. Without being as opaque as it would become in 1897, her "dark night" pushed her with more passion than ever to the Person of Jesus. On August 6, she consecrated herself to the Holy Face (with two novices) in a very loving prayer.

On August 2, her new missionary brother, Fr. Roulland, set sail for China. With him, she "threw herself... into her missionary apostolate."

In Isaiah, on which she was meditating a great deal at this time, she was again discovering recurring harmonies in the prophet's beautiful texts on spiritual childhood (cf. GCII, pp. 993–996). More and more she was yearning to "love like a little child."

She was integrating all these vehement and contrasting desires into the simplicity of one unique vocation (cf. Manuscript B of *Story of a Soul*).

Most of these ideas delicately show through in "Jesus Alone."

On a literary level, readers [who know French] will see that here, for the one time in her "career," Thérèse uses an "aabbccdd" rhyme scheme from beginning to end, giving it a consistent meter. The verses are compact and disciplined. The images are sparse and almost all borrowed from human experience (father, mother, child, warrior), except for "the storm." Adjectives are scarce as well. The poem's regular metric scheme (usually ten syllables per line scanned for the most part 4 + 6) only gives way to passionate enthusiasm in the last verses.

This poem speaks the language of human love, like the Song of Songs. Thérèse's original title, "My Only Love," stressed that even better.

Her heart's natural generosity is given free rein in the first stanza, conveying warmth and fullness. The final recognition of disappointment (v. 5, 7–8) is only for oratorial effect and prepares for verse 6 and the irresistible burst of the refrain, with its progression: "peace, happiness, love" and "only" used three times.

Thérèse chose wisely in reversing stanzas 2 and 3 from the first rough draft (cf. vol. II) to focus on images of childhood. The image of "the warrior" is in a better place at the end of stanza 3. From stanza 2 emerges an atmosphere of tenderness, security, and closeness "at each moment," even in Jesus's game of hide-and-seek (less trying than in PN 31) with his spouse.

The daring third stanza brings out the very Theresian law of *contrasts:* "the child" full of "delicate attentions" who overwhelms the Spouse with "caresses" is also the one whom love leads to the virile fight of the apostolate.

Stanza 4 more directly addresses the spiritual afflictions of Marie of the Eucharist (cf. vol. II), but it is also possible to see the personal trial of Thérèse, whose heart is "assailed by the storm" (SS, p. 198) and who begins to doubt "Heaven" (mentioned twice, once emphatically in v. 8 "for you").

In one of those reversals that Thérèse has a gift for, the last stanza brings on quite a different attitude than the one with which the poem began. At the beginning the creature spoke of her love as an aside: "Who will be able to understand?" "What heart will want?" Now she discovers a Heart more overflowing with tenderness than her own: a love that makes itself poor and pleading, that "begs for" his creature's sighs and tears. No one can resist such a love, so she "surrenders" everything to Him: her heart and her desires and "those whom she loves" (a curious finale, explained only by Marie Guérin's excessive attachment to her family).

Thus Thérèse won over her disciples less by "pious advice" than by the extreme generosity of her own love for Jesus.

[1] [Vol. II of the French edition of the *Poetry* contains historical information on several poems, showing how Thérèse closely studied her subjects to evoke the essence of their personalities.—Trans.]

(Melody: "Près d'un berceau")

Jesus Alone

1   My burning heart wants to give itself unceasingly.
      It needs to prove its tenderness.
      Ah! who will be able to understand my love?
      What heart will want to pay me in return?.....
      But I crave this return in vain.
      Jesus, you alone can satisfy my soul.
      Nothing can charm me here below.
      True happiness cannot be found here.....

My only peace, my only happiness,
My only love is you, Lord!...

2   O you who knew how to create the mother's heart,
I find in you the tenderest of Fathers!
My only Love, Jesus, Eternal Word,
For me your heart is more than maternal.
At each moment, you follow me, you watch over me.
When I call you, ah! you never tarry.
And if sometimes you seem to hide yourself,
It's you who come to help me look for you.

3   It's to you alone, Jesus, that I'm attached.
It's into your arms that I run and hide.
I want to love you like a little child.
I want to fight like a brave warrior.
Like a child full of little attentions,
Lord, I want to overwhelm you with caresses,
And in the field of my apostolate,
Like a warrior I throw myself into the fight!....

4   Your heart that preserves and restores innocence
Won't betray my trust!
In you, Lord, rests my hope.
After this exile, I'll go to see you in Heaven....
When in my heart the storm arises,
To you, Jesus, I lift up my head.
In your merciful look,
I read: "Child, for you I made the Heavens."

5   I know well, my sighs and tears
Are before you, all radiant with charms.
The seraphim in Heaven form your court,
And yet you beg for my love!....
You want my heart, Jesus, I give it to you.
I surrender all my desires to you,
And those whom I love, O my Spouse, my King,
From now on I only want to love them for you.

PN 37-38-39 – For Jeanne and Francis La Néele
(August 21, 1896)

Thérèse's talent for "poems made to order" was beginning to catch on in the Guérin family, where greetings in verse were appreciated. The entry of Francis La Néele— a real "live wire"—into the family revived all the more their old tradition in this area. So of course Thérèse was drafted to compose "some Alexandrines" for her cousin Jeanne's feastday on August 21. But Thérèse only complied halfway with their request: she did not give them any "Alexandrines for Francis."

The first of her three compositions shows how easy it is for her to write poetry when the subject does not require long discussions. For her everything is charming, playful, and very free. Her choice of the octosyllable [in French]—no doubt due to verse 2, 2—doubles her playfulness.

The "worthless quatrains" dedicated to Jeanne (PN 38), who never would be a mother, are really written with "exquisite tenderness." The tone is all the more lively because it introduces a feastday poem that is serious and even sad, and yet is still consoling for Jeanne. In the original French, the octosyllable flows as freely here as in PN 37. Thérèse is less concerned with feastday wishes than with a prayer for her cousin. Jesus answers her with a calming "secret," which seems to confirm a dream Jeanne had had (cf. vol. II, p. 232). Jeanne admitted that she "cried when she read it." But she added, they "were not tears of sorrow, there was something very sweet that made me shed them.... Now I am resigned" (GCII, p. 983).

As for Francis, the Christian doctor, whose giant frame, chivalrous character, and strong faith predisposed him for combat, Thérèse presented him with a well-crafted acrostic poem (PN 39) naming him "defender of the Church." He was "delighted" with it (GCII, p. 983).

So although modest in appearance (the autograph manuscripts are very small in size!), this "feastday bouquet" that Thérèse sent to La Musse is by no means "sad," but has finely nuanced tonalities.

[PN 37]   August 21, 1896

J.M.J.T.

1   These worthless quatrains
    Are a sad feastday bouquet,
    For, alas! your *"Alexandrines"*
    Have stayed in the back of my head!...

2   You had to have, I recollect,
     "Some Alexandrines for Francis."
     I should have keep silent
     Before such a precise order...

3   But knowing well the indulgence
     Of Jeanne and the Learned Doctor,
     I'll step forward *without Alexandrines*
     To fête my Lovable Sister.

                              (Thérèse of the Ch. Jesus)

[PN 38]   August 21, 1896
                    J.M.J.T.

Confidential Message from Jesus to Thérèse

1   Jesus, hear my prayer.
     Grant my ardent desire.
     Exile an angel on earth.
     Give Jeanne a little baby!...

2   This little exiled one from Heaven
     Is really making us wait.....
     But, Lord, you make me understand
     Your mysterious silence.

3   Yes, you tell me by your silence:
     "Your sighs go right up to Heaven.
     I have to force myself
     Not to fulfill your desires.

4   "It's not an ordinary angel
     I want to give your sister.
     And I prefer to form
     Her heart and soul in mystery.

5   "I Myself am adorning this soul.
     I'm giving her the gift of my treasures.
     But in return... ah, I require
     From Jeanne perfect Abandonment...

6   "With exquisite tenderness
        My hand is preparing her,
        Since she is to give to my Church:
        A Pontiff, a great Saint!"

[PN 39]   J.M.J.T.

A Holy and Famous Doctor

F   Francis took this motto:
R   Nothing for man, everything for my God.
A   And so to defend the Church
N   Has he not a heart all on fire?
C   Fighting godless science,
I   He confesses it out loud:
S   His glory is Mary's!...

The child of the seraphic Doctor:
Saint Teresa
August 21, '96

Thérèse as sacristan, with her three sisters and cousin, November, 1896 (see PN 40).
l.r.: Sr. Marie of the Sacred Heart (Marie Martin), Mother Agnes of Jesus (Pauline Martin), Sr. Geneviève of the Holy Face (Céline Martin), Sr. Marie of the Eucharist (Marie Guérin), Sr. Thérèse

PN 40 The Sacristans of Carmel
(November 1896)

[In the French version of this poem] we again see the ease with which
Thérèse uses octosyllabic verse, and she does it very subtly here as she evokes
that mysterious exchange between heaven and earth. The word "heaven"
frames the poem (twice at the beginning, as well as "heavenly," and once at
the end). The sacristans are the untiring agents of this mysterious exchange.
In this poem, they readily call to mind something like Jacob's ladder.

These stanzas are full of "gentleness" (cf. GCII, p. 1081). There is the
discreet gentleness of the "housewife," if we dare call it that: of the spouse
"happier than a queen" (st. 3) whose heart remains attentive to her Hus-
band, while her hands are diligently working for him. There is also the dis-
creet gentleness of the Carmelite nun, who is associated with the apostle at
the altar in the role that is hers, that of the hidden companion. In both
cases, the assistant becomes like the one she assists.

Sister Marie Philomena, for whom this poem was first written, fit this
description perfectly. She was "a true lamb of God, and good batter for
making hosts. She was all God's from head to toe," the nuns wrote about
her in 1893 (cf. CGII, p. 1175). She was the sister in charge of making altar
breads, and "her tall figure was prematurely bent from excessive work"
(Death Notice). "How many recreations she spent turning the iron over and
over on the stove, far from the company of her Sisters whom she loved so
much!" (*ibid.*) To give a spiritual dimension to this everyday task, Marie-
Philomena asked Thérèse, her former companion in the novitiate, to write
a few verses for her. She would sing them afterward when she was alone.

The other sacristans (Sister Marie of the Angels, assisted by Thérèse
and Marie of the Eucharist), and the other altar bread helpers (among
whom at that time were also Thérèse's three blood sisters), used to sing this
canticle too.

In writing this poem, Thérèse knew that the first one to read it would
be her aunt Guérin, for her feastday on November 19. It was easy for
Thérèse to associate with the Carmelites' "ministry" this peacemaker and
devoted wife and mother who had prepared five living hosts for Jesus.

In a very modest way, the second part of the canticle (sts. 7–10) brings
a response to the apparent challenge recorded two months earlier in Manu-
script B of *Story of a Soul*. There Thérèse proclaimed, among other burning
desires, her unrealizable desire for the priesthood. Here she sings of her
concrete way of sharing immediately in the "sublime mission of the Priest."
"Transformed" into Jesus by the Eucharist, "changed" into Him (cf. 6, 4 and

7, 3 var.), does she not then also become an "alter Christus," as a priest was described in her day? She cannot leave her cloister to "preach the Gospel" (SS, p. 193), but Jesus, the first Missionary, walks in her and through her. He "guides her steps" (7, 4), as he does those of the apostles she prays for, loves, and struggles for.

She cannot absolve from sins. But Jesus present in her through the Eucharist gives her a share in his ministry of reconciling sinners (9, 4).

She will never fill the ciborium with consecrated hosts. But she is spending her life "filling Heaven with souls"—living hosts in which Christ lives alone from then on.

Thus, she will never be a priest to consecrate the Eucharist, but in a sense the Eucharist consecrates her a priest then and there.

So Thérèse has no inferiority complex toward "men" or priests. She has no presumption either: For her, it is Jesus who acts in collaboration with men—and women. Even in 1892 she wrote to Céline, "I find that our share is really beautiful, what have we to envy in priests?" (GCII, p. 753).

This privileged part is lived out in the harmony of a little family group (PN 13,1) which is happy to "work together" for Him. In the photo taken to accompany this canticle and sent with it to Mme. Guérin (GCII, p. 916), we see Thérèse with her three sisters and her cousin, each attending to preparing the bread and wine for the altar.[1] Thérèse will soon sing, "How sweet and pleasant it is for brothers to live together in unity" (SS, p. 215). This union, however, will come about "in the midst of sacrifices" (SS, p. 216) and is itself the fruit of "the Sacrifice that gives Heaven to earth!" (1, 3–4).

---

[1] See pp. 190–195 (poses 39, 39A, 40, and 40A) in *The Photo Album of Saint Thérèse of Lisieux*. It is interesting that—according to Sister Marie of the Trinity (letter of 11/ 26/1916 to the Carmel of Angers)—Thérèse thought that the first pose (39, 39A), where she is partially cut off, was one of the best photos of herself.

The Sacristans of Carmel

1   Here below our sweet office
       Is to prepare for the altar
       The bread and wine of the Sacrifice
       Which brings "Heaven" to earth!

2   O supreme mystery, Heaven
       Hides in humble bread,
       For Heaven is Jesus Himself,
       Coming to us each morning.

3   There are no queens on earth
Who are happier than we.
Our office is a prayer
Which unites us to our Spouse.

4   This world's greatest honors
Cannot compare
To the deep, celestial peace
Which Jesus lets us savor.

5   We bring a holy envy
For the work of our hands,
For the little white host
Which is to veil our divine Lamb.

6   But his love has chosen us.
He is our Spouse, our Friend.
We are also hosts
Which Jesus wants to change into Himself.

7   Sublime mission of the Priest,
You become our mission here below.
Transformed by the Divine Master,
It is He who guides our steps.

8   We must help the apostles
By our prayers, our love.
Their battlefields are ours.
For them we fight each day.

9   The hidden God of the tabernacle
Who also hides in our hearts,
O what a miracle! at our voice
Deigns to pardon sinners!

10   Our happiness and our glory
Is to work for Jesus.
His beautiful Heaven is the ciborium
We want to fill with souls!...

PN 41 – How I Want to Love

(end of 1896)

This poem seems to spring from one stroke of the pen, impelled by a rich inner energy. At any rate, there is nothing redundant in it. Thérèse's rushed handwriting seems to support this. Here we see no new ideas, but a great interiority—and that majestic fullness that the decasyllabic meter brings [in the French].

"To delight, to please, to charm, to console" (in stanza 1) are very Theresian verbs. But only the "Savior" (carried over to the end of the last line of the stanza, and thus forcefully resonating after "Spouse" and "Beloved") can transform our "works" into "love."

The tone becomes still more interior in the second stanza with the rich words "love" (three times), "to love" (four times), "to transform," "consuming flame," and "to bless" (two times). There is no awkwardness in those untiring repetitions that embellish a great lyric intensity, reminding us of a blazing but calm furnace. Once this perfect reciprocity is reached, she appropriates the very flame with which her Spouse burns for her (vv. 7–8)—the love with which He loves her "from the Eternal day," she wrote in the first version, with a calm certainty of predestination.

The third stanza is more animated with the desire for and the approach of death: we note the "ah!" and "oh!" and Jesus's repeated call: "Come." Her Spouse is truly a "Savior" in the poem's admirable finale: "Come, all is forgiven"—rare in Thérèse's writings—which precedes the ineffable rest on Jesus' heart: for "you have greatly loved me"...

We know very little about the personality of Sister Saint John of the Cross, for whom this poem was written; and it is probably better that way. Each of us can make this "love song of an unknown Carmelite nun" his or her own. However, here the apostolic dimension is lacking—an unusual omission for Thérèse.

In 1893, the subprioress described Sister Saint John of the Cross as "a passionate lover of prayer and reading, who finds all her happiness before the Tabernacle" (CGII, p. 1175) In the short death notice for this religious who died at age 56 (9/3/1906), she seems not very communicative. It stressed her "unflinching exactitude" in her exclusive quest for God's will. Her secret life was hardly evident. After her death, the nuns were astonished to find in her breviary a prayer "expressing feelings that one would never have suspected" (cf. vol II, pp. 239–240).

Such "perfect observance" is quite different from that of a well-wound clock: Sister Saint John of the Cross was "a faithful spouse" (3, 7) who, no doubt, was too rigid. And Thérèse, to whom she readily came for advice

(PO, p. 313), knew that well. Here Thérèse is reminding this fearful sister, who needs to blossom in trust, of Jesus' welcome to Mary Magdalene: in "tenderness, gentleness, and love."

(Melody: "Je crois au Dieu" J.M.J.T. (To Sr. St. John of the X)

How I Want to Love

1   Divine Jesus, listen to my prayer.
By my love I want to make you rejoice.
You know well, I want to please you alone.
Deign to grant my most ardent desire.
I accept the trials of this sad exile
To delight you and to console your heart.
But change all my works into love,
O my Spouse, my Beloved Savior.

2   It's your love, Jesus, that I crave.
It's your love that has to transform me.
Put in my heart your consuming flame,
And I'll be able to bless you and love you.
Yes, I'll be able to love you and bless you
As they do in Heaven.
I'll love you with that very love
With which you have loved me, Jesus Eternal Word.

3   Divine Savior, at the end of my life
Come get me without the shadow of a delay.
Ah! show me your infinite tenderness
And the sweetness of your divine gaze.
With love, oh! may your voice call me,
Saying: Come, all is forgiven.
Come rest on my heart, my faithful spouse,
You have greatly loved me.

PN 42 "Child, You Know My Name"
(December 1896)

Here is another fresh poem written on request. Thérèse gracefully plays with the balance between "the child" and "the storm," with Jesus calming the tempest. The child who sleeps (or we should say does *not* sleep) during the storm is one of the archetypes of childhood. As for Jesus, he wants to sleep, as he indeed will later in the boat. So all this is a subtle game.

This gentle incantation is particularly appropriate for the Sister to whom the poem was addressed: Sister Marie of Saint Joseph, a companion with a stormy temperament that Thérèse tried to tame, for this violent person was also affectionate, and childlike words would disarm her better than reasoning. Even after she left Carmel in 1909, she very carefully kept the notes she had received from our saint (GCII pp. 989, 990, 1012, 1013, and especially 1033 and 1034, no doubt written around the same time as this poem).

"Music calms the savage beast": That saying proved true in the case of Sister Marie of Saint Joseph, who was gifted with a very beautiful voice. Verses like these could change a stormy sea into a tender mother, "tenderly" rocking the "little blond head" of the Child who surrenders himself to her in order to bring her to surrender herself to him.

In the second stanza (2, 1 and 3), Thérèse gives us a choice: "hand" or "voice." The 1898 edition of *Story of a Soul* (where this poem was first published) preferred to repeat "voice." But our author's freedom as a poet at this time in her life makes the other option more plausible. So that is the one we use. Besides, in the Gospels, the Lord "calms the roaring waves— And the wind" with his hand *and* with his voice!

1   Child, you know my name,
    And your sweet gaze beckons to me.
    It says to me: simple abandonment.
    I want to steer your little boat.

2   With your little child's hand,
        O what wonder!
    With your little child's voice,
    You calm the roaring waves
            And the wind!...

3   If you want to rest
    While the storm is raging,
    Let your little blond head
    Rest on my heart.

4   How delightful your smile is
        While you're asleep!...
    With my sweetest song
    I always want to rock you tenderly,
            Fair child!

PN 43 – The Aviary of the Child Jesus

(December 25, 1896)

A very nice image helps this "Birds' Christmas" take flight. However, the comparison between the aviary and Carmel goes on a little too long. But for a recreation on Christmas Day, the nuns would be indulgent....

There is nothing simpler and freer than the first three stanzas of this poem, which set the stage for Thérèse's poetic comparison. In the following stanzas (4–6), the tone becomes more interior. Jesus is sufficient for the soul whom his smile "captivates" (in both senses of the word). From then on, each one freely sings in its own register: "the dove" (with the Biblical meaning we have already heard in PN 3), or else "the lark, the wren, and the finch" (sts. 7–9). In a later poem (PN 52), Thérèse even goes beyond this for herself, writing of the vertical ascent of "the lark" (PN 52, 16).

Like the bird in the Gospels "who neither sows nor reaps," Carmelites receive "everything from the hand" of Jesus: their livelihood, and no doubt every event in their lives. That is where their cheerfulness and surrender come from—and their consecration to "the one thing necessary: to love" (sts. 10–12). A few couplets remind us of the tone of the "Canticle of Céline" (PN 18). Here once more, "he who has Jesus has everything" (18, 39).

An image of the whole community, which suits the circumstances well, concludes the poem: "all the birds," once freed, together "take flight to Heaven," where they will continue their song of praise.

A happy, concrete experience from Thérèse's childhood is at the origin of this comparison: Ten years before, at Les Buissonnets, an aviary brightened up the "poor attic" that she had transformed into a study. A "large cage enclosed a great number of birds; their melodious song got on the nerves of visitors, but not on those of their little mistress who cherished them very much...." (SS, p. 90).

In Carmel, little birds kept filling Thérèse's dreams: "I see beautiful children almost all the time. I catch butterflies and birds the like of which I've never seen before" (SS, p. 171).

During the summer of 1896, the symbolic value of "the bird" (which she sometimes associates with "the child," as in RP 5) takes on a new dimension in Manuscript B of *Story of a Soul*. Obsessed at this time by forces of both expansion and integration, our Carmelite recognizes herself in the bird, which is the sign par excellence of dynamic unity. True, her own dynamism is shackled by an inborn powerlessness, and that torments her: "To fly is not within its little power!" (SS, p. 198). But isn't a bird as much *song* as flight? Even in the eye of the storm (whether physical or spiritual trials, or both at the same time), Thérèse does not give up on her "work of love" (cf. PN 52, 15 and SS, p. 199). Besides, her "night song" (cf. Lamartine's poem, "To

Kenney   Bancroft

                    ✱ ⑤   copy Eng + French
                                        ✓
        ?   8   ?

    √(8)   10

    ┌─────────────────────────┐
    ✓│   13 F √√   │ copy
    └─────────────────────────┘
neco phons ┌──────────────────────────────┐
opt's poen │ ✓ │ ⑯ + the introd   │
           └──────────────────────────────┘
                    copy
                    parts

        ✓   ⑰F

            ✓   ⑱   nice

          ✓ 23   xerox ?

the Nightingale," which she chose as a melody for this poem) is drawing to a close. This is our Saint's last Christmas on earth.

(Melody: "Au Rossignol")

The Aviary of the Child Jesus

1 For those exiled on earth
 God created birds.
 They chirp away their prayers
 On hill and vale.

2 Happy, flighty children,
 Having chosen their favorite birds,
 Imprison them in cages
 With bars all of gold.

3 O Jesus! our little Brother,
 For us you leave your beautiful Heaven,
 But, Divine Child, you know well,
 Your aviary is Carmel.

4 Our cage is not of gold,
 And yet we love it dearly.
 Never more will we fly
 In the forests or azure plains.

5 Jesus, the groves of this world
 Cannot satisfy us.
 In deep solitude,
 For you alone we want to sing.

6 Your little hand beckons to us.
 Child, how beautiful your charms!
 O Divine Jesus! your smile
 Captivates little birds!.......

7 Here the simple, candid soul
 Finds the object of its love.
 Like the timid dove,
 She no longer fears the vulture.

8   On the wings of prayer,
           We see the fervent heart ascend
           Like the nimble lark
           That rises up so high as it sings.

9   Here we hear the chirping
           Of the wren, of the merry finch.
           O little Jesus! In their cage
           Your birds warble your name.

10   The little bird sings all the time.
           His life doesn't worry him.
           One grain of seed makes him happy.
           He never sows here below.

11   Like him in our aviary,
           We receive everything from your hand.
           The one thing necessary
           Is to love you, Divine Child.

12   We also sing your praises,
           United to the pure spirits of Heaven,
           And we know, all the angels
           Love the birds of Carmel.

13   Jesus, to dry the tears
           That sinners make you shed,
           Your birds keep on singing your charms.
           Their sweet songs win hearts for you.

14   One day far from this sad earth,
           When they will hear your call,
           All the birds in your aviary
           Will take flight to Heaven.

15   With the charming choirs
           Of merry little Cherubim,
           O Divine Child, we will sing
           Your praises in Heaven.

PN 44 – To My Little Brothers in Heaven
(December 28, 1896)

"Merit does not consist in doing or in giving much, but rather in receiving, in loving much," Thérèse had once written (GCII, pp. 794–795).

According to this "order of merit," the Holy Innocents would be in a good position, for they did not *do* anything—except let their new lives be taken. And so they "freely" received "the immense riches of Paradise."

Since the summer of 1896, when she rediscovered Scripture's most beautiful texts on childhood (cf. introduction to PN 36), Thérèse thought a great deal about the Holy Innocents. And during her retreat in September, she painted two holy cards in memory of her four little brothers and sisters who had died as babies. On the back, she copied some very significant Bible verses, these among them:

"Blessed are they to whom God credits justice without requiring deeds, for when a man works, his wages are not regarded as a favor but as his due.... All are now undeservedly justified by the gift of God, through the redemption wrought in Christ Jesus" (St. Paul to the Romans)."[1]

It was Mother Agnes who had the idea to use this text as an epigraph for the 1898 edition of *Story of a Soul*, in which this poem first appeared. These verses put the poem in a powerful light. Thérèse's delight and envy before these "conquerors who achieved glory without fighting" then take on full meaning. They proclaim the gratuitous—and even shocking—mercy shown to children who never used their will and for whom "the Savior" alone "won the victory."

Thérèse sensed that her own situation was similar to theirs. What has she *done* in her "short life" (cf. PN 46, 4)? Nothing, when compared with what she dreamed of doing for her Beloved: "I feel the need and the desire of carrying out the most heroic deeds for You, O Jesus..." (SS, p. 192). Instead of that, she soon realized: "I haven't any works!" (HLC, p. 43). But she feels no bitterness or dread about this realization. Ten years before, her little brothers and sisters in Heaven had freed her from her torment of scruples, bringing her "peace" at last (SS, p. 93). Now, their example was sparing her, as death drew near, the anguish of "empty hands." This even overwhelms her with joy: "It is probably this that makes my joy, for having nothing, I shall receive everything from God" (HLC, p. 67).

She goes even farther. So that this "mystery of mercy"[2] may be known more widely, Thérèse really seems "to wish" that many newly baptized babies "would die," just as she once did for her father and mother in her "outbursts of affection" (SS, p. 17). And that is not primarily "so that they will go to Heaven," but to offer these "newly opened flowers"—which have her preference—to Jesus. As much as she possibly can, she wants to offer him "the sweetness of giving" (GCII, p. 795) by overwhelming these innocent children beyond all measure. Without this viewpoint, it would be impossible to understand stanzas 10 and 11 of the poem. Thérèse is not expressing any morbid instincts here, but rather her "extreme love"[3] for Jesus. Besides, isn't she consenting to her own premature death at the same time? Her health has been declining very rapidly since November.

Once we see clearly this doctrinal background, we better understand this poem, which is, granted, too naively descriptive. No doubt Thérèse willingly lingers to "pamper" these little innocent children throughout the first five stanzas (as her sister, Marie, who on the morning of Thérèse's clothing was so finicky with her curls a few minutes before the ceremony that Thérèse begged her: "Enough! enough!"). But she is not taken in by her own imagery. She would soon wisely remind Mother Agnes, who was too inclined to superficial interpretations (GCII, p. 1099; p. 1119):

"The Holy Innocents will not be little children in heaven; they will only have the indefinable charms of childhood. They are represented as 'children' because we need pictures to understand spiritual things" (HLC, p. 48). It is really to a spiritual universe that these flowers, children, and stars take us, to a universe radiant with freshness, light, and joy.

At the end of the eighth stanza, Thérèse reveals herself: *She* is the one who wants to "caress the Face of Jesus" and even "kiss" it (11, 7). What her tenderness as a *spouse* has never allowed her to do (for in her writings, it is always Jesus who gives the kiss), the "childish daring" of little children, with whom she categorizes herself in a trick of love, at last lets her do. In putting herself on stage from stanza 9 on, she gives real strength to the end of the poem (sts. 9–11).

Always consistent, Thérèse is not satisfied with mere words. Does she really want to "stay little"? She was offered an excellent opportunity for just that on the very evening of December 28, 1896. For the feast of the Holy Innocents (a day when the observance of silence was lifted), the sisters had expressed the desire to hear this newly composed poem sung. Mother Marie de Gonzague at first acquiesced. But while the community was still "under the spell," she lost her temper. She thought this success would only contribute to "bolster up Sister Thérèse's pride."[4] But Thérèse remained calm. She was "so little" that from then on she did not "seem to feel it or suffer from it..." (GCII, p. 1117).

---

[1] Rm 4:6, 4 and 3:24. Other Biblical texts important for an interpretation of this poem are Is 40:11; Mk 10:14,16; Mt 18:10, 4; Rev 14: 2–5.

[2] Cf. St. Bernard's sermon on the Holy Innocents that Thérèse had read in Dom Guéranger's *The Liturgical Year*.

[3] Cf. rough draft 10, 5 in *Poésies*, vol II, p. 248.

[4] From Mother Agnes's "Preparatory Notes for the Apostolic Process."

(Melody: "La rose mousse" or "Le fil de la Vierge")

To My Little Brothers in Heaven

1   Happy little children, with what tenderness
              The King of Heaven
     Once blessed you and covered your joyous heads
              With caresses!
     You were the symbol of all Innocent Children,
              And in you I glimpse
     Blessings the King of kings gives you beyond all measure
              In Heaven.

2   You have contemplated the immense riches
              Of Paradise
     Before having known our bitter sadness,
              Dear little Lilies.
     O fragrant Buds! Harvested just at dawn
              By the Lord,
     Love's sweet Sun knew how to make you blossom:
              It was his Heart!...

3   What ineffable care, what exquisite tenderness,
              And what love
     Our Mother the Church joyfully lavishes on you,
              One-day-old children!...
     In her maternal arms, you were offered to God
              As first fruits.
     For all Eternity, you will be the delight
              Of God's beautiful blue Heaven.

4   Children, you form the virginal procession
              Of the Sweet Lamb,
     And over and over you can sing a new song,
              O astonishing privilege!
     Without fighting you achieved the glory
              Of conquerors;
     The Savior won the victory for you,
              Charming victors!

5   We see no precious stones sparkling
               In your hair.
        The mere golden reflection of your silken locks
               Charms Heaven......
        The treasures of the Elect, their palms, their crowns,
               All is yours.
        Children, in the Holy Homeland your rich thrones
               Are their laps...

6   Together you play with the little angels
               Near the altar,
        And your childish songs, gracious armies,
               Charm Heaven.
        God is teaching you how He makes roses,
               Birds, the winds.
        No genius here below knows as many things
               As you, Children!...

7   Lifting all the mysterious veils,
               From the azure firmament,
        You take the stars of a thousand lights
               In your little hands.
        Running, you often leave a silver trail
               At night.
        When I gaze up in the sky at the white milky way,
               I think I see you......

8   After all your feast days you run
               Into the arms of Mary.
        Hiding your blond heads under her starry veil,
               You doze off.
        Charming little Imps, your childish audacity
               Pleases the Lord.
        You dare to caress his Adorable Face..........
               What a favor!...

9   It's you the Lord gives me as a model,
               Holy Innocents.
        I want to be your faithful likeness here below,
               Little Children.

Ah! deign to obtain for me the virtues of childhood.
    Your candor,
Your perfect surrender, your lovely innocence
    Charm my heart.

10   O Lord! You know the ardent desires
    Of my exiled soul.
Beautiful Lily of the valley, I'd like to harvest
    Brilliant lilies.
These springtime Buds, I seek them and love them
    For your pleasure.
Deign to pour on them the Dew of Baptism.
    Come pluck them......

11   Yes, I want to increase the candid army
    Of Innocents.
My sufferings, my joys, I offer them in exchange
    For Children's Souls.
Among these Innocents, I claim a place,
    King of the Elect.
Like them, in Heaven I want to kiss your Sweet Face,
    O my Jesus!.....

PN 45 – My Joy!

(January 21, 1897)

"My whole soul is in that," Thérèse simply said as she handed "My Joy!" to Mother Agnes on her feastday, January 21, 1897.

This poem is one of the most astonishing and one of the richest that Thérèse wrote, at a time when she was approaching the most terrible straits of her trial of faith and—soon—her agony (cf. General Introduction). Behind apparently naive phrases and images an attitude of faith and a mystical battle are at work here. They are expressed without artistic affectation, but with a surprising inner intensity and vital strength. Each word is weighted heavily with experience and maturity, and the development of the stanzas lets us really enter into Thérèse's "soul," yet she uses a singing meter [the octosyllable in French], as if she wanted to sidetrack us.

We see her soul as it has always been, with all its contradictions: her optimism in the face of life and her understanding of suffering, her burning love for Jesus and her concern to please him in everything, her awareness of her littleness and her magnanimity in her spiritual motherhood.

We see her soul at the time she confided to Sister Teresa of Saint Augustine: "I don't believe in eternal life, it seems to me that after this mortal life there is nothing left... Everything has disappeared for me, love is all I have" (DE, p. 786). How did she get to such a tragic interior state? How did she fix her joy in such an impregnable light? The poem gives an answer.

It already points to the famous June 1897 page of her autobiography: "Lord, you fill me with joy in all that you do" (SS, p. 214). We find identical themes in both texts: joy in suffering, unending struggle, care to hide this suffering from others and if possible from God himself, to offer it all for her brothers and sisters (PN 45, however, does not mention "unbelievers").

But in contrast the poem also brings out the progress Thérèse made in the next few months. In January her joy was still an obstinate act of faith and, when all is said and done, not very joyous. However moving these vestiges of will power may be, they will be swept away in "An Unpetalled Rose" (PN 51), where Thérèse reached the utmost degree of abandonment. Later, in the infirmary, she was completely natural and truly cheerful. Her secret to such "détente" was "the little way," which she clearly affirms in stanzas 3 and 4, and unflaggingly lived out as her trial weighed her down.

So the smile and the flowers in "My Joy!" should not throw us off track. A verse like "I love the night as much as the day" is of astonishing courage and is important theologically and spiritually in her life at this time. Thérèse signed this terrible affirmation with her whole behavior right up to her death. And likewise for the challenge, "What are death or life to me?" which she heroically reiterated in the infirmary (HLC, pp. 128–129; DE, p.

735). Her going from better to worse and to better again finished purifying her impatience to die.

Precious as this poem is as an autobiographical document, it still holds our attention by its very form. The change from quatrains (in the original manuscript) to stanzas of eight verses (in her copy for Maurice Bellière) gives it more inspiration and consistency. There are some beautiful images to enhance what she wants to say, such as (in st. 1) the "springtime rose" combined in an unexpected and poetic way with "not ephemeral," even though the rose conveys precisely the feeling of the ephemeral (cf. Malherbe: "And the rose lived what roses live...") or her "blue sky" that "sinks" into night.

The dynamic succession of images, in a broken line, would in itself deserve an extensive analysis. In the last two stanzas the tempo accelerates and the images are stirred up. The fire of suffering and love has completely stripped Thérèse, who loses herself in joy. She identifies herself with "Jesus, my joy," which sounds like a kind of apposition.

Springing up like a final bouquet, this superb verse ends by *personalizing* the joy that, right from the first stanza, "is found" in Thérèse's heart and "smiles" at her. This joy is no one else but Jesus himself, invisible but present in the heart of her night.

(Melody: "Rêve, parfum ou frais murmure")

My Joy!

1 There are some souls on earth
Who search in vain for happiness,
But for me, it's just the opposite.
Joy is in my heart.
This joy is not ephemeral.
I possess it forever.
Like the springtime rose,
It smiles at me every day.

2 Truly I'm so happy.
I always have my way....
How could I not be joyful
And not show my cheerfulness?
My joy is to love suffering.
I smile while shedding tears.
I accept with gratitude
The thorns mingled with the flowers.

3   When the blue Sky becomes somber
           And begins to abandon me,
           My joy is to stay in the shadow
           To hide and humble myself.
           My joy is the Holy Will
           Of Jesus, my only love,
           So I live without any fear.
           I love the night as much as the day.

4   My joy is to stay little,
           So when I fall on the way,
           I can get up very quickly,
           And Jesus takes me by the hand.
           Then I cover him with caresses
           And tell Him He's everything for me,
           And I'm twice as tender
           When He slips away from my faith.

5   If sometimes I shed tears,
           My joy is to hide them well.
           Oh! how many charms there are in suffering
           When one knows how to hide it with flowers!
           I truly want to suffer without saying so
           That Jesus may be consoled.
           My joy is to see him smile
           When my heart is exiled.....

6   My joy is to struggle unceasingly
           To bring forth spiritual children.
           It's with a heart burning with tenderness
           That I keep saying to Jesus:
           "For you, my Divine Little Brother,
           I'm happy to suffer.
           My only joy on earth
           Is to be able to please you.

7   Lord, I'm willing to live a long time more
           If that is your desire.
           I'd like to follow you to Heaven
           If that would make you happy.
           Love, that fire from the Homeland,
           Never ceases to consume me.
           What do life and death matter to me?
           Jesus, my joy, it's to love you!"

PN 46 – To My Guardian Angel
(January 1897)

This poem's tone of calm fervor is characteristic of the last phase of Thérèse's poetic evolution: it is less visionary, less bathed in sensible consolations, and more deliberate. We find many themes sketched out here, and in the middle of the third stanza it would seem that Thérèse sees herself having passed into another world. Is it just the cloister or already death?

To measure Thérèse's poetic evolution and the state of spiritual deprivation she had reached, we only need to compare this work to the verses she dedicated to Mother Agnes not even eighteen months before, "Fair Angel of My Childhood" (PN 22).

In this present poem, after the beautiful opening vision uniting the brilliant stars, the candle's flame, and the glory of the "Eternal's throne," we come back down to earth. The "Brother" has come down from on high to be a traveling companion to someone "weak." He brings his "help" and "tenderness." The child does not need to worry about the road. She is asked just "to look at Heaven" (which was then so impenetrable to her gaze). There is no question of her flying away! Her part is "the little way," glorified in the second stanza, whose soft atmosphere contrasts with the brightness of the first.

Here there are no flowers to pick, except those of "sacrifices" and "austere poverty" (st. 4). The "child" does not forget the "sinner," who is also her "brother," lost on other roads.

A parenthesis on this little way: We note that the third stanza speaks of consolation (for others...), imploring for those she loves who are still crying on earth. So is Thérèse anticipating her departure? A tone of great tenderness runs through the last three verses of this stanza, where Jesus' goodness, the charms of suffering, and the reminder of little Thérèse ("And softly, whisper my name") create a relieving balm (cf. PN 22, sts. 14–15).

The glorious tone of the beginning comes back again in the final verses, which are almost exultant, like some of the Psalms, with those "For you... For me... For me... With... With..." at the beginning of the verses. [In the French] there are rich sounds in this last stanza: "Royaume, Gloire, Richesse, Roi des rois, ciboire, Croix" ["Kingdom, Glory, Riches, King of kings, ciborium, Cross"]. Eight of these words end in "oi," plus the rhymes "Gloire" and "ciboire" ["Glory" and "ciborium"]. Although the goal of the little way is hidden, Thérèse goes toward it in "peace" as she repeats a kind of "litany of glory" in which so many of the riches of heaven and "joys that will last forever" are concentrated in a few verses.

This poem was probably written for—and at the request of—Sister Marie Philomena. But that information calls for some nuancing.[1] Be that as it may, this poem was well-suited for this religious who was so "humble and little" by nature and grace. "What intelligence in that innocent soul! And what unaffected love of God!", Sister Marie Philomena's spiritual director exclaimed (in 1924 after her death). That love of God especially took the form of a real compassion for the Lord in his sorrow for the sinner: "What a martyrdom such a sight must be for your Divine Heart! Ah! I beg you, give my heart as much of it as it can bear. How sad to know that you are so good and yet so offended!" (Notes, no date.) Another characteristic of Sister Marie Philomena was her attachment to her family. After having delayed entering the cloister, she even had to leave for several years because of it. Later this attachment changed into anxious affection. Finally, it is not necessary to recall her love for "the Host" (cf. the introduction to PN 40).

For all these reasons, it is not surprising that Thérèse, who was very ill in the spring of 1897, wanted to leave this poem as a "remembrance" to the Sister whose "little girl" she called herself, perhaps referring to their year together in the novitiate (1888–1889, cf. GCI, p. 415). That was the time when the mutual respect of these two humble religious blurred the thirty-four–year difference in their ages.

[1] [The "Copy of the Writings" for the Beatification Process lists this poem as written "at the request of Sr. Marie Philomena," but a more recent study reveals that it was probably written spontaneously by Thérèse in January 1897 and then *copied* in May for Sr. Marie Philomena as a goodbye remembrance. Cf. *Poésies*, vol. II, p. 263.—Trans.]

J.M.J.T.

(Melody: "Par les chants les plus magnifiques")

To My Guardian Angel

1   Glorious Guardian of my soul,
        You who shine in God's beautiful Heaven
        As a sweet and pure flame
        Near the Eternal's throne,
        You come down to earth for me,
        And enlightening me with your splendor,
        Fair Angel, you become my Brother,
        My Friend, my Consoler!...

2   Knowing my great weakness,
        You lead me by the hand,
        And I see you tenderly
        Remove the stone from my path.

Your sweet voice is always inviting me
To look only at Heaven.
The more you see me humble and little,
The more your face is radiant.

3   O you! who travel through space
More swiftly than lightning,
I beg you, fly in my place.
Close to those who are dear to me.
With your wing dry their tears.
Sing how good Jesus is.
Sing that suffering has its charms,
And softly, whisper my name....

4   During my short life I want
To save my fellow sinners.
O Fair Angel of the Homeland,
Give me holy fervor.
I have nothing but my sacrifices
And my austere poverty.
With your celestial delights,
Offer them to the Trinity.

5   For you the Kingdom and the Glory,
The Riches of the King of kings.
For me the ciborium's humble Host.
For me the Cross's treasure.
With the Cross, with the Host,
With your celestial aid,
In peace I await the other life,
The joys that will last forever.

To my dear Sister Marie-Philomena
a remembrance of *her little girl.*
Thérèse of the Child Jesus of the Hl. F.
rel. Carm. ind. [unworthy Carmelite religious]

PN 47 – To Théophane Vénard

(February 2, 1897)

"Tell me whom you sing about, and I'll tell you who you are...."

There would be no end to listing the traits of Théophane Vénard (1829–1861) in which Thérèse could spontaneously see herself: youth, cheerfulness, purity of heart, affection for family, but also love full of freshness and poetry for Jesus, the right appreciation of littleness, filial trust in Mary, and, more, offering the missions even one's outpoured blood—in joy. "My soul resembles his," she would later tell her sisters (DE, p. 422). And, as a farewell remembrance, she gave them an anthology of letters from this "little saint."

"Interested and touched more than she could say" (GCII, p. 1071) when she read Théophane's life in November of 1896, right away Thérèse gave this young missionary to Tonkin a special place among her heavenly friendships. She was still being influenced by this grace when she wrote "a few couplets that are quite personal" for the thirty-sixth anniversary of his beheading (February 2, 1897).

So Thérèse took up her "lyre" (1, 8) as she often did on special occasions. To "sing of" her blessed friend, she rediscovered the feelings her "favorite saint," Saint Cecilia, had inspired in the past: singing and flowers, but also suffering and martyrdom, a strenuous apostolate, "the Sword and Fire." Perhaps in the first four stanzas she does not look out enough for redundancies—and even for a certain sentimentality of tone. But then she finds her craft again with the powerful fifth stanza, the great cosmic amplification of the sixth, and the enthusiasm and impatience of the last.

On March 19 when she sent the poem to Fr. Roulland (cf. GCII, p. 1071), she drew his attention to the next to last stanza. That was her way of telling him her secret plan to be a missionary and to join the recent foundation in Hanoi—if her health did not stand in the way. This was really talking nonsense, for "it would be necessary that the sheath be as solid as the sword, and perhaps the sheath would be cast into the sea before reaching Tonkin" (*ibid.*, p. 1072). As a matter of fact, the "sheath" was deteriorating more and more. And Théophane Vénard hardly seemed in a hurry to make her strong again—on the contrary (HLC, p. 52). As for the "sword," Thérèse's spiritual trial, even more than her illness, was only serving to sharpen it all the more for the last battle drawing near. The following poem, "My Weapons," will show the cutting edge of that.

Thérèse's missionary desires to "make Jesus loved" kept growing in her heart, as her signature reminds us.[1] But from then on, she knew that even death would not thwart her plans. After her contact with Théophane, she increasingly experienced that communion of saints that binds earth and heaven in time and space for the salvation of "the universe, one speck" in God's sight. During these same weeks, her confidence that she would "come back to earth" (GCII, pp. 1026–1027) was becoming stronger so that she could work without rest right up to the end of the world (HLC, p. 102).

In the infirmary, Thérèse always kept Théophane's portrait with her. "Pointing to Heaven" (HLC, p. 143) in that picture, he supported his sister in her "painful martyrdom" when "dreadful thoughts were obsessing her" (DE, p. 525). She even suspected a touch of mischievousness in that picture of her brother who "seemed to look at [her] out of the corner of his eye with a kind of mischievous look" (HLC, p. 144). But then *children* understand one another.[2] They have their own way of being heroic.

---

[1] "A very little flower who would like to make Jesus loved!..." Thérèse left out this signature on her final copy of the poem.
[2] Theophane signed one of his last letters to his bishop, "Little child Ven."

(Melody: "Les adieux du Martyr")

To Théophane Vénard

Priest of the Foreign Mission Society,
Martyred at Tonkin at the age of 31.

1   All the Elect celebrate your praises,
O Théophane! Angelic Martyr.
And I know, in the Saintly army
The seraphim aspire to serve you!...
Since, exiled on this earth, I can't
Blend my voice with those of the Elect,
On this foreign shore I too want
To take up my lyre and sing of your virtues.....

2   Your short exile was like a sweet canticle
Whose notes knew how to touch hearts,
And for Jesus your poetic soul
Made flowers spring up at each moment.
In ascending to the Celestial sphere,
Your farewell song again was spring-like.
You whispered: "As for Me, little ephemeral one,
I'm going off first to God's beautiful Heaven!..."

3   Blessed Martyr, at the moment of your death
     You savored the happiness of suffering.
     To you suffering for God seemed a delight.
     Smiling, you knew how to live and to die.....
     You hastened to say to your executioner
     When he offered to shorten your torment:
     "The longer my painful martyrdom lasts,
     The better it will be and the happier I'll be!!!"

4   Virginal Lily, in the springtime of your life
     The King of Heaven heard your desire.
     I see in you: The Flower in bloom
     That the Lord plucked for his good pleasure......
     And now you are no longer exiled.
     The Blessed admire your splendor.
     The Rose of Love, the Immaculate Virgin
     Breathes the freshness of your perfume.

5   Soldier of Christ, ah! lend me your weapons.
     For sinners, here below I want
     To struggle, to suffer in the shadow of your victory palms.
     Protect me, come steady my arm.
     Without stopping the war for them I want
     To storm the Kingdom of God,
     For the Lord cast down on the earth
     Not peace, but the Sword and Fire!....

6   I also love that infidel shore
     That was the object of your burning love.
     I would happily fly to it
     If God called me there some day...
     But in his eyes, there is no distance.
     For Him the whole universe is just one speck.
     My weak love, my little sufferings,
     Blessed by Him, make Him loved far and wide!...

7   Ah! if I were a springtime flower
     That the Lord soon wanted to pluck,
     O Blessed Martyr! I implore you,
     Descend from Heaven at my last hour.
     Come embrace me in this mortal dwelling,
     And I'll be able to fly with the souls
     That will make up your eternal procession!...

PN 48 – My Weapons
(March 25, 1897)

This poem is nervous, warlike, taut, without any poetic fat, and thrown on paper like someone going into battle. This is a poem with no fear or trembling. It shows a Thérèse in the crucible of suffering who, like Joan of Arc at the stake, is sure of herself and sure of God. Thérèse knows she is queen. She is a queen who is fighting, polishing her weapons so as to triumph, and whose first concern is what is effective. The two quotations she uses in the epigraph are very significant: The one from St. Paul (Eph 6:11) is borrowed from the Rule of Carmel and straightaway introduces us to what we might call the "dubbing of a knight." The one from the Song of Songs is astonishing—and very revealing of Thérèse's state of mind at this time: It depicts a queen awesome in her omnipotence, "terrible as an army ranged in battle, like a choir of music in an armed camp." In bringing together these two unrelated verses, Thérèse creates a very strong, dynamic image appropriate for uplifting a religious profession—which was the immediate occasion for this work—as well as the whole poem. One has to have a truly poetic vision to use such dazzling, antithetical quotes in this way as a source of inspiration. Thérèse is also brave to launch into a complete allegory of the vows, an awkward subject for poetry if ever there was one.

Thérèse dedicated "My Weapons" to her cousin Marie Guérin for her profession on March 25, 1897. It was sung that night in community, following the custom (cf. PN 10 and PN 29). Thérèse was asked to write something because of her role as assistant novice mistress.

Both a "little angel" and a "strong woman" (GCII, p. 909), a "little child" and a "valiant warrior" (PN 36), Sister Marie of the Eucharist could see herself in this poem of contrasts, which presents religious vows as the "apparel" and "armor" of the "Spouse of the King" of Heaven.

Beyond Marie, Thérèse was alluding even more to Sister Geneviève, who had felt disappointed the year before about the official poem that she should have had (cf. introduction to PN 27). In the cloister, Céline had kept her enthusiasm for everything that had to do with "ideas of knighthood."

But for Thérèse herself, this poem was much more than a matter of a chivalrous tale, even if the allegorical language gives us that impression. She herself was soon to be more specific about this (GCII, p. 1085, in reply to a letter from Abbé Bellière, GCII, p. 1081). She was waging war among the "realities of life" (SS, p. 72) and—soon—death. The winter that was drawing to a close had been fatal for her. At the beginning of Lent, she had stretched her strength to the limit in order to fast. It was too much for her. She had fever "every day at three o'clock sharp" and "her meals did not go down at all" (GCII, p. 1076). The doctor had prescribed rubdowns with

coarse hair gloves, vesicatories [an extremely painful remedy of hot plas-
ters applied to the skin to induce blistering], tincture of iodine lotion,
and—later—"pointes de feu" [a cauterizing remedy consisting in the re-
peated puncturing of the skin with red-hot needles]. These treatments wore
her out more than they helped her (cf. GCII, p. 1189). She expected to die
within the year. Her struggle with her inner darkness was becoming more
and more bitter (cf. introduction to PN 45).

So the clear willpower of this poem is not a literary device. Even less
is she boasting. This is the accurate reflection of harsh reality, of indispens-
able heroism.

"My Weapons" was Thérèse's last official composition, almost a last
will and testament to her community. "Smiling" (like her friend Théophane
Vénard, PN 47), "singing" (like a loving spouse), she was fighting right up
to the limits of her strength, before falling "with her weapons in hand" (we
note the power of this ending.) Her death, six months later, was a real flour-
ishing signature to this poem.

My Weapons

(Canticle composed for   (Melody: "Partez, Hérauts
   a profession day)   de la bonne nouvelle")

> "Put on the armor of God so that you may be able to stand
> firm against the tactics of the devil."   (St. Paul)

> "The Spouse of the King is terrible as an army ranged in battle, she is
> like a choir of music in an armed camp."   (Song of Songs)

1   I have put on the weapons of the All-Powerful.
         His divine hand has deigned to adorn me.
         Henceforth nothing causes me alarm.
         Who can separate me from his love?
         At his side, rushing into the arena,
         I shall fear neither sword nor fire.
         My enemies will know that I am queen,
             That I am the spouse of a God!
         O my Jesus! I shall keep the armor
         That I put on under your adored eyes.
     Up to the evening of life, my finest adornment
             Will be my sacred Vows!

2   O Poverty, my first sacrifice
Even unto death, you will follow me everywhere,
For I know, to run into the arena
The Athlete must be detached from everything.
People of the world, taste remorse and sorrow,
Those bitter fruits of your vanity.
As for me, in the arena I joyously cut
      The palms of Poverty.
Jesus said: "It is by violence
That one takes the kingdom of Heaven."
So! Poverty will serve as my Lance,
      As my glorious Helmet.

3   Chastity makes me the sister of angels,
Of those pure, victorious Spirits.
One day I hope to fly in their armies,
But during this exile I must fight like them.
I must fight with no rest or truce
For my Spouse, the Lord of hosts,
Chastity is the celestial sword
      That can conquer hearts for him.
Chastity is my invincible armor.
My enemies are vanquished by it.
By it I become, O inexpressible joy!
      Jesus' Spouse!

4   The arrogant angel in the midst of light
Cried out: "I shall not obey!"
As for me, I cry out in the night of this life,
"Here below I always want to obey."
I sense springing up within me a holy audacity.
I face the fury of all hell.
Obedience is my strong Breastplate
      And the Shield of my heart.
Lord God of Hosts, I want no other glory
Than to submit my will in everything.
Since the Obedient One will tell of his victories
      For all Eternity.

5   If I have the powerful armor of the Warrior,
       If I imitate him and fight bravely,
       Like the Virgin of ravishing graces,
       I also want to sing as I fight.
       You make the strings of my lyre vibrate,
       And this lyre, O Jesus, is my heart!
       Then I can sing of the strength and sweetness
              Of your Mercies.
       Smiling, I bravely face the fire.
       And in your arms, O my Divine Spouse,
    I shall die singing on the battlefield,
              My Weapons in hand!...

PN 49 – To Our Lady of Perpetual Help

(March 1897)

Western Catholicism is now familiar with Eastern icons. That was not the case in nineteenth-century France. Devotion to Our Lady of Perpetual Help (probably painted in Crete in the fourteen or fifteenth century, after the Byzantine style of Hodegetria) was one of the rare exceptions to the rule. This devotion developed beautifully from 1866 on after being promoted by the Redemptorists.

Even as a little girl, Marie-Louise Castel (Marie of the Trinity) had felt drawn to this picture. In the mysterious gaze of the Virgin, she saw the mirror of her own childlike conscience: The Virgin would smile at her when she was good, but would be sad when she was naughty.

In 1894 when Marie was an aspirant to the Carmel of Lisieux, she attributed to Our Lady of Perpetual Help the solution to the difficulties delaying her entry.

In 1897, offering her life for priests, this young Carmelite was asking for strength from Our Lady, who, according to the usual interpretation of the miraculous painting, is reassuring and strengthening the Child Jesus, frightened by the vision of the instruments of his Passion.

These thoughts probably kept Sister Marie of the Trinity going during her annual retreat in March. At her request, Thérèse expressed them in a few easy verses. They are a canticle as unaffected as the pictures in a prayer book. And they are a very simple testimony of filial love for Mary.

J.M.J.T.

To Our Lady of Perpetual Help

(1st Couplet)

Dear Mother, from my tender youth
Your sweet picture has delighted my heart.
In your gaze I could read your tenderness,
And near you I found happiness.

(Refrain)

Virgin Mary, after this exile I'll go
To the Celestial shore to see you forever,
But here below your sweet Picture
Is my Perpetual Help!....

(2nd Couplet)
When I was a good girl and very obedient,
It seemed that you were smiling at me;
And if sometimes I was a little naughty,
I thought I could see you crying over me...

(3rd Couplet)
In answering my simple prayers,
You showed me your maternal love.
In contemplating you I found on earth
A foretaste of the good things of Heaven.

(4th Couplet)
When I'm struggling, O my dear Mother,
You strengthen my heart in the fight,
For you know, at the evening of this life
I want to offer Priests to the Lord!...

(5th Couplet)
Always, always, Image of my Mother,
Yes, you will be my happiness, my treasure.
And at my last hour I would like
To fix my gaze on you again.

(Last Refrain)
Then flying away to the Celestial shore,
I'll go to sit on your lap, Mother,
Then I'll be able to receive
Your sweet kisses!...

Remembrance of a blessed retreat—March 1897
                    (Thérèse of the Child Jesus to her little Sister)

PN 50 – To Joan of Arc
(May 1897)

The year of her death, Thérèse felt the need to rediscover the mystery of Joan of Arc,[1] as if to identify with Joan at the threshold of the passion she herself was going through. (Likewise she revised her poem "To Saint Cecilia." In her last days she acknowledged and strengthened her great friendships.) Later in the infirmary she often referred to Joan.

It was not in victory and glory that Joan was fulfilled, but in the "dungeon" and in "betrayal," where she identified with Jesus. And He, by his death, gives every suffering its "charm." Thérèse also felt she was "at the bottom of a black dungeon, laden with heavy chains" in her trial of faith. She was drinking "the bitter cup of the Beloved" in her illness. To us she also seems "more radiant and more beautiful in her dark prison."

Thérèse was not even spared betrayal. As if Compiègne and Rouen were not enough, Joan of Arc had just been the victim of a new treason in the nineteenth century. For years an impostor, Leo Taxil, had used her name and her mission to deceive French Catholics. He all but compromised the Holy See with his disgraceful farce. However, he went beyond the limits of the believable in claiming to launch "a new Joan of Arc" at the very time the Church was encouraging devotion to the real one. Exposed as a fraud, this character flaunted his treacherous act at a well-orchestrated press conference on April 19, 1897, in the heart of Paris. The show he had organized began with a slide of a Joan of Arc in chains.

This profanation of Joan wounded Thérèse too. But she felt betrayed twice over, because it was her *own* photo of Joan as prisoner that had been jeered at that night.[2] There are some sufferings so deep that we have to bear them alone....

[In French] the Alexandrine is a fine metrical support for this sad and profound meditation. This is an excellent poem. It is dense in its simplicity. It moves magnificently from glory to bitterness and death. Then it rises again all the way to the "love" that transfigures and redeems all sorrow into "treasure."

Until very recently, no one paid any attention to the blue sheet of paper on which Thérèse wrote these verses in pencil. In all likelihood, they were written in May 1897. This document was not submitted to the "Process of the Writings."

[1] Joan was Thérèse's companion from childhood; cf. SS, p. 72, RP 1, PN 4 and especially RP 3.

[2] [Thérèse and the Carmelites of Lisieux, like most French Catholics, were completely taken in by the story of the conversion of "Diana Vaughan" from satanism and freemasonry to Catholicism. Thérèse was especially impressed that this conversion had taken place through the intercession of Joan of Arc. She even wrote a short play

about it, entitled *The Triumph of Humility*, in which she showed that the main weapon to defeat Satan is humility. Mother Agnes also asked Thérèse to write a poem for "Diana," but the inspiration would not come. Instead, Thérèse sent her a photograph of herself and Céline (cf. p. 114—pose 14—in *The Photo Album of Saint Thérèse of Lisieux*), taken the previous year for Thérèse's play *Joan of Arc Accomplishing Her Mission*. This photo formed the backdrop for Leo Taxil on the night of April 19, 1897, when he revealed to more than 400 people that he himself was "Diana Vaughan." A few days later the newspaper *Le Normand* described how Taxil had chosen this photo to make fun of devotion to Joan of Arc. Thérèse was deeply humiliated—at the very time she was struggling in her trial of faith and in her illness. For a detailed study of this subject, see the French *Le triomphe de l'humilité: Thérèse mystifiée, L'affaire Léo Taxil et le Manuscrit B* (Paris: Cerf/DDB, 1975)—Trans.]

To Joan of Arc

1   When the Lord God of Hosts gave you the victory,
You drove out the foreigner and had the king crowned.
Joan, your name became renowned in history.
Our greatest conquerors paled before you.

2   But that was only a fleeting glory.
Your name needed a Saint's halo.
So the Beloved offered you his bitter cup,
And, like Him, you were spurned by men.

3   At the bottom of a black dungeon, laden with heavy chains,
The cruel foreigner filled you with grief.
Not one of your friends took part in your pain.
Not one came forward to wipe your tears.

4   Joan, in your dark prison you seem to me
More radiant, more beautiful than at your king's coronation.
This heavenly reflection of eternal glory,
Who then brought it upon you? It was betrayal.

5   Ah! If the God of love in this valley of tears
Had not come to seek betrayal and death,
Suffering would hold no attraction for us.
Now we love it, it is our treasure.

Taken after June 3, 1897. Thérèse with her novices in the cloister courtyard, casting flower petals at the stone crucifix (see PN 51).

PN 51 – An Unpetalled Rose
(May 19, 1897)

Probably few mystics have gone as far as Thérèse—wasted away by illness, at the end of her strength—in offering her "nothingness" by throwing herself under Jesus' feet, in an act of pure and total love. That is how we discover her in "An Unpetalled Rose": She is not asking for anything, she abandons herself, she is already almost beyond death, almost beyond love, we might say.

This poem, really distressing from a biographical point of view—is equally very beautiful from the poetic point of view. There is no nonsense here. The tone is very tender, but very strong, and not insipid in the least. [In the French] the rhythm she chose (an Alexandrine followed immediately by a verse of four syllables) is perfectly suited to her subject, better than the same form in PN 44 (cf. General Introduction).

In the month of May when the roses began to bloom, the novices once again started up their "liturgy of love" for the crucifix in the cloister garden, and they would "strew flowers" at it (PN 34). But that year Thérèse did not join them, except for a last photo in which she looks exhausted.[1] Her tuberculosis was then waging its final offensive. Worn out with fever and coughing, Thérèse was dispensed from community acts one after the other: the choral office, her work in the vestry, her talks with the novices, recreation, and eating in the refectory. From then on, one last task remained: "I must die".... die by being dissolved day after day, like a "rose" that "is unpetalled." This took place in the most absolute self-giving possible: "unreservedly," "naturally," "without regret," without any show ("artlessly"). Thérèse's generosity was only equaled by her delicacy. She wanted her life, "squandered" that way, to be only gentleness ("sweetly," "soften") under the "little feet" of the Child Jesus and the "last steps" of the Man of Sorrows. Jesus alone, "Beauty Supreme," could deserve such a sacrifice.

The symbol of the Saint of Lisieux as the "unpetalled rose" is quite hackneyed today, but it springs up in all its pathetic beauty here, as genuinely as Thérèse really lived it. One might say that the circumstances of the poem matter little. Nevertheless, we need to recall them on account of the poem's epilogue.

It was by way of an amiable challenge that Mother Henriette, an austere Carmelite nun in Paris, asked for a poem for herself in the spring of 1897. After a brief term as prioress, she had become very ill and was prematurely reduced to a state of helplessness (although she was only fifty-five). Fearful and living in dryness, she dreaded death. All this made her rather sceptical of anything having to do with signs and wonders. And here came the prioress of Lisieux, Mother Marie de Gonzague, telling her wonderful things about one of her young religious, whom she was trying to talk out of dying. And besides her, Marie of the Trinity, who herself had lived two years in the Carmel of Paris (Avenue de Messine), was writing to sing the praises of her novice mistress and friend. So Mother Henriette is said to have written words to this effect: "If it is true that this little Sister in Lisieux is such a pearl and writes such beautiful poetry, then let her send me one of her poems, and I shall see for myself." [2] Perhaps she even suggested the theme of the unpetalled rose. At least that is what Sister Marie of the Trinity affirmed. She continued:

"Since the subject of the unpetalled rose spoke to our dear Saint, she put her whole heart into it. Mother Henriette was very pleased with the poem, only she wrote me that it lacked one last verse explaining that at death God would gather together the discarded petals to form a beautiful rose that would shine for all eternity." [3]

She was completely mistaken.... For Thérèse, "To love is to give everything. It's to give oneself" (PN 54, 22), without any hope of return. Thérèse's response to Marie of the Trinity was: "Let that good Mother write those verses herself as she thinks best. As for me, I am not at all inspired to do it. My wish is to be unpetalled forever, to make God happy. Period. That is all!..." [4]

Yes, "that was all." Another spontaneous answer, this time to Mother Agnes, came soon after, like a bold signature attesting to just what point of no return Thérèse had reached: "I don't want to give in order to receive.... It's God whom I love, not myself" (DE, p. 496).

[1] See pp. 208–209 (poses 44 and 44A) in *The Photo Album of Saint Thérèse of Lisieux.* This photo was taken in June 1897.
[2] According to a story told at the Carmel of Boulogne-sur-Seine. But we should add that since Mother Henriette made her profession on May 3, 1864, she would not have celebrated her jubilee that May 19, 1897. [Note error in footnote 2, GCII, p. 1086—Trans.]
[3] Note from Sister Marie of the Trinity to Mother Agnes of Jesus, 1/17/1935.
[4] *Ibid.*

(Melody for "Fil de la Vierge"   J.M.J.T.   May 19, 1897
or "La rose mousse")

An Unpetalled Rose

1   Jesus, when I see you held by your Mother,
         Leaving her arms
   Trying, trembling, *your first steps*
         On our sad earth,
   Before you I'd like *to unpetal a rose*
         In its freshness
   So that your little foot might rest ever so softly
         On a flower!....

2   *This unpetalled rose* is the faithful image,
         Divine Child,
   Of the heart that wants to sacrifice itself for you unreservedly
         at each moment.
   Lord, on your altars more than one new rose
         Likes to shine.
   It gives itself to you..... but I dream of something else:
         To be unpetalled!... "

3   The rose in its splendor can adorn your feast,
         Lovable Child,
   But *the unpetalled rose* is just flung out
         To blow away.
   An unpetalled rose gives itself unaffectedly
         To be no more.
   Like it, with joy I abandon myself to you,
         Little Jesus.

4   One walks *on rose petals* with no regrets,
         And this debris
   Is a simple ornament that one disposes of artlessly,
         That I've understood.
   Jesus, for your love I've squandered my life,
         My future.
   In the eyes of men, a rose forever *withered,*
         I must *die!...*

5   *For you,* I must *die,* Child, Beauty Supreme,
              What a blessed fate!
    In *being unpetalled,* I want to prove to you that I love you,
              O my Treasure!...
    Under your *baby steps,* I want to live here below
              With mystery,
    And I'd like to soften once more on Calvary
              Your last steps!.....

PN 52 – Abandonment Is the Sweet Fruit of Love
(May 31, 1897)

This is an allegory developed for six stanzas—the first third of the poem, from which the rest of the poem stems. It is a song to sing while going through "the storm" (st. 2) and to take heart with, but it is also calm, firm and "in peace" (the word is repeated four times). The assurance of the last four stanzas is not pretense: it is true "abandonment," beyond sensible consolations. Less vibrant and more cautious in trust than in "An Unpetalled Rose"—with which it makes a striking diptych—this poem is just as personal, though carefully avoiding any showiness.

It begins like a fairy tale: "There is on this earth...." The image of the tree whose "roots are in Heaven" is beautiful, like an upside-down image in a painting by Chagall. This "marvelous Tree" makes us think both of Eden and of the Song of Songs, where the lover finds "rest in the shadow of Him whom she had desired" (Song 2:3, a verse Thérèse loved very much). The "fruit" of this Tree of paradise is fragrant and "delectable." It gives eternal "life" (7, 3–4). We note in passing Thérèse's need to "touch, feel, and taste": this is a proof, conversely, of the absence of sensible consolations for her at this time. This fruit is "abandonment" into the arms and "on the heart" of the Beloved (sts. 7–9). It evokes Saint John's surrender at the Last Supper. It does not have the tragic existential element of the abandonment we find in "An Unpetalled Rose," but it is no less an act of faith and will (twice in stanza 9 she repeats "I want").

There is a "daisy" under this fair tree. As soon as the sun appears, she seeks the "Sun of [her] life." A "ray" gives her peace and fixes her in her abandonment. These are beautiful stanzas on the Eucharist (10–12) with the comparison that is so like Thérèse: "the host as little as me"....

She may become forsaken by others and especially by Jesus himself (who "hides" in PN 32, 5 and "steals away" in PN 43,3-4). But she loves to keep repeating that "He is free to act as He likes" (SS, p. 207), and Thérèse keeps "smiling" and singing.

She repeats as an ending (sts. 15–18) what she believes and wants to believe—what she is sure of in her love: she "waits in peace" (sts. 15 and 18). But there is nothing lazy about her waiting. The sudden flight of the "lark," in a straight-up ascent that pierces the "thick fog" (SS, p. 212) says that well enough. Irresistibly, she calls to mind the anagogical act of St. John of the Cross: For the soul assailed by temptation, it is best to soar right up in one leap to God.... Thérèse even flies "higher than the lark": We can see a bird flying up in the sky, but we cannot see Thérèse's soul soaring much higher, right up to the border of that Promised Land where the Tree of Life immerses its roots. This fleeting burst gives all its worth to the hoped-for fruition of happiness, through faith, in the sacrament of Love.

This poem was requested by Sister Teresa of Saint Augustine, the same sister who had urged Thérèse to write her first poem in 1893. As virtuous as she was rigid, this religious had made "the vow to surrender everything to God's good pleasure" (Death Notice, p. 6). Later she admitted that her weak nature got the best of her and spoiled this beautiful fruit: By doing this was she not wanting to assure herself of "some superiority in perfection"?...

For Thérèse, "abandonment" is not "the work of him who wills nor of him who runs, but of God showing mercy" (SS, p. 13). Seeing in herself this total abandonment in the face of death, Thérèse will acknowledge the real Author of it: "Now I'm there. God has put me there. He took me in His arms and put me there" (HLC, p. 77).

J.M.J.T.

May 31, 1897

Abandonment Is the Sweet Fruit of Love

1   There is on this earth
       A marvelous Tree.
       Its root, O mystery!
       Is in Heaven....

2   In its shade
       Never could anything cause pain.
       One can rest there
       Without fearing the storm.

3   Love is the name
       Of this ineffable Tree,
       And its delectable fruit
       Is called Abandonment.

4   Even in this life this fruit
       Gives me happiness.
       My soul delights
       In its divine fragrance.

5   When I touch this fruit,
       It seems a treasure.
       Putting it to my mouth,
       It is sweeter still.

6   It gives me in this world
      An ocean of peace.
      In this deep peace
      I rest forever...

7   Abandonment alone brings me
      Into your arms, O Jesus.
      It alone makes me live
      The life of the Elect.

8   To you I abandon myself,
      O my Divine Spouse,
      And I only yearn for
      Your sweet gaze.

9   Me, I want to smile at you
      As I fall asleep on your heart.
      I want to tell you over and over
      That I love you, Lord!

10   Like the daisy
      With the rosy calyx,
      Me, tiny *little* flower,
      I open up to the sun.

11   O my Lovable King,
      The sweet Sun of my life
      Is your Divine Host,
      Little like me....

12   The bright ray
      Of its Celestial Flame
      Makes perfect Abandonment
      Take life in my soul.

13   Every creature
      Can forsake me.
      Near you I'll know how to do without them
      Without complaining.

14   And if you abandon me,
      O my Divine Treasure,
      Deprived of your caresses,
      I still want to smile.

15 In peace, Sweet Jesus,
    I want to wait for your return,
    Without ever ceasing
    My canticles of love.

16 No, nothing worries me.
    Nothing can trouble me.
    My soul knows how to fly
    Higher than the lark.

17 Above the clouds
    The sky is always blue.
    One touches the shores
    Where God reigns.

18 I await in peace the glory
    Of that Heavenly abode,
    For I find in the Ciborium
    The sweet Fruit of Love!

PN 53 – For Sister Marie of the Trinity

"A Lily Among Thorns," (May 1897)

In spite of its Lamartinian tone, this is a poem of great strength, confirmed by Thérèse's handwriting, and an astonishing energy for someone so ill. This piece has the classical simplicity we saw in "My Weapons" (PN 48). There is a noticeable reduction in adjectives. Here the Normandy meadow has almost become a formal French garden.

Although not very polished (as evidenced by some repetitions, in st. 1, 3–4 and st. 2, 2–3, etc.), the text flows harmoniously. The majestic opening (st. 1, 1–2 with verses in the style of Racine) tells us what calm assurance in faith Thérèse has reached, but without being presumptuous (she is still a "poor little nothing"). This is truly a "song of the mercies of the Lord" (SS, p. 13) that she lends, so to speak, to Sister Marie of the Trinity. That Marie humbly accepts her weakness and lack of virtue makes her a prime candidate for the work of this "consuming and transforming Love" (GCII, p. 999). For Thérèse especially, now more than ever, nothing matters but love (GCII, pp. 1120–1121).

A touch of mischief joyfully brightens up the third stanza: We have a graceful, colorful vignette of "the little lamb far from the sheepfold, frolicking unaware of the danger," like Monsieur Seguin's goat....[1] The Blessed Virgin Mary is the "shepherdess." We see an "alpine antithesis" between "the precipice" and "the summit of Carmel." All that softens beforehand the "austere delights" of the last two verses. Once all reasons for fear of being accepted for profession had passed, Marie of the Trinity often entertained the community with the account of her adolescent escapades among the attractions, stores, and fairs of Paris.

This young disciple of Thérèse was sometimes troubled by scruples about chastity. Here our Saint is giving her more confidence, not in herself, but in the *prevenient* love of the Lord, who alone is able to keep pure this lily "rising from the mire" (st. 4).

This composition brought up to eight the poems Thérèse bequeathed to her favorite novice. For a heart "that needed to love even to the infinite," it is no small privilege that Marie had such a close sister for a friend—and the saint of love for a guide.

[1] [Monsieur Seguin's goat, "of an independent nature, ... seeking fresh air and freedom at any price," ended up being eaten by a wolf! Cf. Alphonse Daudet, *Letters from My Mill*, trans. John P. MacGregor (Toronto: Harrap & Co. Ltd., 1962), pp. 26–27—Trans.]

For Sister Marie of the Trinity

1   Lord, you chose me from my earliest childhood,
And I can call myself the work of your love...
O my God! in my gratitude I would like
Oh! I would like to be able to pay you in return!...
Jesus my Beloved, what is this privilege?
What have I, poor little nothing, done for you?
And I see myself placed in the royal procession
Of the virgins in your court, lovable and Divine King!

2   Alas, I am nothing but weakness itself.
You know that, O my God! I have no virtues...
But you also know, the only friend I love,
That the one who has charmed me is you, my Sweet Jesus!...
When in my young heart was enkindled that flame
Called love, you came to claim it....
And you alone, O Jesus! could satisfy a soul
That needed to love even to the infinite.

3   Like a little lamb far from the sheepfold,
I merrily frolicked unaware of the danger,
But, O Queen of Heaven! my darling Shepherdess,
Your invisible hand knew how to protect me
While I played on the edge of the precipice.
You were already showing me the summit of Carmel.
I understood then the austere delights
That I would have to love to fly away to Heaven.

4   Lord, if you cherish the purity of the angel,
Of that spirit of fire which swims in the blue,
Do you not also love the lily, rising above the mire,
That your love knew how to keep pure?
My God, if the angel with vermillion wings
Who appears before you is happy,
My joy even here below is like his,
Since I have the treasure of virginity!...

PN 54 – Why I Love You, O Mary!

(May 1897)

"There is still one thing I have to do before I die," Thérèse, who was already very sick, confided to her sister Céline: "I have always dreamed of saying in a song to the Blessed Virgin everything I think about her" (PA, p. 268). During May 1897 she was already beginning to sense that her writings, including her poetry, would probably become known. And she regarded her "thoughts" on Mary as an integral part of the "very important work" she was preparing (HLC, p. 126). Perhaps they are even its crowning achievement.

So the request that Sister Marie of the Sacred Heart made for her to write on the Blessed Virgin Mary anticipated a very deep personal desire on Thérèse's part. Sister Geneviève was right in observing that Thérèse wrote this swan song "by herself, in every sense of the word." [1]

For Thérèse, *thoughts* [pensée] are not the same as *ideas* [idée]. [2] Thoughts open up and blossom in her heart, she said poetically a few weeks later (GCII, p. 1160). In fact, Thérèse's thoughts are immersed in her prayer and very quickly become prayer (SS, pp. 74–75). And it is first of all as a prayer that we should understand this long poem. It is a sort of liturgical hymn of 200 Alexandrines [in the French], written during the month of May 1897.

Now more than ever, Thérèse can only "be nourished on truth" (HLC, p. 134). She has to "see things as they really are" (HLC, p. 105). As for the Virgin Mary, all that interests her is "her real life, not her imagined life" (HLC, p. 161). Instinctively, she turns to the Gospels as her only source of inspiration from then on: "The Gospels are enough for me" (HLC, p. 44 and GCII, pp. 1093–1094). She herself tells us about her "method": "The Gospels teach me... and my heart reveals to me..." (st. 15).

She goes to the Gospels to find facts and events: "what Mary did and taught," we would dare say, transposing Acts 1, 1. Thérèse attentively "sees... looks... hears... listens to" what the Evangelists tell. (All the verbs are in the present tense, for *she is really there*). Consequently she omits the "glorious mysteries": Jesus himself is waiting to sing about them in Heaven (cf. st. 24).

And her *heart* makes her "understand" (a very Theresian verb) by a kind of connaturality the hidden meanings of those deeds, their implication for her own present life and soon even for her eternal life. Her understanding has been refined in a thousand ways during these last few months, but especially in two areas: through the mystery of suffering—and tested by it in trial—and through all the demands of charity, in which she has received special lights. All this was wrapped in silence.

Thérèse's personal experience helps her to discover in Mary's life the same law that governed the life of Jesus, her Son: "*It was necessary* for her to suffer so as to enter into her glory" (cf. Lk 24:26). Jesus "wished" it so for his Mother, for mysteriously "it is a blessing to suffer on earth" (16, 3). And Mary was not satisfied with submitting to her "mortal and suffering" condition, like ours (cf. 2, 8). If Thérèse does not say so explicitly, her whole poem implies that Mary *freely chose* her condition, out of solidarity with us. Through her whole life, she had already affirmed, and incomparably better than Thérèse would say one day: "My God, *I choose all* that you will... I'm not afraid to suffer for you" (SS, p. 27). Or again, "I prefer what He wills. It's what He does that I love" (HLC, p. 51). Mary preferred her hidden, poor, and suffering life to any other. At Nazareth, she "wanted nothing more" (st. 17, 2) than "to live by faith just like us" (cf. HLC, p. 161), without anything out of the ordinary. "She liked" to walk "the same ordinary way" that "little ones" also walk (st. 17). When Jesus seemed to neglect her for "the family" of his disciples, she "did not become sad." She even "rejoiced" (st. 21). She lives all that for us: "to draw me to you," Thérèse boldly declares (st. 2).

Yes, "the Blessed Virgin knew what it was to suffer" (HLC, p. 158). She is the maternal replica of the Suffering Servant (cf. Is 53:3, quoted in GCI, p. 631 and RP 2, 3).

And Mary knew the secret of "suffering while loving" (16,4), for her "immense tenderness" is also the response to "Jesus' immense love for us." This love is not so much a question of quantity but of quality. Mary "loves us as Jesus loves us." That is the second basic law of the poem. Thérèse states this with all the more authority because she is still being influenced by a recent illumination: "This year...God has given me the grace to understand what charity is...to love one's neighbor as He, Jesus, loves him..." (SS, pp. 219, 220).

This very bright light not only renewed her relationships with others. It enabled her to "penetrate into the mysterious depths of charity" (SS, p. 233) that animated Mary's whole life, "the secrets of her maternal heart" (22, 6). Those "abysses of love" (18, 4) led her, "like Jesus," to give everything and to give herself" (22, 3). Thus we see the Mother sharing her "treasures" of grace with her children: "her virtues, her love" (5, 1). She also shares with "sinners" her privilege par excellence as the *Mother* of Jesus (sts. 20–21). What is more, she "accepts" losing Him for us, "being separated from Him." And yet what a martyrdom she had already known during those three days in Jerusalem when the Child was separated from her (st. 13)! Mary "wants...to remain our support" (st. 22) right up to the time we meet Him in Heaven. She emptied herself totally for love; she could not go farther. So we can also say about Mary, "For our sake she made herself poor though she was rich, so that we might become rich by her poverty" (2 Cor 8:9). That is why Thérèse, moved by this, protests:

How can we not love you, O my dearest Mother,
On seeing so much love and so much humility? (21, 7–8)

Mary's humble love is wrapped in silence and invites us to silence. This is also a main axis of the poem. For Mary, love is safer than knowledge. She is not afraid of what she does not understand. Whether in her attitude toward Joseph after the Annunciation (st. 8), in her comportment at Bethlehem (sts. 9–10), in her docile acceptance of her Son's mysterious words in the Temple (14–15) or "on the hill" (20–21), in every situation Mary acquiesces in silence. In her faith, so often put to the test, she can fathom and understand everything (according to Thérèse). And the end of her earthly life is immersed in a "deep silence" (st. 24). This is a silence that speaks more eloquently than words. Only *the Word* will reveal its "secrets" to us (*ibid.*).

With her eyes fixed on Mary, Thérèse made silence the great bulwark of her whole contemplative life. Silence was her strength more than ever "in the night of faith." One of the most moving aspects of this poem is the almost total absence of allusion to the physical and moral trials she herself was going through (cf. HLC, May 1897, pp. 40–53). Stanza 16 is the only evidence we have, and it is more intense and personal because of its flat style.

Would Thérèse have seen such depths in her Mother's heart if she herself had not been "her child" to such a striking degree? She was so much like Mary that she has been called "a ravishing miniature of the Most Holy Virgin."[3] She was ravishing and sorrowful, for it was with "anguish of heart" (16, 2) that she ended by "giving everything and giving herself" (st. 22) for her brothers...poor sinners" (SS, p. 213).

Mary and Thérèse are of the same people and of the same blood. They are "Mother" and "child." Thérèse's assurance about this was extremely important not only for her everyday life, but also for the heavenly relationships that are soon to begin for her. The chisel of trial had cut away "everything that could be a natural satisfaction in her desire for heaven" (SS, p. 214). But it did not succeed in shaking her conviction that she was "soon going to Heaven" (st. 25, 2). The anticipation of the marvels of paradise, as Arminjon had once described them to her,[4] no longer "thrilled her heart" (GCII, p. 1142 and DE, p. 721). Her whole attention from then on was focused on people: those she was going to meet (the Holy Family, the angels, all the blessed), and also those she would hurry back to help and to save, right up to the end of the world (HLC, p. 102).

What would her encounter—so close at hand—with Mary be like? Thérèse had no use for the exaggerations of certain spiritual writers. It was unacceptable for her to imagine Mary as a being whose "glorious and powerful splendor appear with so much more brilliance than that of all the angels and saints that it is like the sun, which, by its presence, eclipses all the stars of heaven, as if they were hiding themselves in shame, not daring to appear before such beauty that surpasses theirs beyond all comparison" (text quoted in DE, p. 575). Letting such people "hide in shame," Thérèse knew where she stood. She had suffered with Mary, as Mary had suffered for her (25, 6 and 2, 4). Such love had "banished all her fears" (18, 5). At last she was going to see once more "the ravishing smile of the Blessed Virgin" (SS, p. 66), who is more "Mother than Queen" (HLC, p. 161).

Thérèse put "her whole heart" into writing this last poem (CSG, p. 90).[5] It is the favorite of most of her readers and disciples. Certainly, this long "historical" work, at times too predictable and a little affected, is quite a different poetic *genre* than "An Unpetalled Rose" (PN 51) or "To the Sacred Heart" (PN 23). [In French] the Alexandrines are regular, steady, and almost always divided into two equal hemistichs. This well expresses the apparent "objectivity" with which the author wanted to confine herself. However, a certain restrained emotion does run through the poem, which has some great moments (sts. 8, 16, 22...). It is enriched with some beautiful images (3, 7–8; 7, 5–6...). Concise expressions come forth (10, 4; 16, 4— which is like Thérèse's Credo—and the famous 22, 3). A wonderful stanza concludes the poem.

"Little Thérèse" signed this poem with a faltering hand a short time before her death: What a humble, moving end to her entire poetic work!

[1] Sr. Geneviève, Note on a loose sheet of paper; cf. CSG, p. 122.

[2] Thérèse uses the word "idea" [idée] 23 times in her writings, frequently with the meaning of "project, plan." She uses the word "thought" [pensée] 143 times.

[3] Abbé Hodierne, confessor to the Carmel of Lisieux just after the death of Thérèse. Quoted from a letter to Mother Marie de Gonzague, 1899.

[4] Especially chapter 7 of Abbé Arminjon's *End of the Present World and the Mysteries of the Future Life.*

[5] Thérèse asked for Mother Agnes's help with this poem. The rough draft is very enlightening as to how they worked together.

✛

(Melody: "Pourquoi m'avoir   J.M.J.T.   May 1897
livré l'autre jour, ô ma mère")

Why I Love You, O Mary!

1   Oh! I would like to sing, *Mary, why I love you,*
      Why your sweet name thrills my heart,
      And why the thought of your supreme greatness
      Could not bring fear to my soul.
      If I gazed on you in your sublime glory,
      Surpassing the splendor of all the blessed,
      I could not believe that I am your child.
      O Mary, before you I would lower my eyes!...

2   If a child is to cherish his mother,
      She has to cry with him and share his sorrows.
      O my dearest Mother, on this foreign shore
      How many tears you shed to draw me to you!....
      In pondering *your life in the holy Gospels,*
      I dare look at you and come near you.
      It's not difficult for me to believe I'm your child,
      For I see you human and suffering like me....

3   When an angel from Heaven bids you be *the Mother*
      Of the God who is to reign for all eternity,
      I see you prefer, O Mary, what a mystery!
      The ineffable treasure of *virginity.*
      O Immaculate Virgin, I understand how your soul
      Is dearer to the Lord than his heavenly dwelling.
      I understand how your soul, *Humble and Sweet Valley,*
      Can contain Jesus, the Ocean of Love!...

4   Oh! I love you, Mary, saying you are the servant
      Of the God whom you charm by your humility.
      This hidden virtue makes you all-powerful.
      It attracts *the Holy Trinity* into your heart.
      Then *the Spirit of Love covering you with his shadow,*
      The Son equal to the Father became incarnate in you,
      There will be a great many of his sinner brothers,
      Since he will be called: Jesus, your first-born!...

5   O beloved Mother, despite my littleness,
      Like you I possess The All-Powerful within me.
      But I don't tremble in seeing my weakness:
      The treasures of a mother belong to her child,
      And I am your child, O my dearest Mother.
      Aren't your virtues and your love mine too?
      So when the white Host comes into my heart,
      Jesus, your Sweet Lamb, thinks he is resting in you!...

6   You make me feel that it's not impossible
      To follow in your footsteps, O Queen of the elect.
      You made visible the narrow road to Heaven
      While always practicing the humblest virtues.
      Near you, Mary, I like to stay little.
      I see the vanity of greatness here below.
      At the home of Saint Elizabeth, receiving your visit,
      I learn how to practice ardent charity.

7   There, Sweet Queen of angels, I listen, delighted,
      To the sacred canticle springing forth from your heart.
      You teach me to sing divine praises,
      To glory in Jesus my Savior.
      Your words of love are mystical roses
      Destined to perfume the centuries to come.
      In you the Almighty has done great things.
      I want to ponder them to bless him for them.

8   When good Saint Joseph did not know of the miracle
      That you wanted to hide in your humility,
      You let him cry close by the *Tabernacle*
      Veiling the Savior's divine beauty!.....
      Oh Mary! how I love *your eloquent silence!*
      For me it is a sweet, melodious concert
      That speaks to me of the greatness and power
      Of a soul which looks only to Heaven for help.....

9   Later in Bethlehem, O Joseph and Mary!
      I see you rejected by all the villagers.
      No one wants to take in poor foreigners.
      There's room for the great ones....

There's room for the great ones, and it's in a stable
That the Queen of Heaven must give birth to a God.
O my dearest Mother, how lovable I find you,
How great I find you in such a poor place!....

10 When I see the Eternal God wrapped in swaddling clothes,
When I hear the poor cry of the Divine Word,
O my dearest Mother, I no longer envy the angels,
For their Powerful Lord is my dearest Brother!...
How I love you, Mary, you who made
This Divine Flower blossom on our shores!........
How I love you listening to the shepherds and wisemen
And keeping it all in your heart with care!...

11 I love you mingling with the other women
Walking toward the holy temple.
I love you presenting the Savior of our souls
To the blessed Old Man who pressed Him to his heart.
At first I smile as I listen to his canticle,
But soon his tone makes me shed tears.
Plunging a prophetic glance into the future,
Simeon presents you with a sword of sorrows.

12 O Queen of martyrs, till the evening of your life
That sorrowful sword *will pierce your heart.*
Already you must leave your native land
To flee a king's jealous fury.
Jesus sleeps in peace under the folds of your veil.
Joseph comes begging you to leave at once,
And at once your obedience is revealed.
You leave without delay or reasoning.

13 O Mary, it seems to me that in the land of Egypt
Your heart remains joyful in poverty,
For *is not Jesus the fairest Homeland,*
What does exile matter to you? You hold Heaven...
But in Jerusalem a bitter sadness
Comes to flood your heart like a vast ocean.
For three days, Jesus hides from your tenderness.
That is indeed exile in all its harshness!...

14   At last you find him and you are overcome with joy,
You say to the fair Child captivating the doctors:
"O my Son, why have you done this?
Your father and I have been searching for you in tears."
And the Child God replies (O what a deep mystery!)
To his dearest Mother holding out her arms to him:
"Why were you searching for me? I must be about
My Father's business. Didn't you know?"

15   The Gospel tells me that, growing in wisdom,
Jesus remains subject to Joseph and Mary,
And my heart reveals to me with what tenderness
He always obeys his dear parents.
Now I understand the mystery of the temple,
The hidden words of my Lovable King.
Mother, your sweet Child wants you to be the example
Of the soul searching for Him in the night of faith.

16   Since the King of Heaven wanted his Mother
To be plunged into the night, in anguish of heart,
Mary, is it thus a blessing to suffer on earth?
Yes, *to suffer while loving is the purest happiness!...*
All that He has given me, Jesus can take back.
Tell him not to bother with me.....
He can indeed hide from me, I'm willing to wait for him
Till the day without sunset when my faith will fade away.....

17   Mother full of grace, I know that in Nazareth
You live in poverty, wanting nothing more.
No rapture, miracle, or ecstasy
Embellish your life, O Queen of the Elect!.....
The number of little ones on earth is truly great.
They can raise their eyes to you without trembling.
It's by *the ordinary way,* incomparable Mother,
That you like to walk to guide them to Heaven.

18   While waiting for Heaven, O my dear Mother,
I want to live with you, to follow you each day.
Mother, contemplating you, I joyfully immerse myself,
Discovering in your heart *abysses of love.*

Your motherly gaze banishes all my fears.
It teaches me *to cry*, it teaches me *to rejoice.*
Instead of scorning pure and simple joys,
You want to share in them, you deign to bless them.

19 At Cana, seeing the married couple's anxiety
Which they cannot hide, for they have run out of wine,
In your concern you tell the Savior,
Hoping for the help of his divine power.
Jesus seems at first to reject your prayer:
"Woman, what does this matter," he answers, "to you and to me?"
But in the depths of his heart, He calls you his Mother,
And he works his first miracle for you....

20 One day when sinners are listening to the doctrine
Of Him who would like to welcome them in Heaven,
Mary, I find you with them on the hill.
Someone says to Jesus that you wish to see him.
Then, before the whole multitude, your Divine Son
Shows us the immensity of his love for us.
He says: "Who is my brother and my sister and my Mother,
If not the one who does my will?"

21 O Immaculate Virgin, most tender of Mothers,
In listening to Jesus, you are not saddened.
But you rejoice that He makes us understand
How our souls become *his family* here below.
Yes, you rejoice that He gives us his life,
The infinite treasures of his divinity!...
How can we not love you, O my dear Mother,
On seeing so much love and so much humility?

22 You love us, Mary, as Jesus loves us,
And for us you accept being separated from Him.
To love is to give everything. It's to give oneself.
You wanted to prove this by remaining our support.
The Savior knew your immense tenderness.
He knew the secrets of your maternal heart.
Refuge of sinners, He leaves us to you
When He leaves the Cross to wait for us in Heaven.

23   Mary, at the top of Calvary standing beside the Cross
To me you seem like a priest at the altar,
Offering your beloved Jesus, the sweet Emmanuel,
To appease the Father's justice...
A prophet said, O afflicted Mother,
"There is no sorrow like your sorrow!"
O Queen of Martyrs, while remaining in exile
You lavish on us all the blood of your heart!

24   Saint John's home becomes your only refuge.
Zebedee's son is to replace Jesus.....
That is the last detail the Gospel gives.
It tells me nothing more of the Queen of Heaven.
But, O my dear Mother, doesn't its profound silence
Reveal that *The Eternal Word Himself*
Wants to sing the secrets of your life
To charm *your children*, all the Elect of Heaven?

25   Soon I'll hear that sweet harmony.
Soon I'll go to beautiful Heaven to see you.
You who came *to smile at me* in the morning of my life,
Come smile at me again... Mother.... It's evening now!...
I no longer fear the splendor of your supreme glory.
With you I've suffered, and now I want
To sing on your lap, Mary, why I love you,
And to go on saying that I am your child!......

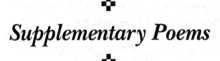

Supplementary Poems

Supplementary Poems (PS)

Because we wanted to be faithful to the purpose of a complete edition, we have included even the least fragments of Thérèse's poetry: those she never finished, along with some humorous verses in her handwriting (if not all written by her). Three of these poems were written while she was ill. They are the last "vibrations from her harp" before the great silence of death.

The second volume of Thérèse's *Letters* ends with some short notes that she wrote in pencil with a trembling hand. The words recorded in *Her Last Conversations* become fewer as weakness overcame her. All the sisters could do was to "watch her suffering, smiling, suffocating, and crying" (HLC, p. 125). In the same way, after the great final canticle, "Why I Love You, O Mary" (PN 54), Thérèse wrote only three very short little poems. But they express the purest love and the most exquisite tenderness: for her prioress (PS 6), for a companion moved by her departure (PS 7), and for Jesus in the Eucharist who had never stopped "lowering himself" toward her "littleness" (PS 8).

And then Thérèse was silent. But she who understood so well and loved so resolutely the "silence of God" had already prepared us for this: Her silence is "the pledge of her inexpressible love" (PN 13, 13) "till the day without sunset when faith will fade away" (PN 54, 16).

PS 1 – O Hidden God

(January 6, 1895 or 1896)

This unfinished piece was probably written for a community evening recreation on Epiphany. Had it been improved and completed, it might have been able to stand in comparison with other poems by Thérèse. A few well-done ten-syllable verses [in the French] and an evocative image ("your bloody halo") already show a certain craftsmanship. For this reason, we could reverse the dates of the two compositions PS 1 and PS 2. However, the themes and especially the deep movement of this fragment are related to those of Thérèse's recreation "Angels at the Crib of Jesus" (RP 2, Christmas 1894).

1   O God hidden under the guise of childhood,
    I see in you the monarch of Heaven.
    I recognize your grandeur and power
    From the soft brightness shining in your eyes.
    If you wished, a thousand legions of angels
    Would come at your call to form your court.
    Sprinkling your humble swaddling clothes with golden stars,
    They would sing of your ineffable love.

R.1   I see on the foreign shore
    My God, my Savior, and my Brother,
    Who cannot yet speak,
    Who has neither scepter or treasure.
    Adoring this deep mystery,
    Divine King, I offer you my gold.

2   O King of Heaven, you come on this earth
    Wanting to save the human race, your brother.
    For your love, Oh! I would like to suffer!
    Since you want to die one day for me,
    I offer you the symbol of your sorrows.
    Seeing your bloody halo shine,
    Ah! I would like to win every heart for you,
    Divine Jesus, to dry your tears.

R.2   Receive myrrh, O King of Heaven,
    Since you want to be a mortal man.
                      [unfinished]

PS 2 – In the Orient
(January 6, 1896? or 1895?)

This is another unfinished composition for a feast of the Epiphany. The short stanzas are reminiscent of the end of PN 28.

1   In the Orient a star appeared,
And we follow its mysterious course.
Blessed star, its brightness discloses to us
That the King of Heaven is born on earth.

2   Heaven protects us,
And our procession
Follows the brilliant star,
Braving rain and snow!...

3   Let each one get ready...
The star is coming to rest!...
Let the celebrating begin,
Let us adore the Child!...

PS 3 – For Fifty Years
(January 15, 1896?)

The quality of these verses is not much better than those of PN 2. Whether they have to do with the entrance anniversary (4/6/1845) of Sister Saint Stanislaus—the senior of the community—or more probably her clothing anniversary (1/15/1846), in any case they are a regression. Their only merit consists in evoking the goodness of Sister Saint Stanislaus (cf. CGII, p. 1172: "of inexhaustible goodness"), which earned her the unanimous affection of her community. A few months later, for her golden jubilee of profession (2/8/1897), Thérèse redeemed herself by writing the little play "Saint Stanislaus Kostka" (RP 8).

1   For fifty years on earth
      You have perfumed with your virtues
      Our humble little monastery,
      The palace of the King of the Elect.

          Refrain

      Let us celebrate, let us celebrate the happy entrance
      Of our senior sister in Carmel.
      All our hearts love her
      As a truly sweet gift from Heaven.

2   You have received us all
      At our entrance into this place.
      Your kindness is well-known to us,
      Along with your tender love.

3   Soon an even more beautiful feast
      Will come to gladden our hearts.
      We shall place new flowers
      On your head as we sing.

PS 4 – Heaven's the Reward

(Summer 1896?)

Are these funny verses, copied in Thérèse's handwriting to the melody of a well-known song, written by her? It is very doubtful. She probably joyously joined in singing them during a recreation in the novitiate. But the idea for them had to have come from Sister Marie of the Eucharist, who is surely the main author.

Be that as it may, Thérèse would have certainly used this opportunity to channel the merriment of her trio (Céline, Marie of the Trinity, and Marie Guérin)—to encourage them to greater generosity.

We have tried to put these rhymes in a logical (if not chronological) order so as to show the typical day of a Carmelite nun in 1896, but written in a style we might find in a student magazine. The following are humorously described: rising in the morning (st. 1); the poverty of the cell (2–4); the wearing apparel, where "armor" (instruments of penance) clearly holds a prominent place... (5–9); the frugal meals (10–14); recreation in common (15–18); taking the discipline (19–20) with each lash tallied up by some laughing young sister. All this was prescribed for the spiritual combat of the apostolate (21), as Saint Teresa of Avila expressly wished for her daughters.

We put the first line back in for each couplet. On the original manuscript it only appeared in the first couplet.

1   Heaven's the reward.
     The clapper resounding
     Before dawn
     Makes me jump out of bed.

2   Heaven's the reward.
     As soon as we're awake,
     We see more wonderful things
     Than what they have in Paris.

3   Heaven's the reward.
     In my poor cell
     There are no fancy curtains
     Or mirrors or carpets.

4   Heaven's the reward.
Nothing, no table or chair.
To feel uncomfortable
Is happiness here.

5   Heaven's the reward.
I notice without alarm
My flashing weapons.
I love their clatter.

6   Heaven's the reward.
Sacrifice is for me.
Cross, chains, and hair-shirt.
These are my weapons.

7   Heaven's the reward.
After a prayer
We have to kiss the floor.
Our rule says so.

8   Heaven's the reward.
I hide my armor
Under my coarse habit
And my blessed veil.

9   Heaven's the reward.
If Mother Nature
Lets out a rumble,
Laughing, I tell her:

10   Heaven's the reward.
Fasting's rather easy.
It makes you nimble.
If you're hungry, too bad!

11   Heaven's the reward.
We don't spare
Turnips, potatoes,
Cabbage, carrots, radishes.

12   Heaven's the reward.
We're never astonished
When at night we're only given
Bread and fruit.

13   Heaven's the reward.
        Often it's only fair,
        The bread passes by and I leave
        The fruit on the plate.

14   Heaven's the reward.
        My plate is made of clay.
        I use my hand for a fork.
        The spoon is made of wood.

15   Heaven's the reward.
        When we finally get together,
        We can all talk
        Of the joys of paradise.

16   Heaven's the reward.
        While we talk we're working.
        One sews, the other cuts out
        Holy vestments.

17   Heaven's the reward.
        We see saintly cheerfulness
        Leave its mark
        On our beaming faces.

18   Heaven's the reward.
        An hour goes by quickly.
        I become a hermit again,
        But without frowning.

19   Heaven's the reward.
        The noise of the discipline
        Interrupts the silence.
        It's deafening.

20   Heaven's the reward.
        I count off
        Sixty-six thousand lashes a year.
        That's the precise number.

21   Heaven's the reward.
        For missionaries
        We make war on ourselves
        Unceasingly, mercilessly.

PS 5 – For a Feast of Saint Martha

(July 29, 1896)

According to an old tradition in the Carmelite Order, the feast of Saint Martha is celebrated by merry-making in honor of the "white veil sisters" (or lay sisters). There is usually a song on the program and gifts as well: useful things for the kitchen and other work areas and something nice that the sisters can later send to their families.

In 1894, the community did not celebrate the feast because the sisters were in mourning for Monsieur Martin, who died that same day. In 1895, Thérèse wrote and played a role in "Jesus at Bethany" (RP 4). In 1896, it was mainly the Guérins who bore the expenses of the day: Their various gifts earned them a thank-you letter signed by Sister Marie of the Incarnation, Sister Saint Vincent de Paul, Sister Martha of Jesus, and Sister Marie-Madeleine. Perhaps they gave some toys too: the "boat," the "pug dog," the "pig," and the "cat" that Thérèse presents to the sisters in funny couplets, several of which barely rhyme [in French].

Refr.

Very noble white veil sisters,
Honoring you makes the heart glad.

1   To Sister Marie of the Incarnation
     We offer navigation
     And this pretty little boat.
     Miss Henrietta[1] will think it's pretty.

2   We offer Sister Saint Vincent
     This smart little pug dog.
     Barking near her garden,
     He will be a good guardian.

3   We offer our very dear Marthon[2]
     This delightful little pig.
     He will be her mount
     When he's chasing after rats.

4   To honor Mélanie Lebon[3]
     It's Baptiste[4] who'll set the tone.
     He'll present her with a little cat
     To lick the dishes clean.

5   What to say to offer this jug?
      Ah! we really don't know.

      ....

      Papa, here's the Master.[5]
      Let's get out of here, he's got that look about him!

[1] Perhaps a sister or niece of Sr. Marie of the Incarnation.
[2] [A masculine nickname for Martha—Trans.]
[3] Sister Marie-Madeleine's legal name.
[4] A reference to a comedy put on by the novitiate in which Sr. Marie of the Eucharist played the part of a gardener named Baptiste.
[5] The father of Sister Marie of the Trinity was a school teacher (or "master"). She herself had played this role in the same comedy referred to in st. 4.

PS 6 – To Mother Marie de Gonzague

(June 21, 1897)

The handwriting of these few lines, though still steady, shows well Thérèse's state of fatigue. She had been on a special milk diet for about twelve days, and she was keeping what strength she had to write the last part of her autobiography (Manuscript C of *Story of a Soul*)—her "little assignment" (HLC, p. 67).

With these few lines so full of tenderness, Thérèse offered her prioress, for her feastday, "the photograph album and some toques she had made with Sr. Marie of Saint Joseph" (note by Mother Agnes).

J.M.J.T.

June 21, 1897

Me too, beloved Mother,
I want to get my little word in,
But you don't have many ideas
When you're just drinking moo-moo![1]...
And yet, my darling mother,
With great happiness I offer you
A photograph album,
My toques,[2] and my little heart.

Thérèse of the Child Jesus
unwor. carm. rel.[3]

[1] [Thérèse uses baby-talk ("lolo") here for the word "milk" —Trans.]
[2] [The one-piece coarse white linen cap and covering of the neck and shoulders that the nuns wore under the veil— Trans.]
[3] [unworthy Carmelite religious—Trans.]

PS 7 – Silence Is the Sweet Language...

(June 1897)

Specialists have wondered if Thérèse really wrote these two quatrains. It is highly probable that she did. These lines overflow with the fraternal charity that is one of the major themes of Manuscript C of *Story of a Soul.* We even see a similarity in an expression used in both (2, 1 and SS, p. 216).

This poem gives us the impression of a very delicate goodbye Thérèse is saying to a sister who is being kept away from her because of her illness: Was it perhaps Sister Marie of Saint Joseph (cf. GCII, p. 1137)?

But the fact that this poem is not specifically dedicated to any one person broadens its scope. Just as we are about to close this collection of poetry, the reader can understand this poem as a personal message from Thérèse telling each one of us that she will see us again "in Heaven." Let us not forget her last will and testament here: "As I have loved you"....

This is my commandment, that you love one another, as I have loved you!... St. John XV, 12.

1　　Silence is the sweet language
　　　Of the angels[1] and all the elect.
　　　It must also be the lot
　　　Of souls who love each other in Jesus.

2　　It is only in the midst of sacrifices
　　　That we can love one another in Carmel.
　　　One day, inebriated with delights,
　　　We'll love each other in Heaven.

---

[1] Painted on a wall of the dormitory of the Lisieux Carmel were the words: "Silence is the language of the angels."

PS 8 – You Who Know My Extreme Littleness
(July 16, 1897)

"During the night she had written this poem for Communion: 'You who know, etc.' Referring to it, she said: 'I wrote it so easily, it's extraordinary. I thought I could no longer write poetry'" (HLC, pp. 91–92).

All things considered, this "night" had to have been July 12–13 (DE, p. 469).

With a "beautiful, strong" voice, Sister Marie of the Eucharist sang this stanza before Thérèse received Holy Communion in the infirmary on July 16 (cf. GCII, p. 1145). After Communion, she sang stanza 14 from "Living for Love" (PN 17): "Dying of love is a truly sweet martyrdom"....

Thérèse wrote no more poetry. Her "martyrdom" reached its completion eleven weeks later (September 30) in a "death of love" like that of Jesus on the cross (HLC, p. 73).

You who know my extreme littleness,
You aren't afraid to lower yourself to me!
Come into my heart, O white Host that I love,
Come into my heart, it longs for you!
Ah! I wish that your goodness
Would let me die of love after this favor.
Jesus! Hear the cry of my affection.
    Come into my heart!

The Poems
in French

PN 1
J.M.J.T.

2 Février 1893

La Rosée Divine, ou Le Lait Virginal de Marie

1   Mon Doux Jésus, sur le sein de ta Mère
     Tu m'apparais, tout rayonnant d'Amour.
     L'Amour, voilà l'ineffable mystère
     Qui t'exila du Céleste Séjour...
     Ah! laisse-moi me cacher sous le voile
     Qui te dérobe à tout regard mortel,
     Et près de toi, ô Matinale Etoile!
     Je trouverai un avant-goût du Ciel.

2   Dès le réveil d'une nouvelle aurore
     Quand du soleil on voit les premiers feux,
     La tendre fleur qui commence d'éclore
     Attend d'en haut un baume précieux.
     C'est du matin la rosée bienfaisante
     Toute remplie d'une douche fraîcheur
     Qui produisant une sève abondante
     Du frais bouton fait entrouvrir la fleur.

3   C'est toi, Jésus, la Fleur à peine éclose,
     Je te contemple à ton premier réveil.
     C'est toi, Jésus, la ravissante Rose,
     Le frais bouton, gracieux et vermeil.
     Les bras si purs de ta Mère chérie
     Forment pour toi berceau, trône royal.
     Ton doux soleil, c'est le sein de Marie
     Et ta Rosée, c'est le Lait Virginal!...

4   Mon Bien-Aimé, mon divin petit Frère,
     Dans ton regard je vois tout l'avenir.
     Bientôt pour moi tu quitteras ta Mère.
     Déjà l'Amour te presse de souffrir.
     Mais sur la croix, ô Fleur Epanouie!
     Je reconnais ton parfum matinal.
     Je reconnais la Rosée de Marie.
     Ton sang divin, c'est le Lait Virginal!...

5   Cette Rosée se cache au sanctuaire,
     L'ange des Cieux la contemple ravi,
     Offrant à Dieu sa sublime prière.
     Comme Saint Jean, il redit: "Le voici."
     Oui, le voici, ce Verbe fait Hostie,
     Prêtre éternel, Agneau sacerdotal,

Le Fils de Dieu, c'est le Fils de Marie,
Le pain de l'Ange est le Lait Virginal.

6   Le séraphin se nourrit de la gloire,
Au Paradis son bonheur est parfait.
Moi faible enfant, je ne vois au ciboire
Que la couleur, la figure du Lait.
Mais c'est le Lait qui convient à l'enfance,
Et de Jésus l'Amour est sans égal.
O tendre Amour! Insondable puissance,
Ma blanche Hostie, c'est le Lait Virginal!...

(Air: "Minuit, chrétiens")

PN 2

A Notre Maîtresse et Mère chérie pour fêter ses 60 ans

1   Oh! Quel joyeux anniversaire
Nous célébrons en ce beau jour!
A notre bonne et tendre Mère,
Chantons, chantons tout notre amour.

2   Depuis soixante ans, sur la terre,
Divin Jésus, vous contemplez
Une fleur qui vous est bien chère,
De vos grâces vous l'arrosez.

3   Jésus, votre fleur embaumée
A pour vous gagné bien des coeurs,
Elle a cueilli dans la vallée
Une belle moisson de fleurs.

4   Divin Jésus, dans la Patrie
Vous saurez la récompenser;
De la moisson qu'elle a cueillie,
Nous vous verrons la couronner.

5   Jésus, votre Rose est la Mère
Qui dirige nos coeurs d'enfants;
Daignez écouter leur prière:
Qu'ils fêtent ses quatre-vingts ans!

Les trois petites novices
Sr. Thérèse de l'Enfant Jésus
Sr. Marthe de Jésus
Sr. Marie-Madeleine
20 Février de l'an de grâce 1894

PN 3

Sainte Cécile

Pendant le son des instruments
Cécile chantait en son coeur...
(Office de l'église)

1 O Sainte bien-aimée, je contemple ravie
 Le sillon lumineux qui demeure après toi.
 Je crois entendre encor ta douce mélodie,
 Oui, ton céleste chant arrive jusqu'à moi.
5 De mon âme exilée écoute la prière.
 Laisse-moi reposer sur ton coeur virginal,
 Ce lys immaculé qui brilla sur la terre
 D'un éclat merveilleux et presque sans égal.

 O très chaste Colombe, en traversant la vie
10 Tu ne cherchas jamais d'autre époux que Jésus.
 Ayant choisi ton âme, Il se l'etait unie
 La trouvant embaumée de toutes les vertus.
 Cependant un mortel, radieux de jeunesse,
 Respira ton parfum, blanche et céleste fleur!
15 Afin de te cueillir, de gagner ta tendresse,
 Valérien voulut te donner tout son coeur.
 Bientôt il prépara des noces magnifiques,
 Son palais retentit de chants mélodieux...
 Mais ton coeur virginal redisait des cantiques
20 Dont l'écho tout divin s'élevait jusqu'aux Cieux!
 Que pouvais-tu chanter, si loin de ta Patrie,
 Et voyant près de toi ce fragile mortel?
 Sans doute tu voulais abandonner la vie
 Et t'unir pour toujours à Jésus dans le Ciel...
25 Mais non... j'entends vibrer ta lyre séraphique,
 Lyre de ton amour dont l'accent fut si doux,
 Tu chantais au Seigneur ce sublime cantique:
 "Conserve mon coeur pur, Jésus mon tendre Epoux!..."
 Ineffable abandon! Divine mélodie!
30 Tu dévoiles l'amour par ton céleste chant.
 L'amour qui ne craint pas, qui s'endort et s'oublie
 Sur le Coeur de son Dieu, comme un petit enfant...

 Dans la voûte azurée parut la blanche étoile
 Qui venait éclairer de ses timides feux
35 La lumineuse nuit qui nous montra sans voile
 Le virginal amour des époux dans les Cieux...

Alors Valérien rêvait la jouissance,
Cécile, ton amour était tout son désir...
Il trouva le bonheur dans ta noble alliance
40   Tu lui montras la vie qui ne doit pas finir.
"Jeune ami, lui dis-tu, près de moi toujours veille
"Un ange du Seigneur qui garde mon coeur pur,
"Il ne me quitte pas, alors que je sommeille,
"Il me couvre avec joie de ses ailes d'azur.
45   "La nuit, je vois briller son aimable visage
"D'un éclat bien plus doux que les feux du matin
"Sa face me paraît la transparente image
"Le pur rayonnement du visage divin."
Valérien reprit: "Montre-moi ce bel Ange,
50   "Afin qu'à ton serment je puisse ajouter foi.
"Autrement, crains déjà que mon amour se change
"En terrible fureur, en haine contre toi..."

O Colombe cachée dans le creux de la pierre!
Tu ne redoutais pas les filets du chasseur.
55   La Face de Jésus te montrait sa lumière,
L'Evangile sacré reposait sur ton coeur...
Tu repris aussitôt avec un doux sourire:
"Mon céleste Gardien exauce ton désir,
"Bientôt tu le verras, il daignera te dire
60   "Que pour voler aux Cieux, tu dois être martyr.
"Mais avant de le voir, il faut que le baptême
"Répande dans ton âme une sainte blancheur,
"Il faut que le vrai Dieu l'habite par Lui-même
"Il faut que l'Esprit-Saint soit la vie de ton coeur.
65   "Le Verbe, Fils de Dieu et le Fils de Marie,
"Dans son immense amour s'immole sur l'autel.
"Tu dois aller t'asseoir au Banquet de la Vie
"Afin de recevoir Jésus le Pain du Ciel.
"Alors le Séraphin t'appellera son frère,
70   "Et voyant dans ton coeur le trône de son Dieu
"Il te fera quitter les plages de la terre.
"Tu verras le séjour de cet esprit de feu."
— "Je sens brûler mon coeur d'une nouvelle flamme,"
S'écria dans sa joie l'ardent patricien.
75   "Je veux que le vrai Dieu habite dans mon âme,
"Cécile, mon amour sera digne du tien!..."

Revêtu de la robe emblème d'innocence,
Valérien put voir le bel ange des Cieux,
Il contempla ravi sa sublime puissance

80   Il vit le doux éclat de son front radieux.
      Le brillant séraphin tenait de fraîches roses
      Mélangées de beaux lys éclatants de blancheur.
      Dans les jardins du Ciel, ces fleurs étaient écloses
      Sous les rayons d'Amour de l'Astre créateur.

85   "Epoux chéris des Cieux, les roses du martyre
      "Couronneront vos fronts, dit l'ange du Seigneur,
      "Il n'y a pas de voix, il n'y a pas de lyre
      "Capables de chanter cette grande faveur!
      "Je m'abîme en mon Dieu, je contemple ses charmes,
90   "Mais je ne puis pour lui m'immoler et souffrir,
      "Je ne puis lui donner ni mon sang ni mes larmes
      "Malgré tout mon amour, je ne saurais mourir...
      "La pureté, de l'ange est le brillant partage
      "Son immense bonheur ne doit jamais finir,
95   "Mais sur le Séraphin, vous avez l'avantage
      "Vous pouvez être purs, et vous pouvez souffrir!
      ....
      "De la virginité vous voyez le symbole
      "Dans ces lys embaumés que vous envoie l'Agneau.
      "Vous serez couronnés de la blanche auréole,
100   "Vous chanterez toujours le cantique nouveau,
      "Votre chaste union enfantera de âmes
      "Qui ne rechercheront d'autre époux que Jésus.
      "Vous les verrez briller comme de pures flammes,
      "Près du trône divin, au séjour des élus..."

105   Cécile, prête-moi ta douce mélodie
      Je voudrais convertir à Jésus tant de coeurs!
      Je voudrais comme toi sacrifier ma vie.
      Je voudrais lui donner et mon sang et mes pleurs...
      Obtiens-moi de goûter sur la rive étrangère
110   Le parfait abandon, ce doux fruit de l'amour.
      O ma Sainte chérie! bientôt, loin de la terre,
      Obtiens-moi de voler près de toi sans retour...

                    28 Avril 1894

PN 4

(Air: "Pitié, mon Dieu")

Cantique pour obtenir la canonisation
de la Vénérable Jeanne d'Arc

1   Dieu des armées, l'Eglise tout entière
    Voudrait bientôt honorer à l'Autel
    Une Martyre, une Vierge guerrière
    Dont le doux nom retentit dans le Ciel.

Refr. 1   Refrain

Par ta Puissance
O Roi du Ciel
Donne à Jeanne de France   } bis
L'Auréole et l'Autel!

2   Un conquérant pour la France coupable,
    Non, ce n'est pas l'objet de son désir.
    De la sauver Jeanne seule est capable.
    Tous les héros pèsent moins qu'un martyr!

3   Jeanne, Seigneur, est ton oeuvre splendide:
    Un coeur de feu, une âme de guerrier,
    Tu les donnas à la Vierge timide
    Que tu voulais couronner de laurier.

4   Jeanne entendit dans son humble prairie
    Des voix du Ciel l'appeler au combat.
    Elle partit pour sauver la patrie.
    La douce Enfant à l'armée commanda.

5   Des fiers guerriers elle gagna les âmes
    L'éclat divin de l'Envoyée des Cieux,
    Son pur regard, ses paroles de flammes
    Surent courber les fronts audacieux...

6   Par un prodige unique dans l'histoire,
    On vit alors un monarque tremblant
    Reconquérir sa couronne et sa gloire
    Par le moyen d'un faible bras d'enfant.

7   Ce ne sont pas de Jeanne les victoires
    Que nous voulons célébrer en ce jour.
    Nous le savons, ses véritables gloires
    Ce sont, mon Dieu, ses vertus, son amour.

8 En combattant, Jeanne sauva la France,
 Mais il fallait que ses grandes vertus
 Fussent marqées du sceau de la souffrance,
 Du sceau divin de son Epoux Jésus!

9 Sur la bûcher sacrifiant sa vie,
 Jeanne entendit la voix des Bienheureux.
 Elle quitta l'exil pour la Patrie.
 L'Ange Sauveur remonta vers les Cieux!...

10 Jeanne, c'est toi notre unique espérance.
 Du haut des Cieux, daigne entendre nos voix.
 Descends vers nous, viens convertir la France.
 Viens la sauver une seconde fois.

Refr. 2   Refrain

    Par la puissance
    Du Dieu Vainqueur,
   Sauve, sauve la France,
   Ange Libérateur!... } bis

11 Chassant l'anglais hors de toute la France,
 Fille de Dieu, que tes pas étaient beaux!
 Mais souviens-toi qu'aux jours de ton enfance,
 Tu ne gardais que de faibles agneaux...

Refr. 3   Refrain

    Prends la défense
    Des impuissants.
   Conserve l'innocence
   En l'âme des enfants } bis

12 Douce Martyre, à toi nos monastères.
 Tu le sais bien, les vierges sont tes soeurs,
 Et comme toi l'objet de leurs prières
 C'est de voir Dieu régner dans tous les coeurs.

Refr. 4   Sauver des âmes
    Est leur désir.
   Ah! donne-leur tes flammes
   D'Apôtre et de Martyre! } bis

13 De tous les coeurs sera bannie la crainte
 Quand nous verrons l'Eglise couronner
 Le front si pur de Jeanne notre Sainte,
 Et c'est alors que nous pourrons chanter:

Refr. 5   Notre espérance
                 Repose en vous
                 Sainte Jeanne de France,   } bis
                 Priez, priez pour nous!

PN 5

(Air: "Dieu de paix et d'amour")

Mon Chant d'Aujourd'hui

1   Ma vie n'est qu'un instant! une heure passagère.
     Ma vie n'est qu'un seul jour qui m'échappe et qui fuit.
     Tu le sais, ô mon Dieu! pour t'aimer sur la terre
           Je n'ai rien qu'aujourd'hui!...

2   Oh! je t'aime. Jésus! vers toi mon âme aspire.
     Pour un jour seulement reste mon doux appui.
     Viens régner dans mon coeur, donne-moi ton sourire
           Rien que pour aujourd'hui!

3   Que m'importe, Seigneur, si l'avenir est sombre!
     Te prier pour demain, oh non, je ne le puis!...
     Conserve mon coeur pur, couvre-moi de ton ombre
           Rien que pour aujourd'hui.

4   Si je songe à demain, je crains mon inconstance,
     Je sens naître en mon coeur la tristesse et l'ennui.
     Mais je veux bien, mon Dieu, l'épreuve, la souffrance
           Rien que pour aujourd'hui!

5   Je dois te voir bientôt sur la rive éternelle
     O Pilote Divin! dont la main me conduit.
     Sur les flots orageux guide en paix ma nacelle
           Rien que pour aujourd'hui!

6   Ah! laisse-moi, Seigneur, me cacher en ta Face.
     Là je n'entendrai plus du monde le vain bruit.
     Donne-moi ton amour, conserve-moi ta grâce
           Rien que pour aujourd'hui!

7   Près de ton Coeur divin, j'oublie tout ce qui passe.
     Je ne redoute plus les craintes de la nuit.
     Ah! donne-moi, Jésus, dans ce Coeur une place
           Rien que pour aujourd'hui!

8   Pain Vivant, Pain du Ciel, divine Eucharistie,
O Mystère sacré! que l'Amour a produit.
Viens habiter mon coeur, Jésus, ma blanche Hostie
Rien que pour aujourd'hui!

9   Daigne m'unir à toi, Vigne Sainte et sacrée,
Et mon faible rameau te donnera son fruit.
Et je pourrai t'offrir une grappe dorée,
Seigneur, dès aujourd'hui.

10   Cette grappe d'amour, dont les grains sont des âmes,
Je n'ai pour la former que ce jour qui s'enfuit.
Ah! donne-moi, Jésus, d'un Apôtre les flammes
Rien que pour aujourd'hui!

11   O Vierge Immaculée! C'est toi ma Douce Etoile
Qui me donnes Jésus et qui m'unis à Lui.
O Mère! laisse-moi reposer sous ton voile
Rien que pour aujourd'hui!

12   Mon Saint Ange gardien, couvre-moi de ton aile.
Eclaire de tes feux la route que je suis.
Viens diriger mes pas...aide-moi, je t'appelle
Rien que pour aujourd'hui!

13   Seigneur, je veux te voir, sans voile, sans nuage,
Mais encore exilée, loin de toi, je languis.
Qu'il ne me soit caché, ton aimable visage,
Rien que pour aujourd'hui!

14   Je volerai bientôt, pour dire tes louanges
Quand le jour sans couchant sur mon âme aura lui.
Alors je chanterai sur la lyre des Anges
L'Eternel Aujourd'hui!...

PN 6

Fête du Sacré Coeur   1er Juin 1894

Le Portrait d'une Ame que j'Aime

Marie du Sacré Coeur

M   oi je connais un coeur, une âme très aimante,
A   yant reçu du Ciel une sublime Foi,
R   ien ne peut ici-bas ravir cette âme ardente:
I   l n'y a que Jésus qu'elle nomme son Roi.
E   nfin, cette belle âme est grande et généreuse,

D   ouce et vive à la fois, toujours humble de coeur.
U   n horizon lointaine... l'étoile lumineuse

S   uffisent bien souvent pour l'unir au Seigneur.
A   utrefois je la vis aimant l'indépendance,
C   hercher le bonheur pur et la vraie liberté...
R   épandre des bienfaits était sa jouissance
E   t s'oublier toujours, sa seule volonté!...

C   e fut le Coeur divin qui captiva cette âme,
OE   uvre de son amour, digne du Créateur.
U   n jour je la verrai comme une pure flamme
R   ayonner dans le Ciel auprès du Sacré Coeur.

Un coeur d'enfant reconnaissant

PN 7
Chant de Reconnaissance à Notre-Dame du Mont-Carmel

1   Aux premiers instants de ma vie,
           Vous m'avez prise entre vos bras;
           Depuis ce jour, Mère chérie,
           Vous me protegez ici-bas.
           Pour conserver mon innocence,
           Vous m'avez mise en un doux nid,
           Vous avez gardé mon enfance
           A l'ombre d'un cloître béni.

2   Plus tard, aux jours de ma jeunesse,
           De Jésus j'entendis l'appel!...
           Dans votre ineffable tendresse,
           Vous m'avez montré le Carmel.
           "Viens t'immoler pour ton Sauveur.
           Me disiez-vous avec douceur;
           "Près de moi, tu seras heureuse,
           "Viens t'immoler pour ton Sauveur.

           ....

3   Près de vous, ô ma tendre Mère!
           J'ai trouvé le repos du coeur;
           Je ne veux plus rien sur la terre,
           Jésus seul est tout mon bonheur.
           Si parfois je sens la tristesse,
           La crainte qui vient m'assaillir,
           Toujours, soutenant ma faiblesse,
           Mère, vous daignez me bénir.

4   Accordez-moi d'être fidèle
      A mon divin Epoux Jésus.
      Qu'un jour, sa douce voix m'appelle
      A voler parmi les élus.
      Alors, plus d'exil, de souffrance;
      Je vous redirai dans le Ciel
      Le chant de ma reconnaissance,
      Aimable Reine du Carmel!

                            16 Juillet 1894

PN 8

                                                    Août 1894
Prière de l'Enfant d'un Saint

1   Rappelle-toi qu'autrefois sur la terre
         Ton seul bonheur était de nous chérir.
         De tes enfants exauce la prière.
         Protège-nous, daigne encor nous bénir.
      Tu retrouves là-Haut notre Mère chérie
      Qui t'avait précédé dans la Sainte Patrie.
               Maintenant dans les Cieux
               Vous régnez tous les deux.
                  Veillez sur nous!...

2   Rappelle-toi ta bien-aimée Marie,
         Ta fille aînée, la plus chère à ton coeur.
         Rappelle-toi qu'elle remplit ta vie
         Par son amour, de charme et de bonheur...
      Pour Dieu tu renonças à sa douce présence,
      Et tu bénis la main qui t'offrait la souffrance...
               Oh! de ton Diamant
               Toujours plus scintillant
                  Rappelle-toi!...

3   Rappelle-toi ta belle perle fine
         Que tu connus faible et timide agneau.
         Vois-la remplie d'une force divine
         Et du Carmel conduisant le troupeau.
      De tes autres enfants elle est devenue Mère.
      O Papa! viens guider celle qui t'est si chère!...
               Et sans quitter le Ciel
               De ton petit Carmel
                  Rappelle-toi!...

4   Rappelle-toi de l'ardente prière
     Que tu formas pour ta troisième enfant.
     Dieu t'exauça, car elle est sur la terre
     Comme ses soeurs, un beau Lys très brillant.
La Visitation la cache aux yeux du monde
Mais elle aime Jésus, c'est sa paix qui l'inonde.
     De ses ardents désirs
     Et de tous ses soupirs
     Rappelle-toi!...

5   Rappelle-toi de ta chère Céline
     Qui fut pour toi comme un ange des Cieux,
     Lorsqu'un regard de la Face Divine
     Vint t'éprouver par un choix glorieux...
Tu règnes dans le Ciel.... sa tâche est accomplie.
Maintenant à Jésus elle donne sa vie....
     Protège ton enfant
     Qui redit bien souvent
     Rappelle-toi!...

6   Rappelle-toi de ta petite reine,
     L'orpheline de la Bérésina.
     Rappelle-toi que sa marche incertaine,
     Ce fut toujours ta main qui la guida.
O Papa! souviens-toi qu'aux jours de son enfance
Tu voulus pour Dieu seul garder son innocence!...
     Et de ses blonds cheveux
     Qui ravissaient tes yeux
     Rappelle-toi!...

7   Rappelle-toi que dans le belvédère
     Tu l'asseyais toujours sur tes genoux,
     Et murmurant alors une prière
     Tu la berçais par ton refrain si doux.
Elle voyait du Ciel un reflet sur ta face
Quand ton regard profond se plongeait dans l'espace,
     Et de l'Eternité
     Tu chantais la beauté
     Rappelle-toi!...

8   Rappelle-toi du radieux Dimanche
     Où la pressant sur ton coeur paternel,
     Tu lui donnas une fleurette blanche,
     Lui permettant de voler au Carmel.

O Papa! souviens-toi qu'en ses grandes épreuves
Du plus sincère amour tu lui donnas les preuves.
A Rome et à Bayeux
Tu lui montras les Cieux
Rappelle-toi!...

9   Rappelle-toi que la main du Saint-Père
Au Vatican sur ton front se posa,
Mais tu ne pus comprendre le mystère
Du sceau Divin qui sur toi s'imprima...
Maintenant tes enfants t'adressent leur prière
Ils bénissent ta Croix et ta douleur amère!...
Sur ton front glorieux
Rayonnent dans les Cieux
Neuf Lys en fleur.

L'Orpheline de la Bérésina

PN 9
Prière d'une enfant exilée

A   uprès de vous, mon Dieu, je me souviens d'un Père,
L   'apôtre bien-aimé de votre Sacré-Coeur.
M   ais il est exilé sur la rive étrangère...
I   l en est temps enfin, ramenez mon Pasteur!
R   endez à vos enfants leur guide et leur lumière,
E   n France, rappelez votre apôtre, Seigneur.

11 Septembre 1894

PN 10
(Air: "Tombé du nid")   20 Novembre 1894
Histoire d'une Bergère devenue Reine

A ma Sr Marie-Madeleine le jour de sa Profession,
faite entre les mains de Mère Agnès de Jésus.

1   En ce beau jour, ô Madeleine!
Nous venons chanter près de vous
La merveilleuse et douce chaîne
Qui vous unit à votre Epoux,
Ecoutez la charmante histoire
D'une bergère qu'un grand Roi

Voulut un jour combler de gloire
Et qui répondit à sa voix.

Refrain

Chantons la Bergère,
Pauvre sur la terre,
Que le Roi du Ciel
Epouse en ce jour au Carmel.

2 Une petite bergerette
En filant gardait ses agneaux.
Elle admirait chaque fleurette,
Ecoutait le chant des oiseaux,
Comprenant bien le doux langage
Des grands bois et du beau Ciel bleu.
Tout pour elle était une image
Qui lui révélait le Bon Dieu.

3 Elle aimait Jésus et Marie
Avec une bien grande ardeur.
Ils aimaient aussi Mélanie
Et vinrent lui parler au coeur.
"Veux-tu, disait la Douce Reine,
"Près de moi, sur le Mont Carmel
"Veux-tu devenir Madeleine,
"Et ne plus gagner que le Ciel?

4 "Enfant, quitte cette campagne,
"Ne regrette pas ton troupeau,
"Là-bas, sur ma sainte montagne,
"Jésus sera ton seul Agneau."
"Oh! viens, ton âme m'a charmé,
Redisait Jésus à son tour.
"Je te prends pour ma fiancée,
"Tu seras à moi sans retour."

5 "Avec bonheur l'humble bergère,
Répondant à ce doux appel,
Soutenue par Marie, sa Mère,
Parvint au sommet du Carmel."
....
C'est vous, ô Marie-Madeleine!
Que nous fêtons en ce grand jour.
La Bergère est devenue Reine
Près du Roi Jésus, son amour!...

6   Vous le savez, Soeur très chérie,
        Servir notre Dieu, c'est régner.
        Le Doux Sauveur pendant sa vie
        Ne cessait de nous l'enseigner:
        "Si dans la Céleste Patrie
        "Vous voulez être le premier,
        "Il faudra toute votre vie
        "Vous cacher...Etre le dernier."

7   Heureuse êtes-vous, Madeleine,
        Priant Jésus sur le Carmel.
        Serait-il pour vous quelque peine
        Etant si rapprochée du Ciel?...
        Vous imitez Marthe et Marie:
        Prier, servir le doux Sauveur,
        Voilà le but de votre vie.
        Il vous donne le vrai bonheur.

8   Si parfois l'amère souffrance
        Venait visiter votre coeur,
        Faites-en votre jouissance:
        Souffrir pour Dieu... quelle douceur!...
        Alors les tendresses Divines
        Vous feront bien vite oublier
        Que vous marchez sur des épines,
        Et vous croirez plutôt voler...

9   Aujourd'hui l'ange vous envie.
        Il voudrait goûter le bonheur
        Que vous possédez, ô Marie!
        Etant l'épouse du Seigneur.
        Oui, vous êtes dès cette vie
        L'épouse du Roi des élus.
        Un jour en la sainte Patrie
        Vous régnerez près de Jésus.

                        Dernier refrain

                Bientòt la Bergère,
                Pauvre sur la terre,
                S'envolant au Ciel
        Régnera près de l'Eternel.

A nos Vénérées Mères.

10   C'est à vous, bonnes, tendres Mères,
Que Madeleine, notre Soeur,
C'est à vos soins et vos prières
Qu'elle doit sa paix, son bonheur.
Elle saura bien reconnaître
Votre amour tendre et maternel,
Demandant à son Divin Maître
De vous combler des biens du Ciel.

Refrain

Et dans vos couronnes,
O Mères si bonnes,
Brillera la fleur
Que vous offrez au Dieu Sauveur.

[PN 11]

[Pour la prise d'habit de Marie-Agnès de la Sainte Face]

1

Vierge Marie, malgré mon impuissance
Je veux chanter au soir de ce beau jour
Le cantique de la reconnaissance
Et mon espoir d'être à Dieu sans retour.
Ah! si longtemps, bien loin de l'arche sainte,
Mon pauvre coeur désirait le Carmel.
Je l'ai trouvé, maintenant plus de crainte.
Je goûte ici les prémices du Ciel!...

Refrain

Il est enfin passé le temps des larmes.
J'ai revêtu la toison du troupeau.
Pour moi se lève un horizon nouveau.
Divine Mère, en ce jour plein de charmes
Oh! cachez bien le pauvre agneau
Sous votre manteau!

2

Je suis bien jeune, et déjà la souffrance,
L'épreuve amère a visité mon coeur.
Vierge Marie, mon unique espérance,
A votre agneau vous rendez le bonheur.

Vous me donnez le Carmel pour famille.
De vos enfants je suis aussi la Soeur.
Mère chérie, je deviens votre fille,
La fiancée de Jésus mon Sauveur.

3

De votre Fils le regard ineffable
Sur ma pauvre âme a daigné s'abaisser.
J'ai recherché son Visage adorable,
Et c'est en Lui que je veux me cacher.
Il me faudra rester toujours petite
Pour mériter les regards de ses yeux,
Mais en vertu je grandirai bien vite
Sous les ardeurs de cet astre des Cieux.

4

Douce Marie, je ne crains pas l'ouvrage,
Vous connaissez ma bonne volonté.
J'ai des défauts, mais aussi du courage,
Et de mes soeurs grande est la charité.
En attendant le beau jour de mes noces,
J'imiterai leurs sublimes vertus,
Car je le sens, vous me donnez des forces
Pour devenir l'épouse de Jésus.

Dernier Refrain

Daignez bénir les Mères Vénérées
Dont la bonté m'a rendu le Carmel.
Auprès de vous sur un trône immortel
Vierge Marie, que je les voie placées,
Et que votre coeur maternel
Les couronne au Ciel.

[PN 12]

J.M.J.T.

18 Décembre 1894

1   C'est près de vous, Vierge Marie,
Que nous venons chanter ce soir,
Vous priant pour l'enfant chérie
Dont vous êtes l'unique espoir.

2   Au jour béni de votre attente
Vous rendez son coeur bien heureux

Elle dresse au Carmel sa tente
Et n'attend plus que les Saints Voeux.

3 Ce beau jour, ô tendre Marie,
Lui rappelle un doux souvenir.
En un autre jour de sa vie
Votre manteau vint la couvrir.

4 La bure enfin lui et rendue.
Deux fois elle a pris votre habit.
Qu'elle soit aussi revêtue,
Mère, de votre double esprit.

5 Elle a chanté: "J'ai du courage!…"
– C'est vrai, nous l'avons dit tout bas.
Elle a chanté: "J'aime l'ouvrage!"
– L'ouvrage ici ne manque pas!…

6 Mais la force est très bonne chose
Pour travailler avec ardeur.
Sur ses joues, mettez d'une rose,
Mère, la brillante couleur!…

7 Pour elle l'attente est passée.
Son coeur goûte la paix de Ciel.
Avec l'habit de Fiancée
Jésus veut la voir à Noël.

8 Qu'Il daigne cacher en sa Face,
Tendre Mère, votre humble agneau.
C'est là qu'il réclame une place,
Ne voulant pas d'autre berceau.

9 Daignez exaucer, ô Marie!
Les voeux de votre pauvre agneau.
Pendant la nuit de cette vie
Cachez-le sous votre manteau.

10 Ecoutez toutes ses prières,
Et que votre coeur Maternel
Lui garde bien longtemps les Mères
Qui lui rendent son cher Carmel!…

PN 13
J.M.J.T.
La Reine du Ciel à son enfant bien-aimée
Marie de la Ste Face

1   Je cherche une enfant qui ressemble
A Jésus, mon unique agneau
Afin de les garder ensemble,
Tous deux en un même berceau.

2   L'Ange de la Sainte Patrie
De ce bonheur serait jaloux!...
Mais je le donne à toi, Marie,
L'Enfant Dieu sera ton Epoux!...

3   C'est toi-même que j'ai choisie
Pour être de Jésus la soeur.
Veux-tu Lui tenir compagnie?...
Tu reposeras sur mon coeur...

4   Je te cacherai sous le voile
Où s'abrite le Roi des Cieux,
Mon Fils sera la seule étoile
Désormais brillante à tes yeux.

5   Mais pour que toujours je t'abrite,
Sous mon voile près de Jésus,
Il te faudra rester petite,
Parée d'enfantines vertus...

6   Je veux que sur ton front rayonne
La douceur et la pureté
Mais la vertu que je te donne
Surtout, c'est la Simplicité.

7   Le Dieu, L'Unique en trois personnes
Qu'adorent les anges tremblants,
L'Eternel veut que tu lui donnes
Le simple nom de Fleur des champs.

8   Comme une blanche pâquerette
Qui toujours regarde le Ciel,
Sois aussi la simple fleurette
Du petit Enfant de Noël!...

9   Le monde méconnaît les charmes
Du Roi qui s'exile des Cieux.

Bien souvent, tu verras des larmes
Briller en ses doux petits yeux.

10   Il faudra qu'oubliant tes peines
Pour réjouir l'Aimable Enfant
Tu benisses tes douces chaines
Et que tu chantes doucement!...

11   Le Dieu dont la toute-puissance
Arrête le flot qui mugit,
Empruntant les traits de l'enfance,
Veut devenir faible et petit.

12   La Parole incréée du Père
Qui pour toi s'exile ici-bas,
Mon doux Agneau, ton petit Frère,
Marie, ne te parlera pas!...

13   Ce silence est le premier gage
De son inexprimable amour.
Comprenant ce muet langage,
Tu l'imiteras chaque jour.

14   Et si parfois Jésus sommeille,
Tu reposeras près de Lui.
Son coeur Divin qui toujours veille
Te servira de doux appui.

15   Ne t'inquiète pas, Marie,
De l'ouvrage de chaque jour,
Car ton travail en cette vie
Doit être uniquement: "L'Amour!"

16   Mais si quelqu'un vient à redire
Que tes oeuvres ne se voient pas,
"J'aime beaucoup, pourras-tu dire.
"Voilà ma richesse ici-bas!..."

17   Jésus tressera ta couronne,
Si tu ne veux que son amour.
Si ton coeur en Lui s'abandonne,
Il te fera régner toujours.

18   Après la nuit de cette vie
Invitée par Son doux Regard,
Dans le Ciel ton âme ravie
Volera sans aucun retard!...

La nuit de Noël 1894

(Air de cantique: "Sur le grand mât d'une corvette")

PN 14
A Notre Père Saint Joseph

1

Joseph, votre admirable vie
S'est passée dans la pauvreté,
Mais, de Jésus et de Marie
Vous contempliez la beauté.

Refrain

Joseph, ô tendre Père,
Protégez le Carmel.
Que vos enfants sur cette terre
Goûtent toujours la paix du Ciel!   } bis

2

Le Fils de Dieu, dans son enfance,
Plus d'une fois avec bonheur,
Soumis à votre obéissance
S'est reposé sur votre coeur.

3

Comme vous dans la solitude,
Nous servons Marie et Jésus.
Leur plaire est notre seule étude
Nous ne désirons rien de plus...

4

Sainte Thérèse notre Mère
Vous invoquait avec amour.
Elle assure que sa prière,
Vous l'avez exaucée toujours.

5

Après l'exil de cette vie,
Nous en avons le doux expoir,
Avec notre Mère chérie,
Saint Joseph, nous irons vous voir.

Dernier Refrain

Bénissez, tendre Père,
Notre petit Carmel.
Après l'exil de cette terre
Réunissez-nous dans le Ciel.   } bis

(Air: "Nous voulons Dieu")

PN 15
L'atome du Sacré-Coeur

Refrain

Ton atome, Divin Coeur,
Te donne sa vie.
Voilà sa paix, son bonheur,
Te charmer, Seigneur.

1

Je suis à ta porte
La nuit et le jour.
Ta grâce me porte.
Vive ton amour!...

2

O cache ta gloire.
Fais-moi un doux nid
Dans le saint Ciboire
Le jour et la nuit.

3

Ton aile, ô merveille!
Devient mon abri.
Quand je me réveille,
Jésus, tu souris...

4

Ton regard m'enflamme.
Mon unique amour,
Consume mon âme.
Jésus, sans retour.

5

Remplie de tendresse,
Ta voix me ravit;
Et ton coeur me presse,
O mon doux Ami!...

6

Ta main me soulage
Et me sert d'appui.
Tu rends le courage
Au coeur qui gémit.

7

De toute fatigue
Console mon coeur.
Et pour le prodigue
Sois le Bon Pasteur.

8

Oh! le doux spectacle,
Prodige d'amour,
Dans le tabernacle
Je reste toujours.

9

Dégagée du monde
Et sans nul appui,
Ta grâce m'inonde,
Mon unique ami!...

10

Oh! quel doux martyre.
Je brûle d'amour.
Vers toi je soupire,
Jésus, chaque jour!...

PN 16
Chant de Reconnaissance de la Fiancée de Jésus

(Air: "Oh! saint Autel")

1   Tu m'as cachée pour toujours en ta Face!...
Divin Jésus, daigne écouter ma voix.
Je viens chanter l'inexprimable grâce
D'avoir souffert...d'avoir porté la Croix...

2   J'ai bu longtemps au calice des larmes.
J'ai partagé ta coupe de douleurs,
Et j'ai compris que souffrir a des charmes,
Que par la Croix on sauve les pécheurs.

3   C'est par la Croix que mon âme agrandie
A vu s'ouvrir un horizon nouveau.
Sous les rayons de ta Face Bénie,
Mon faible coeur s'est élevé bien haut.

4   Mon Bien-Aimé, ta douce voix m'appelle.
Viens, me dis-tu, déjà l'hiver a fui.

Pour toi commence une saison nouvelle.
Enfin le jour va remplacer la nuit.

5   Lève les yeux vers la Sainte Patrie,
Et tu verras sur des trônes d'honneur
Un Père aimé... Une Mère chérie...
Auxquels tu dois ton immense bonheur!...

6   Comme un instant s'écoulera ta vie.
Sur le Carmel on est tout près des Cieux.
Ma bien-aimée, mon amour t'a choisie
Je te réserve un trône glorieux!...

                                 (5 février 1895)

PN 17

                          (Air du cant. - "Il est à moi")

Vivre d'Amour!...

1   Au soir d'Amour, parlant sans parabole,
Jésus disait: "Si quelqu'un veut m'aimer
"Toute sa vie, qu'il garde ma Parole.
"Mon Père et moi viendrons le visiter,
"Et de son coeur faisant notre demeure,
"Venant à lui, nous l'aimerons toujours!...
"Rempli de paix, nous voulons qu'il demeure
          "En notre Amour!..."

2   Vivre d'Amour, c'est te garder Toi-Même,
Verbe incréé, Parole de mon Dieu.
Ah! tu le sais, Divin Jésus, je t'aime.
L'Esprit d'Amour m'embrase de son feu.
C'est en t'aimant que j'attire le Père.
Mon faible coeur le garde sans retour.
O Trinité! vous êtes Prisonnière
          De mon Amour!...

3   Vivre d'Amour, c'est vivre de ta vie,
Roi glorieux, délice des élus.
Tu vis pour moi, caché dans une hostie.
Je veux pour toi me cacher, ô Jésus!
A des amants, il faut la solitude,
Un coeur à coeur qui dure nuit et jour.
Ton seul regard fait ma béatitude.
          Je vis d'Amour!...

4   Vivre d'Amour, ce n'est pas sur la terre
     Fixer sa tente au sommet du Thabor.
     Avec Jésus, c'est gravir le Calvaire,
     C'est regarder la Croix comme un trésor!...
     Au Ciel je dois vivre de jouissance.
     Alors l'épreuve aura fui pour toujours,
     Mais exilée je veux dans la souffrance
               Vivre d'Amour.

5   Vivre d'Amour, c'est donner sans mesure
     Sans réclamer de salaire ici-bas.
     Ah! sans compter je donne étant bien sûre
     Que lorqu'on aime, on ne calcule pas!...
     Au Coeur Divin, débordant de tendresse,
     J'ai tout donné... légèrement je cours.
     Je n'ai plus rien que ma seule richesse:
               Vivre d'Amour.

6   Vivre d'Amour, c'est bannir toute crainte,
     Tout souvenir des fautes du passé.
     De mes péchés je ne vois nulle empreinte,
     En un instant l'amour a tout brûlé...
     Flamme divine, ô très douce Fournaise!
     En ton foyer je fixe mon séjour.
     C'est en tes feux que je chante à mon aise:
               "Je vis d'Amour!..."

7   Vivre d'Amour, c'est garder en soi-même
     Un grand trésor en un vase mortel.
     Mon Bien-Aimé, ma faiblesse est extrême.
     Ah, je suis loin d'être un ange du ciel!...
     Mais si je tombe à chaque heure qui passe,
     Me relevant tu viens à mon secours,
     A chaque instant tu me donnes ta grâce.
               Je vis d'Amour.

8   Vivre d'Amour, c'est naviguer sans cesse
     Semant la paix, la joie dans tous les coeurs.
     Pilote Aimé, la Charité me presse,
     Car je te vois dans les âmes mes soeurs.
     La Charité voilà ma seule étoile.
     A sa clarté je vogue sans détour.
     J'ai ma devise écrite sur ma voile:
               "Vivre d'Amour."

9 Vivre d'Amour, lorsque Jésus sommeille
  C'est le repos sur les flots orageux.
  Oh! ne crains pas, Seigneur, que je t'éveille.
  J'attends en paix le rivage des cieux...
  La Foi bientôt déchirera son voile.
  Mon Espérance est de te voir un jour.
  La Charité enfle et pousse ma voile.
    Je vis d'Amour!...

10 Vivre d'Amour, c'est, ô mon Divin Maître,
  Te supplier de répandre tes Feux
  En l'âme sainte et sacrée de ton Prêtre.
  Qu'il soit plus pur qu'un séraphin des cieux!...
  Ah! glorifie ton Eglise Immortelle.
  A mes soupirs, Jésus, ne sois pas sourd.
  Moi son enfant, je m'immole pour elle.
    Je vis d'Amour!...

11 Vivre d'Amour, c'est essuyer ta Face.
  C'est obtenir des pécheurs le pardon.
  O Dieu d'Amour! qu'ils rentrent dans ta grâce,
  Et qu'à jamais ils bénissent ton Nom.....
  Jusqu'à mon coeur retentit le blasphème.
  Pour l'effacer, je veux chanter toujours:
  "Ton Nom Sacré, je l'adore et je l'Aime.
    Je vis d'Amour!..."

12 Vivre d'Amour, c'est imiter Marie,
  Baignant de pleurs, de parfums précieux,
  Tes pieds divins, qu'elle baise ravie,
  Les essuyant avec ses longs cheveux...
  Puis se levant, elle brise le vase.
  Ton Doux Visage elle embaume à son tour.
  Moi, le parfum dont j'embaume ta Face,
    C'est mon Amour!...

13 "Vivre d'Amour, quelle étrange folie!"
  Me dit le monde, "Ah! cessez de chanter,
  "Ne perdez pas vos parfums, votre vie,
  "Utilement sachez les employer!..."
  T'aimer, Jésus, quelle perte féconde!...
  Tous mes parfums sont à toi sans retour.
  Je veux chanter en sortant de ce monde:
    "Je meurs d'Amour!"

14   Mourir d'Amour, c'est un bien doux martyre,
     Et c'est celui que je voudrais souffrir.
     O Chérubins! accordez votre lyre,
     Car je le sens, mon exil va finir!...
     Flamme d'Amour, consume-moi sans trêve.
     Vie d'un instant, ton fardeau m'est bien lourd!
     Divin Jésus, réalise mon rêve:
               Mourir d'Amour!...

15   Mourir d'Amour, voilà mon espérance.
     Quand je verrai se briser me liens,
     Mon Dieu sera ma Grande Récompense.
     Je ne veux point posséder d'autres biens.
     De son Amour je veux être embrasée.
     Je veux Le voir, m'unir à Lui toujours.
     Voilà mon Ciel.... voilà ma destinée:
               Vivre d'Amour!!!...

PN 18
Le Cantique de Céline

1   Oh! que j'aime la souvenance
           Des jours bénis de mon enfance...
       Pour garder la fleur de mon innocence
           Le Seigneur m'entoura toujours
               D'amour!...

2   Aussi malgré ma petitesse
           J'étais bien remplie de tendresse,
       Et de mon coeur s'échappa la promesse
           D'épouser le Roi des élus,
               Jésus!...

3   J'aimais au printemps de ma vie
           Saint Joseph, la Vierge Marie.
       Déjà mon âme se plongeait ravie
           Quand se reflétaient dans mes yeux
               Les Cieux!...

4   J'aimais les champs de blé, la plaine.
           J'aimais la colline lointaine.
       Oh! dans ma joie je respirais à peine
           En moissonnant avec mes soeurs
               Les fleurs.

5   J'aimais à cueillir les herbettes,
            Les bluets... toutes les fleurettes.
      Je trouvais le parfum des violettes
         Et surtout celui des coucous
            Bien doux...

6   J'aimais la pâquerette blanche,
            Les promenades du Dimanche,
     Les petits oiseaux chantant sur la branche,
         Et l'azur toujours radieux
            Des Cieux.

7   J'aimais à poser chaque année
            Mon soulier dans la cheminée.
      Accourant dès que j'étais éveillée,
         Je chantais la fête du Ciel:
            Noël!...

8   De Maman j'aimais le sourire:
            Son regard profond semblait dire:
     "L'Eternité me ravit et m'attire...
         Je vais aller dans le Ciel bleu
            Voir Dieu!

9   "Je vais trouver en la Patrie
            "Mes anges...la Vierge Marie.
     "De mes enfants que je laisse en la vie
         "A Jésus j'offrirai les pleurs...
            "Les coeurs!..."

10   Oh! que j'aimai Jésus-Hostie
            Qui vint au matin de ma vie
      Se fiancer à mon âme ravie
         Oh! que j'ouvris avec bonheur
            Mon coeur!...

11   Plus tard j'aimai la créature
            Que me paraissait être pure.
     Cherchant partout le Dieu de la nature,
         En Lui je trouvai pour jamais
            La paix!...

12   Oh! que j'aimais au belvédère,
            Inondée de joie, de lumière,
     A recevoir les caresses d'un Père,
         A contempler ses blancs cheveux
            Neigeux...

13   Sur ses genoux étant placée
       Avec Thérèse à la veillée,
Je m'en souviens, j'étais longtemps bercée.
     J'entends encor de son doux chant
         L'accent!...

14   O souvenir! tu me reposes.
     Tu me rappelles bien des choses...
Les soupers du soir... le parfum des roses!...
      Les buissonnets pleins de gaîté
         L'été!...

15   J'aimais à l'heure où le jour baisse
      A pouvoir confondre à mon aise
Mon âme avec celle de ma Thérèse.
     Je ne formais avec ma soeur
        Qu'un coeur...

16   Alors nos voix étaient mêlées,
     Nos mains l'une à l'autre enchaînée.
Ensemble chantant les Noces Sacrées,
     Déjà nous rêvions le Carmel...
        Le Ciel!...

17   De la Suisse et de l'Italie
     Ciel bleu, fruits d'or m'avaient ravie.
J'aimais surtout le regard plein de vie
     Du Saint Viellard pontife-roi
        Sur moi...

18   Avec amour je t'ai baisée,
     Terre bénie du Colysée!...
Des catacombes la voûte sacrée
     A répété bien doucement
        Mon chant.

19   Après les joies vinrent les larmes!...
     Bien grandes furent mes alarmes...
De mon Epoux je revêtis les armes,
     Et sa Croix devint mon soutien,
        Mon bien...

20   Ah! longtemps je fus exilée,
     Privée de ma famille aimée;
Et je n'avais, pauvre biche blessée,
     Que le seul églantier fleuri,
        D'abri!...

21   Mais un soir mon âme attendrie
   Vit le sourire de Marie,
  Et de son sang une goutte bénie
   Pour moi se changea (quel bienfait!)
    En lait!...

22   Alors j'aimai, fuyant le monde,
   Que l'écho lointain me réponde!...
  En la vallée solitaire et féconde,
   Je cueillais à travers mes pleurs
    Les fleurs!...

23   J'aimais de la lointaine église
   Entendre la cloche indécise.
  Pour écouter les soupirs de la brise
  Dans les champs j'aimais à m'asseoir
    Le soir.

24   J'aimais le vol des hirondelles,
   Le chant plaintif des tourterelles.
  J'écoutais des insectes les bruits d'ailes,
   Aimant de leur bourdonnement
    Le chant.

25   J'aimais la rosée matinale
   Et la gracieuse cigale.
  J'aimais à voir l'abeille virginale
   Qui préparait dès son réveil
    Le miel.

26   J'aimais à cueillir la bruyère
   Courant sur la mousse légère.
  Je prenais voltigeant sur la fougère
   Les papillons au reflet pur
    D'azur.

27   J'aimais le ver luisant dans l'ombre.
   J'aimais les étoiles sans nombre.
  Surtout j'aimais l'éclat en l'azur sombre
   De la lune au disque d'argent
    Brillant.

28   J'aimais à combler de tendresse
   Mon petit Père en sa vieillesse
  Il m'était tout... bonheur... enfant... richesse!...
   Ah! je l'embrassais tendrement
    Souvent.

29   Nous aimions le doux bruit de l'onde,
              Entendre l'orage que gronde
       Le soir en la solitude profonde.
           Du rossignol au fond du bois,
                La voix!...

30   Mais un matin son beau visage
              Du Crucifix chercha l'image...
       De son amour il me laissa le gage,
           Me donnant son Dernier regard...
                "Ma part!..."

31   Et de Jésus la main divine
              Prit le seul trésor de Céline;
       Et l'emportant bien loin de la colline,
           Le plaça près de l'Eternel
                Au Ciel!...

32   Maintenant je suis prisonnière.
              J'ai fui les bosquets de la terre.
       J'ai vu que tout en elle est éphémère...
           J'ai vu mon bonheur se flétrir,
                Mourir!...

33   Sous mes pas l'herbe s'est meurtrie!...
              La fleur en mes mains s'est flétrie!...
       Jésus, je veux courir en ta prairie.
           Sur elle ne marqueront pas
                Mes pas....

34   Comme un cerf en sa soif ardente
              Soupire après l'eau jaillissante,
       O Jésus! vers toi j'accours défaillante.
           Il faut pour calmer mes ardeurs
                Tes pleurs!...

35   C'est ton amour seul qui m'entraine.
              Mon troupeau je laisse en la plaine.
       De le garder je ne prends pas la peine,
           Je veux plaire à mon seul Agneau
                Nouveau.

36   Jésus, c'est toi, l'Agneau que j'aime.
              Tu me suffis, ô bien suprême!
       En toi, j'ai tout, la terre et le Ciel même.
           La Fleur que je cueille, ô mon Roi,
                C'est toi!...

37   Jésus, beau Lys de la vallée,
Ton doux parfum m'a captivée.
Bouquet de myrrhe, ô corolle embaumée!
Sur mon coeur je veux te garder,
T'aimer...

38   Toujours ton amour m'accompagne.
En toi, j'ai les bois, la campagne.
J'ai les roseaux, la prairie, la montagne,
Les pluies et le flocon neigeux
Des Cieux.

39   En toi, Jésus, j'ai toutes choses.
J'ai les blés, les fleurs demi-closes,
Myosotis, bouton d'or, belles roses.
Du blanc muguet j'ai la fraîcheur,
L'odeur!...

40   J'ai la lyre mélodieuse,
La solitude harmonieuse,
Fleuves, rochers, cascade gracieuse,
Daim léger, gazelle, écureuil,
Chevreuil.

41   J'ai l'arc-en-ciel, la neige pure,
Le vaste horizon, la verdure,
Les îles lointaines... La moisson mûre,
Les papillons, le gai printemps,
Les champs.

42   En ton amour, je trouve encore
Les palmiers que le soleil dore,
La nuit pareille au lever de l'aurore,
Le doux murmure du ruisseau,
L'oiseau.

43   J'ai les grappes délicieuses,
Les libellules gracieuses,
La forêt vierge aux fleurs mystérieuses.
J'ai tous les blonds petits enfants,
Leurs chants.

44   En toi, j'ai sources et colline,
Lianes, pervenche, aubépine,
Frais nénuphars, chèvrefeuille, églantine,
Le frisilis du peuplier
Léger.

45   J'ai l'avoine folle et tremblante,
            Des vents la voix grave et puissante,
       Le fil de la Vierge, la flamme ardente,
            Le zéphir, les buissons fleurs,
                 Les nids.

46   J'ai le beau lac, j'ai la vallée
            Solitaire et toute boisée.
       De l'océan j'ai la vague argentée,
            Poissons dorés, trésors divers
                 Des mers.

47   J'ai le vaisseau fuyant la plage,
            Le sillon d'or et le rivage.
       J'ai du soleil festonnant le nuage
            Alors qu'il disparaît des Cieux
                 Les feux.

48   En toi, j'ai la colombe pure.
            En toi, sous ma robe de bure
       Je trouve bague, colliers et parure:
            Joyaux, perles et diamants
                 Brillants.

49   En toi j'ai la brillante étoile,
            Souvent ton amour se dévoile;
       Et j'aperçois comme à travers un voile,
            Quand le jour est sur son déclin,
                 Ta main.

50   Toi dont la main soutient les mondes
            Qui plantes les forêts profondes,
       Toi qui d'un seul coup d'oeil les rends fécondes,
            Tu me suis d'un regard d'amour
                 Toujours.

51   J'ai ton Coeur, ta Face adorée,
            Ton doux regard qui m'a blessée.
       J'ai le baiser de ta bouche sacrée.
            Je t'aime et ne veux rien de plus,
                 Jésus.

52   J'irai chanter avec les anges
            De l'amour sacré les louanges.
       Fais-moi voler bientôt en leurs phalanges,
            O Jésus! que je meure un jour
                 D'amour!...

53   Attiré par la douce flamme
       Le papillon vole et s'enflamme.
Ainsi ton amour attire mon âme.
       C'est en lui que je veux voler
          Brûler!...

54   Je l'entends déjà qui s'apprête,
       Mon Dieu, ton éternelle fête....
Aux saules prenant ma harpe muette,
       Sur tes genoux je vais m'asseoir
          Te voir!...

55   Près de Toi, je vais voir Marie...
       Les Saints... ma famille chérie!...
Je vais après l'exil de cette vie
       Retrouver le toit Paternel
          Au Ciel!...

PN 18 bis

Plusieurs pensées sont prises dans le cant.
spirituel de s. J. de la +   (Air: "Combien j'ai douce souvenance")

Qui a Jésus a Tout

1   Méprisant les joies de la terre,
       Je suis devenue prisonnière.
J'ai vu que tout plaisir est éphémère.
       C'est toi mon unique bonheur,
          Seigneur!...

2   Sous mes pas l'herbe s'est meurtrie,
       La fleur en ma main s'est flétrie!...
Jésus, je veux courir en ta prairie.
       Sur elle ne marqueront pas
          Mes pas!...

3   C'est ton amour seul qui m'entraine.
       Mon troupeau je laisse en la plaine.
De le garder je ne prends pas la peine.
       Je veux plaire à mon seul Agneau
          Nouveau.

4   Jésus, c'est toi l'Agneau que j'aime.
       Tu me suffis, ô Bien suprême!
En toi j'ai tout, la terre et le Ciel même.
       La Fleur que je cueille, ô mon Roi!
          C'est Toi!...

5   En toi, j'ai la belle nature.
       J'ai l'arc-en-ciel, la neige pure,
Les îles lointaines, la moisson mûre,
     Les papillons, le gai printemps,
       Les champs.

6   J'ai le vaisseau fuyant la plage,
       Le sillon d'or et le rivage.
J'ai du soleil festonnant le nuage
     Alors qu'il disparaît des cieux
       Les feux.

7   Toi dont la main soutient les mondes,
       Qui plantes les forêts profondes,
Toi qui d'un seul coup d'oeil les rends fécondes,
     Tu me suis d'un regard d'Amour
       Toujours.

8   Attiré par la douce flamme,
       Le papillon vole et s'enflamme.
Ainsi ton amour attire mon âme,
     C'est en lui que je veux voler
       Brûler!...

9   Je l'entends déjà qui s'apprête,
       Mon Dieu, ton éternelle fête.
Aux saules prenant ma harpe muette,
     Tout près de Toi je vais m'asseoir
       Te voir.

10   Avec Toi, je vais voir Marie,
       Les Saints, ma famille chérie...
Je vais après l'exil de cette vie
     Retrouver le toit paternel
       Au Ciel!...

PN 19
L'atome de Jésus-Hostie

(Pensées de Sr. Saint Vincent de Paul mises en vers à sa demande)

1   Je ne suis qu'un grain de poussière,
     Mais je veux fixer mon séjour
     Dans les ombres du sanctuaire
     Avec le Prisonnier d'Amour.
     Ah! vers l'hostie mon âme aspire.
     Je l'aime et ne veux rien de plus.

C'est le Dieu caché qui m'attire,
Je suis l'atome de Jésus...

2   Je veux rester dans l'ignorance
Dans l'oubli de tout le crée
Et consoler par mon silence
L'Hôte du ciboire sacré.
Oh! je voudrais sauver les âmes,
Des pécheurs faire des élus...
D'un apôtre donnez les flammes
A votre atome, doux Jésus!...

3   Si je suis méprisée du monde,
S'il me regarde comme un rien,
Une paix divine m'inonde,
Car j'ai l'hostie pour mon soutien.
Quand je m'approche du ciboire,
Tous mes soupirs sont entendus...
Etre un néant, voilà me gloire,
Je suis l'atome de Jésus...

4   Parfois lorsque le Ciel est sombre,
L'atome ne pouvant voler,
Il aime se cachant dans l'ombre
A la porte d'or s'attacher,
Alors la Divine lumière
Qui réjouit tous les élus
Vient réchauffer sur cette terre
Le pauvre atome de Jésus...

5   Sous les chauds rayons de la grâce,
L'atome devient scintillant.
Quand la légère brise passe,
Il se balance doucement...
Oh! quel ineffable délice.
Quels bienfaits n'a-t-il pas reçus?...
Jusqu'auprès de l'hostie se glisse
Le pauvre atome de Jésus...

6   Se consumant près de l'hostie
Dans le tabernacle d'amour,
Ainsi s'écoulera ma vie.
En attendant le dernier jour
Quand l'épreuve sera finie
Volant au séjour des élus,
L'Atome de l'Eucharistie
Brillera près de son Jésus!...

                 (Air: "Par les chants les plus magnifiques")

PN 20

J.M.J.T.

(Air: "Mignon sur la rive étrangère")

Mon Ciel ici-bas!...

1   Jésus, ton ineffable image
    Est l'astre qui guide mes pas.
    Ah! tu le sais, ton doux Visage
    Est pour moi le Ciel ici-bas.
    Mon amour découvre les charmes
    De ta Face embellie de pleurs.
    Je souris à travers mes larmes
    Quand je contemple tes douleurs...

2   Oh! je veux pour te consoler,
    Vivre ignorée sur cette terre!...
    Ta beauté que tu sais voiler
    Me découvre tout son mystère.
    Vers toi je voudrais m'envoler!...

3   Ta Face est ma seule Patrie.
    Elle est mon Royaume d'amour.
    Elle est ma riante Prairie,
    Mon doux Soleil de chaque jour.
    Elle est le Lys de la vallée
    Dont le parfum mystérieux
    Console mon âme exilée,
    Lui fait goûter la paix des Cieux.

4   Elle est mon Repos, ma Douceur,
    Et ma mélodieuse Lyre...
    Ton Visage, ô mon doux Sauveur,
    Est le Divin bouquet de Myrrhe
    Que je veux garder sur mon coeur!...

5   Ta Face est ma seule richesse.
    Je ne demande rien de plus.
    En elle me cachant sans cesse,
    Je te ressemblerai, Jésus...
    Laisse en moi la Divine empreinte
    De tes Traits remplis de douceurs,
    Et bientôt, je deviendrai sainte.
    Vers toi j'attirerai les coeurs.

6 Afin que je puisse amasser
  Une belle moisson dorée,
  De tes feux daigne m'embraser.
  Bientôt de ta Bouche adorée
  Donne-moi l'éternel Baiser!...

PN 21

J.M.J.T.

(Air: "Connais-tu le pays")

Cantique d'une âme ayant trouvé le lieu de son repos!...

1 O Jésus! en ce jour, tu brises mes liens...
  C'est dans l'ordre béni de la Vierge Marie
  Que je pourrai trouver les véritables biens.
  Seigneur, si j'ai quitté ma famille chérie,
  Tu sauras la combler de célestes faveurs...
  A moi, tu donnes le pardon des pécheurs...

2   Jésus, au Carmel je veux vivre
  Puisqu'en cet oasis ton amour m'appela.
    C'est là (bis) que je veux te suivre
    T'aimer, t'aimer et mourir.
    C'est là que je veux te suivre.
    C'est là, oui, c'est là!...

3 O Jésus! en ce jour, tu combles tous mes voeux.
  Je pourrai désormais, près de l'Eucharistie,
  M'immoler en silence, attendre en paix les Cieux.
  M'exposant aux rayons de la Divine Hostie,
  A ce foyer d'amour, je me comsumerai;
  Et comme un séraphin, Seigneur, je t'aimerai.

4   Jésus, bientôt je dois te suivre
  Au rivage éternel, quand finiront mes jours.
    Toujours (bis) au Ciel je dois vivre.
    T'aimer et ne plus mourir...
    Toujours au Ciel je dois vivre,
    Toujours, oui, toujours...

PN 22

J.M.J.T.

Le 7 Septembre 1895

A ma Mère Chérie, le Bel Ange de mon enfance.

1   Bien loin du beau Ciel ma Patrie,
       Je ne suis pas seule ici-bas.
       Car en l'exil de cette vie
       Un bel Ange guide mes pas.

2   Ce bel Ange, ô Mère chérie!
       A chanté près de mon berceau,
       Et l'accent de sa mélodie
       Me paraît encor tout nouveau.

3   Il chantait de Jésus les charmes,
       Il chantait la joie d'un coeur pur.
       De son aile séchant mes larmes,
       Il chantait le beau Ciel d'azur.

4   Il chantait la Toute-Puissance
       Qui fit l'astre d'or et la fleur.
       Il chantait le Dieu de l'enfance
       Qui des lys garde la blancheur.

5   Il chantait la Vierge Marie,
       L'azur de son vaste manteau,
       Et la colline et la prairie
       Où les vierges suivent l'Agneau.

6   Ce bel Ange, ô profond mystère!
       M'appelait sa petite soeur...
       Il avait les traits d'une Mère,
       Et je reposais sur son coeur!...

7   A l'ombre de ses blanches ailes,
       Je grandissais rapidement.
       Déjà les rives éternelles
       Avaient ravi mes yeux d'enfant.

8   J'aurais voulu quittant la terre,
       Avec l'Ange voler aux Cieux
       Et voir la Divine lumière
       Nous environner tous les deux.

9   Mais, hélas! un jour le bel Ange,
       Au lieu de m'emporter au Ciel,
       Cherchant des vierges la phalange,
       Prit son essor vers le Carmel!...

10 Ah! que j'aurais voulu le suivre
    Contempler de près ses vertus.
    De sa vie je désirais vivre,
    Comme lui, m'unir à Jésus.

11 Oh! bonheur sans aucun mélange,
    Jésus exauça tous mes voeux.
    Au Carmel près de mon bel Ange
    Je n'attends plus rien que les Cieux!...

12 Et maintenant sa mélodie,
    Je puis l'entendre chaque jour.
    A sa voix, mon âme ravie
    S'embrase du feu de l'Amour.

13 Mère, l'Amour donne des ailes...
    Bientôt je pourrai m'envoler
    Vers les Collines Eternelles
    Où Jésus daigne m'appeler...

14 Mais sur cette plage étrangère
    Sans quitter la Céleste Cour
    Je descendrai près de ma Mère
    Pour être son ange à mon tour.

15 Pour moi le Ciel serait sans charmes
    Si je ne puis vous consoler.
    En sourires changer vos larmes...
    Tous mes secrets vous dévoiler!...

16 De la joie Céleste et profonde
    Sans vous je ne saurais jouir.
    Vous laisser longtemps en ce monde,
    Oh! je ne pourrais le souffrir!...

17 Nous volerons dans la Patrie
    De l'autre côté du Ciel bleu.
    Ensemble, ô ma Mère chérie!
    Toujours, nous verrons le Bon Dieu!!!...

PN 23
Au Sacré Coeur de Jésus

(Air: "Quand viendra Noël")

1   Au sépulcre saint, Marie-Madeleine,
Cherchant son Jésus, se baissait en pleurs.
Les anges voulaient adoucir sa peine,
Mais rien ne pouvait calmer ses douleurs.
Ce n'était pas vous, lumineux archanges,
Que cette âme ardente venait chercher.
Elle voulait voir Le Seigneur des anges,
Le prendre en ses bras, bien loin l'emporter...

2   Auprès du tombeau, restée la dernière,
Elle était venue bien avant le jour.
Son Dieu vint aussi, voilant sa lumière.
Marie ne pouvait le vaincre en amour!
Lui montrant d'abord sa Face Bénie,
Bientôt un seul mot jaillit de son Coeur.
Murmurant le nom si doux de: Marie,
Jésus lui rendit la paix, le bonheur.
....

3   Un jour, ô mon Dieu, comme Madeleine,
J'ai voulu te voir, m'approcher de toi.
Mon regard plongeait dans l'immense plaine
Dont je recherchais le Maître et le Roi;
Et je m'écriais, voyant l'onde pure,
L'azur étoilé, la fleur et l'oiseau:
"Si je ne vois Dieu, brillante nature,
"Tu n'es rien pour moi, qu'un vaste tombeau.

4   "J'ai besoin d'un coeur brûlant de tendresse
"Restant mon appui sans aucun retour,
"Aimant tout en moi, même ma faiblesse...
"Ne me quittant pas, la nuit et le jour.
"Je n'ai pu trouver nulle créature
Qui m'aimât toujours, sans jamais mourir.
Il me faut un Dieu prenant ma nature,
Devenant mon frère et pouvant souffrir!

5   Tu m'as entendue, seul Ami que j'aime,
Pour ravir mon coeur, te faisant mortel,
Tu versas ton sang, mystère suprême!...
Et tu vis encor pour moi sur l'Autel.
Si je ne puis voir l'éclat de ta Face,

Entendre ta voix remplie de douceur,
Je puis, ô mon Dieu, vivre de ta grâce,
Je puis reposer sur ton Sacré Coeur!

6   O Coeur de Jésus, trésor de tendresse,
C'est toi mon bonheur, mon unique espoir,
Toi qui sus charmer ma tendre jeunesse,
Reste auprès de moi jusqu'au dernier soir.
Seigneur, à toi seul j'ai donné ma vie,
Et tous mes désirs te sont bien connus.
C'est en ta bonté toujours infinie
Que je veux me perdre, ô Coeur de Jésus!

7   Ah! je le sais bien, toutes nos justices
N'ont devant tes yeux aucune valeur.
Pour donner du prix à mes sacrifices,
Je veux les jeter en ton Divin Coeur.
Tu n'as pas trouvé tes anges sans tache
Au sein des éclairs tu donnas ta loi!...
En ton Coeur Sacré, Jésus, je me cache.
Je ne tremble pas, ma vertu, c'est Toi!...

8   Afin de pouvoir contempler ta gloire,
Il faut, je le sais, passer par le feu;
Et moi je choisis pour mon purgatoire
Ton Amour brûlant, ô Coeur de mon Dieu!
Mon âme exilée quittant cette vie
Voudrait faire un acte de pur amour,
Et puis s'envolant au Ciel sa Patrie
Entrer dans ton Coeur sans aucun détour.

....

PN 24

(Air: "Rappelle-toi")

Jésus mon Bien-Aimé, rappelle-toi!...

"Ma fille, recherche celles de mes paroles qui respirent le plus d'amour; écris-
les, et puis les gardant précieusement comme des reliques, aie soin de les
relire souvent. Quand un ami veut réveiller au coeur de son ami la vivacité
première de son affection, il lui dit: Souviens-toi de ce que tu éprouvais,
quand tu me dis un jour telle parole, ou bien: Te rappelles-tu de tes senti-
ments à telle époque, en un tel jour, en un tel lieu?... Crois-le donc, les plus
précieuses reliques de moi sur la terre sont les paroles de mon amour, les
paroles sorties de mon très doux Coeur."

(Paroles de Notre Seigneur à Sainte Gertrude.)

1   Rappelle-toi de la gloire du Père.
      Rappelle-toi des divines splendeurs
      Que tu quittas t'exilant sur la terre
      Pour racheter tous les pauvres pécheurs.
O Jésus! t'abaissant vers la Vierge Marie,
Tu voilas ta grandeur et ta gloire infinie.
      Ah! du sein maternel
      Qui fut ton second Ciel
      Rappelle-toi.

2   Rappelle-toi qu'au jour de ta naissance,
      Quittant le Ciel les Anges ont chanté:
      "A notre Dieu, gloire, honneur et puissance
      "Et paix aux coeurs de bonne volonté.
"Depuis dix-neuf cents ans as tu tiens à ta promesse.
Seigneur, de tes enfants la paix est la richesse.
      Pour goûter à jamais
      Ton ineffable paix,
      Je viens à toi.

3   Je viens à toi, cache-moi dans tes langes.
      En ton berceau je veux rester toujours.
      Là je pourrai chantant avec les anges,
      Te rappeler tes joies des premiers jours.
O Jésus! souviens-toi des bergers et des mages
Qui t'offrirent, joyeux, leurs coeurs et leurs hommages.
      Du cortège innocent
      Qui te donna son sang
      Rappelle-toi.

4   Rappelle-toi que les bras de Marie
      Tu préféras à ton trône royal.
      Petit Enfant, pour soutenir ta vie
      Tu n'avais rien que le lait virginal.
A ce festin d'amour que te donne ta Mère
Oh! daigne m'inviter, Jésus mon petit Frère.
      Que ta petite soeur
      A fait battre ton coeur
      Rappelle-toi.

5   Rappelle-toi que tu nommas ton père
      L'humble Joseph qui par l'ordre du Ciel
      Sans t'éveiller, sur le sein de ta mère
      Sut t'arracher aux fureurs d'un mortel.
....Verbe Dieu, souviens-toi de ce mystère étrange.

Tu gardas le silence et fis parler un ange!
De ton lointain exil
Sur les rives du Nil
Rappelle-toi.

6   Rappelle-toi que sur d'autres rivages
Les astres d'or et la lune d'argent
Que je contemple en l'azur sans nuages
Ont réjoui, charmé tes yeux d'Enfant.
De ta petite main qui caressait Marie
Tu soutenais le monde et lui donnais la vie.
Et tu pensais à moi,
Jésus, mon petit Roi,
Rappelle-toi...

7   Rappelle-toi que dans la solitude
Tu travaillais de tes divines mains.
Vivre oublié fut ta plus douce étude;
Tu rejetas le savoir des humains.
O Toi! qui d'un seul mot pouvais charmer le monde,
Tu te plus à cacher ta sagesse profonde.
Tu parus ignorant,
O Seigneur Tout-Puissant!
Rappelle-toi....

8   Rappelle-toi qu'étranger sur la terre,
Tu fus errant, toi Le Verbe Eternel,
Tu n'avais rien.... non, pas même une pierre,
Pas un abri, comme l'oiseau du ciel...
O Jésus! viens en moi, viens reposer ta Tête,
Viens, à te recevoir mon âme est toute prête.
Mon Bien-Aimé Sauveur,
Repose dans mon coeur.
Il est à Toi....

9   Rappelle-toi des divines tendresses
Dont tu comblas les plus petits enfants.
Je veux aussi recevoir tes caresses.
Ah! donne-moi tes baisers ravissants.
Pour jouir dans les Cieux de ta douce présence,
Je saurai pratiquer les vertus de l'enfance.
N'as-tu pas dit souvent:
"Le Ciel est pour l'enfant?...
Rappelle-toi.

10   Rappelle-toi qu'au bord de la fontaine,
      Un Voyageur fatigué du chemin
      Fit déborder sur la Samaritaine
      Les flots d'amour que renfermait son sein.
  Ah! je connais Celui qui demandait à boire.
  Il est Le Don de Dieu, la source de la gloire.
          C'est Lui, L'Eau qui jaillit,
          C'est Lui, qui nous a dit:
          "Venez à moi."

11   "Venez à moi, pauvres âmes chargées,
      "Vos lourds fardeaux bientôt s'allégeront;
      "Et pour jamais étant désaltérées
      "De votre sein des sources jailliront.
  "J'ai soif, ô mon Jésus! cette Eau je la réclame.
  De ses torrents divins daigne inonder mon âme.
          Pour fixer mon séjour
          En l'Océan d'Amour,
          Je viens à toi.

12   Rappelle-toi qu'enfant de la lumière
      Souvent j'oublie de bien servir mon Roi.
      Oh! prends pitié de ma grande misère.
      Dans ton amour, Jésus, pardonne-moi.
  Aux affaires du Ciel daigne me rendre habile.
  Montre-moi les secrets cachés dans l'Evangile.
          Ah! que ce Livre d'or
          Est mon plus cher trésor
          Rappelle-toi.

13   Rappelle-toi que ta divine Mère
      A sur ton Coeur un pouvoir merveilleux.
      Rappelle-toi qu'un jour à sa prière
      Tu changeas l'eau en vin délicieux.
  Daigne aussi transformer mes oeuvres imparfaites.
  A la voix de Marie, Seigneur, rends-les parfaites.
          Que je suis son enfant,
          O Jésus! bien souvent
          Rappelle-toi.

14   Rappelle-toi que souvent les collines
      Tu gravissais au coucher de soleil.
      Rappelle-toi tes oraisons divines,
      Tes chants d'amour à l'heure du sommeil.
  Ta prière, ô mon Dieu, je l'offre avec délice.

Pendant mes oraisons, et puis au saint Office.
Là tout près de ton Coeur
Je chante avec bonheur:
Rappelle-toi!...

15   Rappelle-toi que voyant la campagne,
Ton Divin Coeur devançait les moissons.
Levant les yeux vers la sainte montagne,
De tes élus tu murmurais les noms...
Afin que ta moisson soit bientôt recueillie,
Chaque jour, ô mon Dieu, je m'immole et je prie.
Que mes joies et mes pleurs
Sont pour tes Moissonneurs
Rappelle-toi...

16   Rappelle-toi de la fête des Anges,
Rappelle-toi de l'harmonie des Cieux
Et de la joie des sublimes phalanges
Lorsqu'un pécheur vers toi lève les yeux.
Ah! je veux augmenter cette grande allégresse,
Jésus, pour les pécheurs, ju veux prier sans cesse.
Que je vins au Carmel
Pour peupler ton beau Ciel
Rappelle-toi....

17   Rappelle-toi de la très douce Flamme
Que tu voulais allumer dans les coeurs.
Ce Feu du Ciel, tu l'as mis en mon âme.
Je veux aussi répandre ses ardeurs.
Une faible étincelle, ô mystère de vie,
Suffit pour allumer un immense incendie.
Que je veux, ô mon Dieu,
Porter au loin ton Feu
Rappelle-toi.

18   Rappelle-toi de ce festin splendide
Que tu donnas à ton fils repentant.
Rappelle-toi que pour l'âme candide,
Tu la nourris Toi-Même à chaque instant.
Jésus, avec amour tu reçois le prodigue,
Mais les flots de ton Coeur pour moi n'ont pas de digue.
Mon Bien-Aimé, mon Roi,
Que tes biens sont à moi
Rappelle-toi.

19   Rappelle-toi que méprisant la gloire
En prodiguant tes miracles divins,
Tu t'écriais: "Comment pouvez-vous croire,
"Vous qui cherchez l'estime des humains?...
"Les oeuvres que je fais vous semblent surprenantes
"Mes amis en feront de bien plus éclatantes...
      "Que tu fus humble et doux,
      Jésus, mon tendre Epoux,
      Rappelle-toi.

20   Rappelle-toi qu'en une sainte ivresse
L'Apôtre-Vierge approcha de ton Coeur.
En son repos il connut ta tendresse.
Tous tes secrets, il les comprit, Seigneur...
De ton disciple aimé je ne suis point jalouse.
Je connais tes secrets, car je suis ton épouse.
      O mon divin Sauveur,
      Je m'endors sur ton Coeur.
      Il est à moi!...

21   Rappelle-toi qu'au soir de l'agonie
Avec ton sang se mêlèrent tes pleurs.
Rosée d'amour, sa valeur infinie
A fait germer de virginales fleurs
Un ange te montrant cette moisson choisie,
Fit renaître la joie sur ta Face bénie.
      Jésus, que tu me vis
      Au milieu de tes lys
      Rappelle-toi.

22   Rappelle-toi que ta Rosée féconde,
Virginisant les corolles des fleurs,
Les a rendues capables dès ce monde
De t'enfanter un grand nombre de coeurs.
Je suis vierge, ô Jésus! cependant quel mystère,
En m'unissant à toi, des âmes je suis mère.
      Des virginales fleurs
      Qui sauvent les pécheurs
      Rappelle-toi.

23   Rappelle-toi qu'abreuvé de souffrance,
Un Condamné se tournant vers les Cieux
S'est écrié: "Bientôt, dans ma puissance
"Vous me verrez paraître glorieux.
"Qu'Il fût le Fils de Dieu, nul ne voulait le croire,

Car elle était cachée son ineffable gloire...
          O Prince de la Paix,
          Moi je te reconnais
              Je crois en toi!...
24   Rappelle-toi que ton divin Visage
       Parmi les tiens fut toujours inconnu;
       Mais tu laissas pour moi ta douce image,
       Et tu le sais, je t'ai bien reconnu...
Oui, je te reconnais, toute voilée de larmes.
Face de l'Eternel, je découvre tes charmes.
          Jésus, de tous les coeurs
          Qui recueillent tes pleurs
              Rappelle-toi.

25   Rappelle-toi de l'amoureuse plainte
       Qui sur la croix s'échappa de ton Coeur.
       Ah! dans le mien, Jésus, elle est empreinte,
       Et de ta soif je partage l'ardeur.
Plus je me sens brûlée de tes divines flammes,
Plus je suis altérée de te donner des âmes.
          Que d'une soif d'amour
          Je brûle nuit et jour
              Rappelle-toi.

26   Rappelle-toi, Jésus, Verbe de Vie,
       Que tu m'aimas jusqu'à mourir pour moi.
       Je veux aussi t'aimer à la folie.
       Je veux aussi vivre et mourir pour Toi.
Tu le sais, ô mon Dieu! tout ce que je désire,
C'est de te faire aimer et d'être un jour martyre.
          D'amour je veux mourir,
          Seigneur, de mon désir
              Rappelle-toi.

27   Rappelle-toi qu'au jour de ta victoire
       Tu nous disais: "Celui qui n'a pas vu
       "Le Fils de Dieu tout rayonnant de gloire
       "Il est heureux, si quand même il a cru!"
Dans l'ombre de la Foi, je t'aime et je t'adore.
O Jésus! pour te voir, j'attends en paix l'aurore.
          Que mon désir n'est pas
          De te voir ici-bas
              Rappelle-toi....

28   Rappelle-toi que montant vers Le Père,
        Tu ne pouvais nous laisser orphelins.
        Et te faisant prisonnier sur la terre,
        Tu sus voiler tous tes rayons divins.
     Mais l'ombre de ton voile est lumineuse et pure.
      Pain Vivant de la foi, Céleste Nourriture,
          O mystère d'amour!
          Mon Pain de chaque jour
            Jésus, c'est Toi!...

29   Jésus, c'est toi qui malgré les blasphèmes
        Des ennemis du Sacrement d'Amour,
        C'est toi qui veux montrer combien tu m'aimes,
        Puisqu'en mon coeur tu fixes ton séjour.
    O Pain de l'exilé! Sainte et Divine Hostie,
    Ce n'est plus moi qui vis, mais je vis de ta vie.
         Ton ciboire doré
         Entre tous préferé,
           Jésus, c'est moi!

30   Jésus, c'est moi, ton vivant sanctuaire
        Que les mechants ne peuvent profaner.
        Reste en mon coeur, n'est-il pas un parterre
        Dont chaque fleur vers toi veut se tourner?
    Mais si tu t'éloignais, ô blanc Lys des vallées,
    Tu le sais bien, mes fleurs seraient vite effeuillées.
         Toujours, mon Bien-Aimé,
         Jésus, Lys embaumé,
           Fleuris en moi!...

31   Rappelle-toi que je veux sur la terre
        Te consoler de l'oubli des pécheurs.
        Mon seul Amour, exauce ma prière.
        Ah! pour t'aimer, donne-moi mille coeurs.
    Mais c'est encor trop peu, Jésus, Beauté suprême,
    Donne-moi pour t'aimer ton divin Coeur Lui-Même.
         De mon désir brûlant,
         Seigneur, à chaque instant
           Rappelle-toi.

32   Rappelle-toi que ta volonté sainte
        Est mon repos, mon unique bonheur.
        Je m'abandonne et je m'endors sans crainte
        Entre tes bras, ô mon divin Sauveur.
    Si tu t'endors aussi lorsque l'orage gronde,

Je veux rester toujours dans une paix profonde.
Mais pendant ton sommeil,
Jésus, pour le réveil
Prépare-moi!....

33 Rappelle-toi que souvent je soupire
Après le jour du grand avènement.
Envoie bientôt l'ange qui doit nous dire:
"Réveillez-vous, il n'y a plus de temps!...
"Alors rapidement je franchirai l'espace.
Seigneur, tout près de toi, j'irai prendre ma place.
Qu'au séjour Eternel
Tu dois être mon Ciel
Rappelle-toi...

PN 25
Mes Désirs auprès de Jésus caché dans sa Prison d'Amour

1 Petite Clef, oh je t'envie!
Car tu peux ouvrir chaque jour
La prison de l'Eucharistie
Où réside le Dieu d'Amour.
Mais je puis, ô quel doux miracle!
Par un seul effort de ma foi
Ouvrir aussi le tabernacle
M'y cacher près du Divin Roi...

2 Je voudrais dans le sanctuaire,
Me consummant près de mon Dieu,
Toujours briller avec mystère
Comme la Lampe du Saint Lieu...
Oh! bonheur... en moi j'ai des flammes,
Et je puis gagner chaque jour
A Jésus un grand nombre d'âmes,
Les embrasant de son amour...

3 A chaque aurore, je t'envie,
O Pierre Sacrée de l'Autel!
Comme dans l'étable bénie,
Sur toi veut naître l'Eternel...
Ah! daigne exaucer ma prière.
Viens en mon âme, Doux Sauveur...
Bien loin d'être une froide pierre,
Elle est le soupir de ton Coeur!...

4   O Corporal entouré d'anges!
         Qu'il est enviable ton sort.
         Sur toi comme en ses humbles langes,
         Je vois Jésus mon seul trésor.
         Change mon coeur, Vierge Marie,
         En un Corporal pur et beau
         Pour recevoir la blanche hostie,
         Où se cache ton Doux Agneau.

5   Sainte Patène, je t'envie.
         Sur toi Jésus vient reposer.
         Oh! que sa grandeur infinie
         Jusqu'à moi daigne s'abaisser...
         Jésus, comblant mon espérance,
         De ma vie n'attend pas le soir
         Il vient en moi; par sa présence
         Je suis un vivant Ostensoir!...

6   Oh! que j'envie l'heureux Calice
         Où j'adore le Sang divin...
         Mais je puis au Saint Sacrifice
         Le recueillir chaque matin.
         Mon âme à Jésus est plus chère
         Que les précieux Vases d'or.
         L'Autel est un nouveau Calvaire
         Où pour moi son Sang coule encor...

7   Jésus, Vigne sainte et sacrée,
         Tu le sais, ô mon Divin Roi,
         Je suis une grappe dorée
         Qui doit disparaître pour toi...
         Sous le pressoir de la souffrance
         Je te prouverai mon amour.
         Je ne veux d'autre jouissance
         Que de m'immoler chaque jour.

8   Ah! quelle joie, je suis choisie
         Parmi les grains de pur Froment
         Qui pour Jésus perdent la vie...
         Bien grand est mon ravissement!...
         Je suis ton épouse chérie,
         Mon Bien-Aimé, viens vivre en moi.
         Oh! viens, ta beauté m'a ravie.
         Daigne me transformer en Toi!...

PN 26
Les Répons de Ste Agnès

(Air: "Dieu de paix et d'amour")

1   Le Christ est mon Amour, Il est toute ma vie.
Il est le Fiancé qui seul ravit mes yeux.
Aussi j'entends déjà de sa douce harmonie
    Les sons mélodieux.

2   Il a paré ma main de perles sans pareilles,
Il a paré mon cou de colliers d'un grand prix.
Les riches diamants qu'on voit à mes oreilles
    Sont un présent du Christ.

3   Il m'a toute parée de pierres précieuses,
Déjà brille à mon doigt son anneau nuptial.
Il a daigné couvir de perles lumineuses
    Mon manteau virginal.

4   Je suis la fiancée de Celui que les anges
Serviront en tremblant toute l'éternité.
La lune et le soleil racontent ses louanges,
    Admirent sa beauté.

5   Son empire est le Ciel, sa nature est divine;
La Vierge Immaculée pour Mère Il se choisit,
Son Père est le vrai Dieu qui n'a pas d'origine.
    Il est un pur Esprit...

6   Lorsque j'aime le Christ et lorsque je le touche,
Mon coeur devient plus pur, je suis plus chaste encor.
De la virginité le baiser de sa bouche
    M'a donné le trésor.

7   Il a déjà posé son signe sur ma face
Afin que nul amant n'ose approcher de moi.
Je me sens soutenue par la divine grâce
    De mon Aimable Roi.

8   De son sang précieux mes joues sont colorées.
Je crois goûter déjà les délices du Ciel,
Car je puis recueillir sur ses lèvres sacrées
    Et le lait et le miel.

9   Aussi je ne crains rien, ni le fer ni la flamme.
Non, rien ne peut troubler mon ineffable paix,
Et le feu de l'amour qui consumme mon âme
    Ne s'éteindra jamais!...

PN 27

J.M.J.T.

(Air: "Sur terre tout n'est pas rose")

Souvenir du 24 Février 1896

1er C.

O souvenir ineffable
Du beau jour entre les jours.
Ta douceur incomparable,
Je la garderai toujours...

2e C.

A Jésus je suis unie
Par les liens de l'Amour
Et sa Grandeur infinie
En moi fixe son séjour.

1er Refrain

Oh! quelle inexprimable ivresse
Je sens palpiter en moi,
Le coeur brûlant de tendresse
De mon Epoux, de mon Roi.

3e C.

L'exil, je souffre sans peine,
Vivant avec mon Epoux...
Elle est bien douce la chaîne
Qui m'unit au Dieu *Jaloux!*...

4e C.

O Divine *Jalousie,*
Vous avec blessé mon coeur!...
Vous serez toute ma vie
Mon repos et mon bonheur.

2e Refrain

Daignez consumer tout mon être.
Jésus seul doit vivre en moi.
Désormais je ne veux être
Que le voile de mon Roi!...

(Thérèse de l'Enfant Jésus de la Se Face
à sa petite Soeur mille fois chérie)

PN 28

J.M.J.T.

1er Mars 1896

Le cantique éternel chanté dès l'exil

1   Ton épouse exilée, sur la rive étrangère,
Peut chanter de l'Amour le cantique éternel,
Puisque, mon Doux Jésus, tu daignes sur la terre
Du feu de ton Amour l'embraser comme au Ciel.

2   Mon Bien-Aimé, Beauté suprême,
A moi tu te donnes toi-même;
     Mais en retour,
     Jésus, je t'aime,
Et ma vie n'est qu'un seul acte d'amour!

3   Oubliant ma grande misère
Tu viens habiter en mon coeur.
Mon faible Amour, ah quel mystère   } bis
Suffit pour t'enchainer, Seigneur.

Mon Bien-Aimé, etc.....

4   Amour qui m'enflamme,
Pénètre mon âme.
Viens, je te réclame,
Viens, consume-moi.

5   Ton ardeur me presse
Et je veux sans cesse,
Divine fournaise,
M'abîmer en toi.

6   Seigneur, la souffrance
Devient jouissance
Quand l'âme s'élance
Vers toi sans retour.

7   Céleste Patrie,
Joies de l'autre vie,
Mon âme ravie
Vous goûte toujours.

8   Céleste Patrie,
Joies de l'autre vie,
Vous n'êtes que l'Amour!

PN 29
J.M.J.T.
Souvenir du 30 Avril 1896

A notre chère petite Soeur Marie de la Trinité et de la Sainte Face.

1   Qu'il nous est doux, ô Soeur Chérie!
       De chanter ce jour radieux,
       Le plus beau jour de votre vie,
       Qui vous unit au Roi des Cieux.

2   Ce matin votre âme exilée
       S'est vue revêtue de splendeur,
       D'une parure immaculée
       En s'immolant pour le Seigneur.

3   Autrefois regardant votre âme,
       La Bienheureuse Trinité
       Vous avait marquée de sa Flamme
       En vous dévoilant sa beauté.

4   Contemplant la Divine Face,
       Vous avez senti le désir
       De mépriser tout ce qui passe,
       Tout ce qui doit bientôt finir.

5   Du monde craignant le déluge,
       Vous avez invoqué le Ciel.
       Il vous fit trouver un refuge
       Dans l'arche bénie du Carmel.

6   Mais hélas! pauvre fugitive,
       De l'arche il vous fallut sortir.
       Comme la colombe plaintive,
       Longtemps vous avez dû gémir...

7   De l'olivier le vert feuillage
       Vint enfin briller à vos yeux.
       Il vous a désigné l'ombrage
       Du petit Carmel de Lisieux.

8   Aussitôt franchissant l'espace,
       Vous êtes venue réclamer
       Parmi nous la dernière place,
       Voulant souffrir, voulant aimer!...

9   Jésus, en s'immolant Lui-Même,
Nous a dit à son dernier jour:
"Donner sa vie pour ceux qu'on aime
"Il n'est pas de plus grand amour."

10   A cette parole bénie,
Votre coeur s'est tout enflammé.
Vous avez donné vie pour vie
A Jésus votre Bien-Aimé.

11   Maintenant, heureuse victime
Qui vous immolez à l'Amour,
Goûtez la joie, la paix intime
De vous consummer chaque jour.

12   Vers l'Amour votre âme soupire
Il est votre astre lumineux.
L'Amour sera votre martyre.
L'Amour vous ouvrira les Cieux.

(A notre Mère)

13   C'est par vous, ô Mère chérie,
Que nous avons vu ce matin
Cette blanche et nouvelle hostie
S'immoler à L'Agneau Divin.

14   Cette hostie sera votre gloire.
Jésus la fera resplendir
Dans le mystérieux ciboire
Que votre coeur a su remplir.

PN 30
Glose sur le Divin

Composée par N.P. St. Jean de la Croix et mise en vers par la plus petite
de ses filles pour fêter la Profession de sa chère Soeur Marie de la Trinité
et de la Sainte Face.

Appuyée sans aucun Appui
Sans Lumière et dans les Ténèbres
Je vais me consumant d'Amour...

1   Au monde (quel bonheur extrême)
J'ai dit un éternel adieu!.......
......Elevée plus haut que moi-même
Je n'ai d'autre Appui que mon Dieu.
Et maintenant je le proclame,
Ce que j'estime près de Lui,
C'est de voir et sentir mon âme
Appuyée sans aucun appui!...

2   Bien que je souffre sans Lumière
En cette vie qui n'est qu'un jour,
Je possède au moins sur la terre
La vie Céleste de l'Amour...
Dans le chemin qu'il me faut suivre
Se rencontre plus d'un péril,
Mais par Amour je veux bien vivre
Dans les Ténèbres de l'exil.

3   L'Amour, j'en ai l'expérience
Du bien, du mal qu'il trouve en moi,
Sait profiter (quelle puissance)
Il transforme mon âme en soi.
Ce Feu qui brûle dans mon âme
Pénètre mon coeur sans retour
Ainsi dans sa charmante flamme
Je vais me consumant d'Amour!...

30 Avril 1986. Thérèse de l'Enf. Jésus, de la Ste Face
rel. carm. ind.

PN 31

J.M.J.T.

Le Cantique de Soeur Marie de la Trinité et de la Ste Face

Composé par sa petite Sr Th. de l'Enf. J.

1   Dans ton amour, t'exilant sur la terre,
Divin Jésus, tu t'immolas pour moi!
Mon Bien-Aimé, prends ma vie tout entière.
Je veux souffrir, je veux mourir pour toi...

R.1   Seigneur, tu nous l'as dit Toi-Même:
"L'on ne peut rien faire de plus
Que de mourir pour ceux qu'on aime.
"Et mon Amour suprême,
C'est toi, Jésus!...

2   Il se fait tard, déjà le jour décline.
Viens me guider, Seigneur, dans le chemin.
Avec ta croix, je gravis la colline,
Reste avec moi, Céleste Pèlerin....

R.2   Ta voix trouve écho dans mon âme.
Je veux te ressembler, Seigneur.
La souffrance, je la réclame.
Ta parole de flamme
Brûle mon coeur!...

3   Elle est à toi, l'éternelle victoire,
En la chantant, les anges sont ravis,
Mais pour entrer dans ta sublime gloire,
Il a fallu, Seigneur, que tu souffris!...

R.3   Pour moi sur la rive étrangère,
Quels mépris n'as-tu pas reçus?...
Je veux me cacher sur la terre,
Etre en tout la dernière
Pour toi, Jésus!...

4   Mon Bien-Aimé, ton example m'invite
A m'abaisser, à mépriser l'honneur.
Pour te ravir, je veux rester petite.
En m'oubliant, je charmerai ton Coeur.

R.4   Ma paix est dans la solitude.
Je ne demande rien de plus...
Te plaire est mon unique étude,
Et ma béatitude,
C'est toi, Jésus!...

5   Toi le Grand Dieu, que tout le Ciel adore,
         Tu vis en moi, Prisonnier nuit et jour.
         Ta douce voix à toute heure m'implore.
         Tu me redis: "J'ai soif... j'ai soif d'Amour!..."

R.5   Je suis aussi ta prisonnière,
         Et je veux redire à mon tour
         Ta tendre et divine prière:
              "Mon Bien-Aimé, mon Frère,
                   J'ai soif d'Amour!..."

6   J'ai soif d'Amour, comble mon espérance.
         Augmente en moi, Seigneur, ton Divin Feu.
         J'ai soif d'Amour, bien grande est ma souffrance.
         Ah! je voudrais voler vers toi, mon Dieu!...

R.6   Ton Amour est mon seul martyre.
         Plus je le sens brûler en moi
         Et plus mon âme te désire...
              Jésus, fais que j'expire
                   D'Amour pour Toi !!!...

                                                    31 Mai 1896

PN 32
J.M.J.T.
Fête du St. Sacrement. 7 Juin 1896
(Air: "Dieu de paix et d'amour")

Mon Ciel à Moi!...

1   Pour supporter l'exil de la vallée des larmes,
         Il me faut le regard de mon Divin Sauveur.
         Ce regard plein d'amour m'a dévoilé ses charmes.
         Il m'a fait pressentir le Céleste bonheur.
         Mon Jésus me sourit quand vers Lui je soupire.
         Alors je ne sens plus l'épreuve de la foi.
         Le Regard de mon Dieu, son ravissant Sourire,
              Voilà mon Ciel à moi!...

2   Mon Ciel est de pouvoir attirer sur les âmes,
         Sur l'Eglise ma mère et sur toutes mes soeurs
         Les grâces de Jésus et ses Divines flammes
         Qui savent embraser et réjouir les coeurs.
         Je puis tout obtenir lorsque dans le mystère
         Je parle coeur à coeur avec mon Divin Roi.
         Cette douce Oraison tout près du Sanctuaire,
              Voilà mon Ciel à moi!...

3   Mon Ciel, il est caché dans la petite Hostie
       Où Jésus, mon Epoux, se voile par amour.
       A ce Foyer Divin je vais puiser la vie,
       Et là mon Doux Sauveur m'écoute nuit et jour.
       "Oh! quel heureux instant lorsque dans ta tendresse
       "Tu viens, mon Bien-Aimé, me transformer en toi.
       "Cette union d'amour, cette ineffable ivresse,
                Voilà mon Ciel à moi!...

4   Mon Ciel est de sentir en moi la ressemblance
       Du Dieu qui me créa de son Souffle Puissant.
       Mon Ciel est de rester toujours en sa présence,
       De l'appeler mon Père et d'être son enfant.
       Entre ses bras Divins, je ne crains pas l'orage.
       Le total abandon voilà ma seule loi.
       Sommeiller sur son Coeur, tout près de son Visage,
                Voilà mon Ciel à moi!...

5   Mon Ciel, je l'ai trouvé dans la Trinité Sainte
       Qui réside en mon coeur, prisonnière d'amour.
       Là, contemplant mon Dieu, je lui redis sans crainte
       Que je veux le servir et l'aimer sans retour.
       Mon Ciel est de sourire à ce Dieu que j'adore
       Lorsqu'Il veut se cacher pour éprouver ma foi
       Souffrir en attendant qu'Il me regarde encore,
                Voilà mon Ciel à moi!...

                (Pensées de Soeur St. Vincent de Paul mises en vers
                par sa toute petite soeur Thérèse de l'Enfant Jésus.)

                        PN 33
                        J.M.J.T.
                                Fête du Sacré Coeur de Jésus
                                          12 Juin 1896

       Ce que je verrai bientôt pour la Première fois!...

1   Je suis encor sur la rive étrangère,
       Mais pressentant le bonheur éternel,
       Oh! je voudrais déjà quitter la terre
       Et contempler les merveilles du Ciel...
       Lorsque je rêve aux joies de l'autre vie,
       De mon exil je ne sens plus le poids,
       Puisque bientôt vers ma seule Patrie
       Je volerai pour la première fois!...

2   Ah! donne-moi, Jésus, de blanches ailes
Pour que vers toi, je prenne mon essor.
Je veux voler aux rives Eternelles.
Je veux te voir, ô mon Divin Trésor!
Je veux voler dans les bras de Marie,
Me reposer sur ce trône de choix,
Et recevoir de ma Mère chérie
Le doux Baiser pour la première fois!...

3   Mon Bien-Aimé, de ton premier sourire
Fais-moi bientôt entrevoir la douceur,
Et laisse-moi, dans mon divin délire,
Ah! laisse-moi me cacher en ton Coeur!...
Oh! quel instant! quel bonheur ineffable
Quand j'entendrai le doux son de ta voix,
Quand je verrai de ta Face Adorable
L'éclat divin pour la première fois!...

4   Tu le sais bien, mon unique martyre,
C'est ton amour, Coeur Sacré de Jésus.
Vers ton beau Ciel, si mon âme soupire,
C'est pour t'aimer, t'aimer de plus en plus!...
Au Ciel, toujours enivrée de tendresse,
Je t'aimerai sans mesure et sans lois,
Et mon bonheur me paraîtra sans cesse
Aussi nouveau que la première fois!!!...

La petite soeur de l'Enfant Jésus

PN 34

(Air: "Oui, je le crois")

Jeter des Fleurs

1   Jésus, mon seul Amour, au pied de ton Calvaire
Que j'aime chaque soir à te jeter des Fleurs!...
En effeuillant pour toi la rose printanière,
        Je voudrais essuyer tes pleurs....

R.1   Jeter des Fleurs, c'est t'offrir en prémices
Les plus légers soupirs, les plus grandes douleurs.
Mes peines et mes joies, mes petits sacrifices,
        Voilà mes fleurs!...

2 Seigneur, de ta beauté mon âme s'est éprise.
   Je veux te prodiguer mes parfums et mes fleurs.
   En les jetant pour toi sur l'aile de la brise,
     Je voudrais enflammer les coeurs!...

R.2   Jeter des Fleurs, Jésus, voilà mon arme
   Lorsque je veux lutter pour sauver les pécheurs.
   La victoire est à moi... toujours je te désarme
     Avec mes fleurs!!!...

3 Les pétales des fleurs, caressant ton Visage,
   Te disent que mon cœur est à toi sans retour.
   De ma rose effeuillée tu comprends le langage,
     Et tu souris à mon amour.

R.3   Jeter des Fleurs, redire tes louanges,
   Voilà mon seul plaisir en la vallée des pleurs...
   Au Ciel j'irai bientôt avec les petits anges
     Jeter des Fleurs!...

PN 35

16 Juillet 1896

A Notre-Dame des Victoires
Reine des Vierges, des Apôtres et des Martyrs

1 Vous qui comblez mon espérance,
   O Mère! écoutez! l'humble chant
   D'amour et de reconnaissance
   Qui vient du coeur de votre enfant...

2 Aux oeuvres d'un Missionnaire
   Vous m'avez unie sans retour,
   Par les liens de la prière,
   De la souffrance et de l'amour.

3 A lui, de traverser la terre
   De prêcher le nom de Jésus.
   A moi, dans l'ombre et le mystère,
   De pratiquer d'humbles vertus.

4 La souffrance, je la réclame,
   J'aime et je désire la Croix...
   Pour aider à sauver une âme
   Je voudrais mourir mille fois!...

5   Ah! pour le Conquérant des âmes
       Je veux m'immoler au Carmel,
       Et par Lui répandre les flammes
       Que Jésus apporta du Ciel.

6   Par Lui, quel ravissant mystère,
       Jusqu'au Su-tchuen oriental
       Je pourrai de ma tendre Mère
       Faire aimer le nom virginal!...

7   Dans ma solitude profonde,
       Marie... je veux gagner des coeurs.
       Par votre Apôtre, au bout du monde
       Je convertirai les pécheurs...

8   Par Lui, l'eau sainte du baptême
       Du tout petit enfant d'un jour
       Fera le temple où Dieu Lui-Même
       Daigne habiter dans son amour.

9   Je veux peupler de petits anges
       Le brillant séjour éternel...
       Par Lui, d'enfantines phalanges
       Prendront leur essor vers le Ciel!...

10   La palme que mon âme envie,
       Par Lui, je pourrai la cueillir,
       Oh quel espoir! Mère Chérie,
       Je serai la soeur d'un Martyr!!!
       ....

11   Après l'exil de cette vie
       Au soir du glorieux combat,
       Nous jouirons dans la Patrie
       Des fruits de notre apostolat.

12   A Lui l'honneur de la Victoire
       Devant l'armée des Bienheureux.
       A moi... le reflet de sa Gloire
       Eternellement dans les Cieux!...

                          La petite soeur d'un Missionnaire.

In loving memory
Frances Salucci

Born November 25, 1904
Died July 7, 1992

carmel of Reno   S-18

PN 36

(Air: "Près d'un berceau")

Jésus Seul

1 Mon coeur ardent veut se donner sans cesse.
Il a besoin de prouver sa tendresse.
Ah! qui pourra comprendre mon amour?
Quel coeur voudra me payer de retour?...
Mais ce retour, en vain je le réclame.
Jésus, toi seul peux contenter mon âme
Rien ne saurait me charmer ici-bas.
Le vrai bonheur ne s'y rencontre pas...
Ma seule paix, mon seul bonheur,
Mon seul Amour, c'est toi, Seigneur!...

2 O toi qui sus créer le coeur des mères,
Je trouve en toi le plus tendre des Pères!
Mon seul Amour, Jésus, Verbe Eternel,
Pour moi ton coeur est plus que maternel.
A chaque instant, tu me suis, tu me gardes.
Quand je t'appelle, ah! jamais tu ne tardes;
Et si parfois tu sembles te cacher,
C'est toi qui viens m'aider à te chercher.

3 C'est à toi seul, Jésus, que je m'attache.
C'est en tes bras que j'accours et me cache.
Je veux t'aimer comme un petit enfant;
Je veux lutter comme un guerrier vaillant.
Comme un enfant plein de délicatesses,
Je veux, Seigneur, te combler de caresses;
Et dans le champ de mon apostolat,
Comme un guerrier je m'élance au combat!...

4 Ton Coeur qui garde et qui rend l'innocence
Ne saurait pas tromper ma confiance!
En toi, Seigneur, repose mon espoir.
Après l'exil, au Ciel j'irai te voir...
Lorsqu'en mon coeur s'élève la tempête,
Vers toi, Jésus, je relève la tête.
En ton regard miséricordieux,
Je lis: "Enfant, pour toi, j'ai fait les Cieux."

5   Je le sais bien, mes soupirs et mes larmes
     Sont devant toi, tout rayonnants de charmes.
     Les séraphins au Ciel forment ta cour,
     Et cependant, tu mendies mon amour!...
     Tu veux mon coeur, Jésus, je te la donne.
     Tous mes désirs, je te les abandonne;
     Et ceux que j'aime, ô mon Epoux, mon Roi,
     Je ne veux plus les aimer que pour toi.

PN 37-38-39
(Pour Jeanne et Francis La Néele)

[PN 37]   J.M.J.T.   21 Août 1896

1   C'est un triste bouquet de fête,
     Que ces misérables quatrains...
     Mais, hélas! au fond de ma tête,
     Sont restés les *Alexandrins!*...

2   Il fallait, j'en ai souvenance:
     "Des Alexandrins pour Francis."
     Je devrais garder le silence
     Devant un ordre aussi précis...

3   Mais connaissant bien l'indulgence
     De Jeanne et du Savant Docteur,
     Sans Alexandrins, je m'avance,
     Pour fêter mon Aimable Soeur.
                              (Thérèse de l'Enf. Jésus)

[PN 38]   J.M.J.T.   21 Août 1896
Confidence de Jésus à Thérèse

1   Jésus, écoute ma prière,
     Exauce mon désir ardent.
     Exile un ange sur la terre,
     Donne à Jeanne un petit enfant!...

2   Il se fait bien longtemps attendre,
     Ce petit exilé des Cieux...
     Mais, Seigneur, tu me fais comprendre
     Ton silence mystérieux.

3   Oui, tu me dis, par ton silence:
     "Jusqu'au Ciel montent tes soupirs,

"Je dois me faire violence
"Pour ne pas combler tes désirs.

4   "Ce n'est pas un ange ordinaire
"Que je veux donner à ta soeur
"Aussi j'aime dans le mystère
"A former son âme et son coeur.

5   "Moi-même, j'embellis cette âme,
"De mes trésors je lui fais don
"Mais en retour... ah, je réclame!
"De Jeanne un parfait Abandon...

6   "Avec une tendresse exquise
"Je la dispose de ma main,
"Puisqu'elle doit à mon Eglise
"Donner: Un Pontife, un grand Saint!"

PN 39   J.M.J.T.

Un Docteur Saint et Célèbre

F rancis a pris cette devise:
R ien pour l'homme, tout pour mon Dieu.
A ussi, pour défendre l'Eglise
N 'a-t-il pas un coeur tout de feu?...
C ombattant la science impie
I l en a fait bien haut l'aveu:
S a Gloire est celle de Marie!...

L'enfant du Docteur séraphique:
Sainte Thérèse
21 Août 96

PN 40
Les Sacristines du Carmel

1   Ici-bas notre doux office
Est de préparer pour l'autel
Le pain, le vin du Sacrifice
Qui donne à la terre: "Le Ciel!"

2   Le Ciel, ô mystère suprême!
Se cache sous un humble pain;
Car le Ciel, c'est Jésus Lui-Même,
Venant à nous chaque matin.

3   Il n'est pas de reines sur terre
    Qui soient plus heureuses que nous.
    Notre office est une prière
    Qui nous unit à notre Epoux.

4   Les plus grands honneurs de ce monde
    Ne peuvent pas se comparer
    A la paix céleste et profonde
    Que Jésus nous fait savourer.

5   Nous portons une sainte envie
    A l'ouvrage de notre main,
    A la petite et blanche hostie
    Qui doit voiler l'Agneau divin.

6   Mais son amour nous a choisies.
    Il est notre Epoux, notre Ami.
    Nous sommes aussi des hosties
    Que Jésus veut changer en Lui.

7   Mission sublime du Prêtre,
    Tu deviens la nôtre ici-bas.
    Transformées par le Divin Maître,
    C'est Lui qui dirige nos pas.

8   Nous devons aider les apôtres
    Par nos prières, notre amour.
    Leurs champs de combats sont les nôtres.
    Pour eux nous luttons chaque jour.

9   Le Dieu caché du tabernacle
    Qui se cache aussi dans nos coeurs,
    A notre voix, ô quel miracle!
    Daigne pardonner aux pécheurs!

10 Notre bonheur et notre gloire,
    C'est de travailler pour Jésus.
    Son beau Ciel voilà le ciboire
    Que nous voulons combler d'élus!...

PN 41

(Air: "Je crois au Dieu")   J.M.J.T.   (A Sr St Jean de la X)

Comment je veux aimer

1   Divin Jésus, écoute ma prière:
Par mon amour je veux te réjouir.
Tu le sais bien, à toi seul je veux plaire.
Daigne exaucer mon plus ardent désir.
Du triste exil j'accepte les épreuves
Pour te charmer et consoler ton coeur,
Mais en amour change toutes mes oeuvres
O mon Epoux, mon Bien-Aimé Sauveur.

2   C'est ton amour, Jésus, que je réclame.
C'est ton amour qui doit me transformer.
Mets en mon coeur ta consumante flamme,
Et je pourrai te bénir et t'aimer.
Oui, je pourrai t'aimer comme l'on aime
Et te bénir comme on le fait au Ciel.
Je t'aimerai de cet amour lui-même
Dont tu m'aimas, Jésus, Verbe Eternel.

3   Divin Sauveur, à la fin de ma vie
Viens me chercher, sans l'ombre d'un retard.
Ah! montre-moi ta tendresse infinie
Et la douceur de ton divin regard.
Avec amour, oh! que ta voix m'appelle
En me disant: "Viens, tout est pardonné.
Repose-toi, mon épouse fidèle.
Viens sur mon coeur, tu m'as beaucoup aimé."

PN 42
Enfant, Tu Connais Mon Nom

1   Enfant, tu connais mon nom,
Et ton doux regard m'appelle.
Il me dit: Simple abandon.
Je veux guider ta nacelle.

2   De ta petite main d'enfant,
O quelle merveille!
De ta petite voix d'enfant,
Tu calmes le flot mugissant
Et le vent!...

3   Si tu veux te reposer
        Alors que l'orage gronde,
        Sur mon coeur daigne poser
        Ta petite tête blonde...

4   Que ton sourire est ravissant
            Lorsque tu sommeilles!...
        Toujours avec mon plus doux chant
        Je veux te bercer tendrement,
            Bel Enfant!...

PN 43

(Air: "Au Rossignol")

La Volière de l'Enfant Jésus

1   Pour les exilés de la terre
        Le Bon Dieu créa les oiseaux.
        Ils vont gazouillant leur prière
        Dans les vallées, sur les coteaux.

2   Les enfants joyeux et volages,
        Ayant choisi leurs préférés,
        Les emprisonnent dans des cages
        Dont les barreaux sont tout dorés.

3   O Jésus! notre petit Frère,
        Pour nous tu quittes le beau Ciel;
        Mais tu le sais bien, ta volière,
        Divin Enfant, c'est le Carmel.

4   Notre cage n'est pas dorée,
        Cependant nous la chérissons.
        Dans les bois, la plaine azurée
        Plus jamais nous ne volerons.

5   Jésus, les bosquets de ce monde
        Ne peuvent pas nous contenter.
        Dans la solitude profonde
        Pour toi seul nous voulons chanter.

6   Ta petite main nous attire,
        Enfant, que tes charmes sont beaux!
        O Divin Jésus! ton sourire
        Captive les petits oiseaux!...

7   Ici l'âme simple et candide
    Trouve l'objet de son amour.
    Comme la colombe timide,
    Elle ne craint plus le vautour.

8   Sur les ailes de la prière
    On voit monter le coeur ardent,
    Comme l'alouette légère
    Qui bien haut s'élève en chantant.

9   Ici l'on entend le ramage
    Du roitelet, du gai pinson.
    O petit Jésus! dans leur cage
    Tes oiseaux gazouillent ton nom.

10 Le petit oiseau toujours chante.
    Sa vie ne l'inquiète pas,
    Un grain de millet le contente;
    Jamais il ne sème ici-bas.

11 Comme lui dans notre volière,
    Nous recevons tout de ta main.
    L'unique chose nécessaire,
    C'est de t'aimer, Enfant Divin.

12 Aussi nous chantons tes louanges,
    Unies aux purs esprits du Ciel.
    Et nous le savons, tous les anges
    Aiment les oiseaux du Carmel.

13 Jésus, pour essuyer les larmes
    Que te font verser les pécheurs,
    Tes oiseaux redisent tes charmes.
    Leurs doux chants te gagnent des coeurs.

14 Un jour loin de la triste terre
    Lorsqu'ils entendront ton appel,
    Tous les oiseaux de ta volière
    Prendront leur essor vers le Ciel.

15 Avec les charmantes phalanges
    Des petits Chérubins joyeux,
    O Divin Enfant, tes louanges
    Nous les chanterons dans les Cieux.

PN 44

(Air: "La rose mousse" ou bien: "Le fil de la Vierge.")

A mes Petits Frères du Ciel

1   Heureux petits Enfants, avec quelles tendresses
         Le Roi des Cieux
     Vous bénit autrefois et combla de caresses
         Vos fronts joyeux!
     De tous les Innocents vous étiez la figure,
         Et j'entrevois
     Les biens que dans le Ciel vous donne sans mesure
         Le Roi des rois.

2   Vous avez contemplé les immenses richesses
         Du Paradis
     Avant d'avoir connu nos amères tristésses,
         Chers petits Lys.
     O Boutons parfumés! moissonnés dès l'aurore
         Par Le Seigneur,
     Le doux Soleil d'Amour qui sut vous faire éclore,
         Ce fut son Coeur!...

3   Quels ineffables soins, quelle tendresse exquise,
         Et quel amour,
     Vous prodigue avec joie notre Mère l'Eglise,
         Enfants d'un jour!...
     Dans ses bras maternels, vous fûtes en prémices
         Offerts à Dieu.
     Toute l'Eternité, vous ferez les délices
         Du beau Ciel bleu.

4   Enfants, vous composez le virginal cortège
         Du doux Agneau;
     Et vous pouvez redire, étonnant privilège,
         Un chant nouveau!
     Vous êtes sans combats parvenus à la gloire
         Des conquérants;
     Le Sauveur a pour vous remporté la victoire,
         Vainqueurs charmants!

5   On ne voit point briller de pierres précieuses
         Dans vos cheveux.
     Seul le reflet doré de vos boucles soyeuses
         Ravit les Cieux...
     Les trésors des Elus, leurs palmes, leurs couronnes,
         Tout est à vous.

Dans la Sainte Patrie, Enfants, vos riches trônes
Sont leurs genoux...

6   Ensemble vous jouez avec les petits anges
Près de l'Autel,
Et vos chants enfantins, gracieuses phalanges,
Charment le Ciel.
Le Bon Dieu vous apprend comment Il fait les roses,
L'oiseau, les vents.
Ici-bas nul génie ne sait autant de choses
Que vous, Enfants!...

7   Du firmament d'azur soulevant tous les voiles
Mystèrieux,
En vos petites mains vous prenez les étoiles
Aux mille feux.
En courant vous laissez une trace argentée.
Souvent le soir
Quand je contemple au ciel la blanche voie lactée
Je crois vous voir...

8   Dans les bras de Marie après toutes vos fêtes
Vous accourez.
Sous son voile étoilé cachant vos blondes têtes
Vous sommeillez.
Charmants petit Lutins, votre enfantine audace
Plaît au Seigneur.
Vous osez caresser son Adorable Face....
Quelle faveur!...

9   C'est vous que Le Seigneur me donna pour modèle,
Saints Innocents.
Je veux être ici-bas votre image fidèle,
Petits Enfants.
Ah! daignez m'obtenir les vertus de l'enfance.
Votre candeur,
Votre abandon parfait, votre aimable innocence
Charment mon coeur.

10   O Seigneur! tu connais de mon âme exilée
Les voeux ardents.
Je voudrais moissonner, beau Lys de la vallée,
Des Lys brillants.
Ces Boutons printaniers, je les cherche et les aime.
Pour ton plaisir
Sur eux daigne verser la Rosée du Baptême.
Viens les cueillir...

11   Oui, je veux augmenter la candide phalange
         Des Innocents.
      Mes souffrances, mes joies, je les offre en échange
         D'âmes d'Enfants.
      Parmi ces Innocents, je réclame une place,
         Roi des Elus.
      Comme eux, je veux au Ciel, baiser ta Douce Face,
         O mon Jésus!...

PN 45

(Air: "Rêve, parfum ou frais murmure")

Ma Joie!

1   Il est des âmes sur la terre
      Qui cherchent en vain le bonheur,
      Mais pour moi, c'est tout le contraire:
      La joie se trouve dans mon coeur.
      Cette joie n'est pas éphémère.
      Je la possède sans retour.
      Comme une rose printanière,
      Elle me sourit chaque jour.

2   Vraiment je suis par trop heureuse,
      Je fais toujours ma volonté....
      Pourrais-je n'être pas joyeuse
      Et ne pas montrer ma gaîté?...
      Ma joie, c'est d'aimer la souffrance,
      Je souris en versant des pleurs.
      J'accepte avec reconnaissance
      Les épines mêlées aux fleurs.

3   Lorsque le Ciel bleu devient sombre
      Et qu'il semble me délaisser,
      Ma joie, c'est de rester dans l'ombre,
      De me cacher, de m'abaisser.
      Ma joie, c'est la Volonté Sainte
      De Jésus mon unique amour.
      Ainsi je vis sans nulle crainte.
      J'aime autant le nuit que le jour.

4   Ma joie, c'est de rester petite.
      Aussi quand je tombe en chemin,
      Je puis me relever bien vite
      Et Jésus me prend par la main.

Alors le comblant de caresses,
Je Lui dis qu'Il est tout pour moi,
Et je redouble de tendresses
Lorsqu'Il se dérobe à ma foi.

5 Si parfois je verse des larmes,
Ma joie, c'est de les bien cacher.
Oh! que la souffrance a de charmes
Quand de fleurs on sait la voiler!
Je veux bien souffrir sans le dire
Pour que Jésus soit consolé.
Ma joie, c'est de le voir sourire
Lorsque mon coeur est exilé...

6 Ma joie, c'est de lutter sans cesse
Afin d'enfanter des élus.
C'est le coeur brûlant de tendresse
De souvent redire à Jésus:
"Pour toi, mon Divin petit Frère,
"Je suis heureuse de souffrir.
"Ma seule joie sur cette terre,
"C'est de pouvoir te réjouir.

7 "Longtemps encor je veux bien vivre,
"Seigneur, si c'est là ton désir.
"Dans le Ciel je voudrais te suivre
"Si cela te faisait plaisir.
"L'amour, ce feu de la Patrie,
"Ne cesse de me consumer.
"Que me font la mort ou la vie?
"Jésus, ma joie, c'est de t'aimer!"

PN 46
J.M.J.T.
(Air: "Par les chants les plus magnifiques")

A mon Ange Gardien

1 Glorieux Gardien de mon âme,
Toi qui brilles dans le beau Ciel
Comme une douce et pure flamme
Près du trône de l'Eternel,
Tu descends pour moi sur la terre
Et m'éclairant de ta splendeur,
Bel Ange, tu deviens mon Frère,
Mon Ami, mon Consolateur!...

2   Connaissant ma grande faiblesse,
Tu me diriges par la main;
Et je te vois avec tendresse
Oter la pierre du chemin.
Toujours ta douce voix m'invite
A ne regarder que les Cieux.
Plus tu me vois humble et petite,
Et plus ton front est radieux.

3   O toi! qui traverses l'espace
Plus promptement que les éclairs,
Je t'en supplie, vole à ma place
Auprès de ceux qui me sont chers.
De ton aile sèche leurs larmes;
Chante combien Jésus est bon.
Chante que souffrir a des charmes,
Et tout bas, murmure mon nom...

4   Je veux pendant ma courte vie
Sauver mes frères les pécheurs.
O Bel Ange de la Patrie,
Donne-moi tes saintes ardeurs.
Je n'ai rien que mes sacrifices
Et mon austère pauvreté.
Avec tes célestes délices,
Offre-les à la Trinité.

5   A toi le Royaume et la Gloire,
Les Richesses du Roi des rois.
A moi l'humble Hostie du ciboire,
A moi le trésor de la Croix.
Avec la Croix, avec l'Hostie,
Avec ton céleste secours,
J'attends en paix de l'autre vie
Les joies qui dureront toujours.

A ma chère Soeur Marie-Philomène
souvenir de sa *petite fille.*
Thérèse de l'Enfant Jésus de la Ste F.
rel. carm. ind.

PN 47

(Air: "Les adieux du Martyr")

A Théophane Vénard

Prêtre des Missions étrangères,
Martyrisé au Tonkin à l'âge de 31 ans.

1   Tous les Elus célèbrent tes louanges,
O Théophane! Angélique Martyr;
Et je le sais, dans les Saintes phalanges
Le séraphin aspire à te servir!...
Ne pouvant pas, exilée sur la terre,
Mêler ma voix à celle des Elus,
Je veux aussi sur la rive étrangère
Prendre ma lyre et chanter tes vertus...

2   Ton court exil fut comme un doux cantique
Dont les accents savaient toucher les coeurs;
Et pour Jésus, ton âme poétique
A chaque instant faisait naître des fleurs.
En t'élevant vers la Céleste sphère,
Ton chant d'adieu fut encor printanier.
Tu murmurais: "Moi, petit éphémère,
"Dans le beau Ciel, je m'en vais le premier!..."

3   Heureux Martyr, à l'heure du supplice
Tu savourais le bonheur de souffrir.
Souffrir pour Dieu te semblait un délice.
En souriant, tu sus vivre et mourir...
A ton bourreau, tu t'empressas de dire
Lorsqu'il t'offrit d'abréger ton tourment:
"Plus durera mon douloureux martyre,
"Mieux ça vaudra, plus je serai content!!!"

4   Lys Virginal, au printemps de ta vie
Le Roi du Ciel entendit ton désir,
Je vois en toi: La Fleur épanouie
Que Le Seigneur cueillit pour son plaisir...
Et maintenant tu n'es plus exilée.
Les Bienheureux admirent ta splendeur.
Rose d'Amour, La Vierge Immaculée,
De ton parfum respire la fraîcheur.

5   Soldat du Christ, ah! prête-moi tes armes
Pour les pécheurs, je voudrais ici-bas

Lutter, souffrir à l'ombre de tes palmes,
Protège-moi, viens soutenir mon bras.
Je veux pour eux ne cessant pas la guerre,
Prendre d'assault le Royaume de Dieu;
Car le Seigneur apporta sur la terre
Non pas la paix, mais le Glaive et le Feu!...

6   Je l'aime aussi, cette plage infidèle
Qui fut l'objet de ton ardent amour.
Avec bonheur, je volerais vers elle
Si le Bon Dieu m'y appelait un jour...
Mais à ses yeux, il n'est pas de distances.
Tout l'univers devant Lui n'est qu'un point.
Mon faible amour, mes petites souffrances,
Bénies par Lui, Le font aimer au loin!...

7   Ah! si j'étais une fleur printanière
Que Le Seigneur voudrait bientôt cueillir,
Descends du Ciel à mon heure dernière
Je t'en conjure, ô Bienheureux Martyr!
De ton amour aux virginales flammes,
Viens m'embraser en ce séjour mortel;
Et je pourrai voler avec les âmes
Qui formeront ton cortège éternel!...

PN 48
Mes Armes

(Cantique composé pour   (Air: "Partez, Hérauts
le jour d'une profession)   de la bonne nouvelle")

"Revêtez-vous des armes de Dieu, afin que vous puissiez résister
aux embûches de l'ennemi."   (St Paul.)
"L'Epouse du Roi est terrible comme une armée rangée en
bataille, elle est semblable à un choeur de musique dans un
camp d'armée."   (Cant. des cant.)

1   Du Tout-Puissant j'ai revêtu les armes.
Sa main divine a daigné me parer.
Rien désormais ne me cause d'alarmes.
De son amour qui peut me séparer?
A ses côtés, m'élançant dans l'arène,
Je ne craindrai ni le fer ni le feu.
Mes ennemis sauront que je suis reine,
Que je suis l'épouse d'un Dieu!

O mon Jésus! je garderai l'armure
Que je revêts sous tes yeux adorés.
Jusqu'au soir de la vie, ma plus belle parure
 Seront mes Voeux sacrés!

2 O Pauvreté, mon premier sacrifice,
Jusqu'à la mort tu me suivras partout;
Car je le sais, pour courir dans la lice,
L'Athlète doit se détacher de tout.
Goûtez, mondains, le remords et la peine,
Ces fruits amers de votre vanité.
Joyeusement, moi, je cueille en l'arène
 Les palmes de la Pauvreté.
Jésus a dit: "C'est par la violence
Que l'on ravit le royaume des Cieux.
"Eh bien! la Pauvreté me servira de Lance,
 De Casque glorieux.

3 La Chasteté me rend la soeur des anges,
De ces Espirits purs et victorieux.
J'espère un jour voler en leurs phalanges,
Mais dans l'exil je dois lutter comme eux.
Je dois lutter sans repos et sans trêve
Pour mon Epoux le Seigneur des seigneurs.
La Chasteté, c'est le céleste Glaive
 Qui peut lui conquérir les coeurs.
La Chasteté c'est mon arme invincible;
Mes ennemis par elle sont vaincus.
Par elle je deviens, ô bonheur indicible!
 L'Epouse de Jésus.

4 L'ange orgueilleux au sein de la lumière
S'est écrié: "Je n'obéirai pas!
"Moi, je m'écrie dans la nuit de la terre,
"Je veux toujours obéir ici-bas.
Je sens en moi naître une sainte audace.
De tout l'enfer je brave la fureur.
L'Obéissance est ma forte Cuirasse
 Et le Bouclier de mon coeur.
Dieu des Armées, je ne veux d'autres gloires
Que de soumettre en tout ma volonté,
Puisque l'Obéissant redira ses victoires
 Toute l'Eternité.

5   Si du Guerrier j'ai les armes puissantes,
    Si je l'imite et lutte vaillamment,
    Comme la Vierge aux grâces ravissantes
    Je veux aussi chanter en combattant.
    Tu fais vibrer de ta lyre les cordes;
    Et cette lyre, ô Jésus, c'est mon coeur!
    Alors je puis de tes Miséricordes
     Chanter la force et la douceur.
    En souriant je brave la mitraille,
    Et dans tes bras, ô mon Epoux Divin,
   En chantant je mourrai, sur le champ de bataille,
     Les Armes à la main!...

PN 49

J.M.J.T.

A Notre Dame du Perpétuel Secours

(1ᵉʳ Couplet)

Mère chérie, dès ma tendre jeunesse
Ta douce Image a su ravir mon coeur.
En ton regard je lisais ta tendresse,
Et près de toi je trouvais le bonheur.

(Refrain)

Vierge Marie, au Céleste rivage
Après l'exil j'irai te voir toujours;
Mais ici-bas ta douce Image,
C'est mon Perpétuel Secours!...

(2ᵉ Couplet)

Quand j'étais sage et bien obéissante,
Il me semblait que tu me souriais;
Et si parfois j'étais un peu méchante,
Je croyais voir que sur moi tu pleurais...

(3ᵉ Couplet)

En exauçant ma naïve prière,
Tu me montrais ton amour maternel.
Te contemplant je trouvais sur la terre
Un avant-goût des délices du Ciel.

(4ᵉ Couplet)

Lorsque je lutte, ô ma Mère chérie,
Dans le combat tu fortifies mon coeur;
Car tu le sais, au soir de cette vie
Je veux offrir des Prêtres au Seigneur!...

(5ᵉ Couplet)

Toujours, toujours Image de ma Mère
Oui, tu seras mon bonheur, mon trésor.
Et je voudrais à mon heure dernière
Que mon regard sur toi se fixe encor.

(Dernier refrain)

Puis m'envolant au Céleste rivage,
J'irai m'asseoir, Mère, sur tes genoux.
Alors je pourrai sans partage
Recevoir tes baisers si doux!...

Souvenir d'une retraite bénie – Mars 1897
(Thérèse de l'Enfant Jésus à sa petite Soeur)

PN 50
A Jeanne d'Arc

1 Quand le Dieu des armées te donnant la victoire,
Tu chassas l'étranger et fis sacrer le roi.
Jeanne, ton nom devint célèbre dans l'histoire.
Nos plus grands conquérants pâlirent devant toi.

2 Mais ce n'était encor qu'une gloire éphémère.
Il fallait à ton nom l'auréole des Saints.
Aussi le Bien-Aimé t'offrit sa coupe amère,
Et tu fus comme Lui rejetée des humains.

3 Au fond d'un noir cachot, chargée de lourdes chaines,
Le cruel étranger t'abreuva de douleurs.
Pas un de tes amis ne prit part à tes peines;
Pas un ne s'avança pour essuyer tes pleurs.

4 Jeanne, tu m'apparais plus brillante et plus belle
Qu'au sacre de ton roi, dans ta sombre prison.
Ce céleste reflet de la gloire éternelle,
Qui donc te l'apporta? Ce fut la trahison.

5   Ah! si le Dieu d'amour en la vallée des larmes
N'était venu chercher la trahison, la mort,
La souffrance pour nous aurait été sans charmes.
Maintenant nous l'aimons, elle est notre trésor.

PN 51

(Air: "Le fil de la Vierge"   J.M.J.T.   19 Mai 1897
ou bien: "La rose mousse")

Une Rose effeuillée

1   Jésus, quand je te vois soutenu par ta Mère,
Quitter ses bras,
Essayer en tremblant sur notre triste terre
Tes premiers pas,
Devant toi je voudrais *effeuiller une rose*
En sa fraîcheur
Pour que ton petit pied bien doucement repose
Sur une fleur!...

2   *Cette rose effeuillée,* c'est la fidèle image,
Divin Enfant,
Du coeur qui veut pour toi s'immoler sans partage
A chaque instant.
Seigneur, sur tes autels plus d'une fraîche rose
Aime à briller.
Elle se donne à toi... mais je rêve autre chose:
"C'est m'effeuiller!..."

3   La rose en son éclat peut embellir ta fête,
Aimable Enfant;
Mais *la rose effeuillée,* simplement on la jette
Au gré du vent.
Une rose effeuillée sans recherche se donne
Pour n'être plus.
Comme elle avec bonheur à toi je m'abandonne,
Petit Jésus.

4   L'on marche sans regret sur *des feuilles de rose,*
Et ces débris
Sont un simple ornement que sans art on dispose,
Je l'ai compris.
Jésus, pour ton amour j'ai prodigué ma vie,
Mon avenir.

Aux regards des mortels, *rose* à jamais *flétrie*
Je dois *mourir!*...
5 *Pour toi,* je dois *mourir,* Enfant, Beauté Suprême,
Quel heureux sort!
Je veux en *m'effeuillant* te prouver que je t'aime,
O mon Trésor!...
Sous tes *pas enfantins,* je veux avec mystère
Vivre ici-bas;
Et je voudrais encor adoucir au Calvaire
Tes derniers pas!...

PN 52
J.M.J.T.
31 Mai 1897

L'Abandon est le fruit délicieux de L'Amour

1 Il est sur cette terre
Un Arbre merveilleux.
Sa racine, ô mystère,
Se trouve dans les Cieux...

2 Jamais sous son ombrage
Rien ne saurait blesser.
Là sans craindre l'orage
On peut se reposer.

3 De cet Arbre ineffable
L'Amour, voilà le nom,
Et son fruit délectable
S'appelle L'Abandon.

4 Ce fruit dès cette vie
Me donne le bonheur.
Mon âme est réjouie
Par sa divine odeur.

5 Ce fruit quand je le touche
Me paraît un trésor.
Le portant à ma bouche,
Il m'est plus doux encor.

6 Il me donne en ce monde
Un océan de paix.
En cette paix profonde
Je repose à jamais...

7   Seul l'Abandon me livre
         En tes bras, ô Jésus.
         C'est lui qui me fait vivre
         De la vie des Elus.

8   A toi je m'abandonne,
         O mon Divin Epoux;
         Et je n'ambitionne
         Que ton regard si doux.

9   Moi, je veux te sourire,
         M'endormant sur ton coeur.
         Je veux encore redire
         Que je t'aime, Seigneur!

10   Comme la pâquerette
         Au calice vermeil,
         Moi, petite fleurette,
         Je m'entrouvre au soleil.

11   Mon doux Soleil de vie,
         O mon Aimable Roi,
         C'est ta Divine Hostie,
         Petite comme moi....

12   De sa Céleste Flamme,
         Le lumineux rayon
         Fait naître dans mon âme
         Le parfait Abandon.

13   Toutes les créatures
         Peuvent me délaisser.
         Je saurai sans murmures
         Près de toi m'en passer.

14   Et si tu me délaisses,
         O mon Divin Trésor,
         Privée de tes caresses,
         Je veux sourire encor.

15   En paix je veux attendre,
         Doux Jésus, ton retour;
         Et sans jamais suspendre
         Mes cantiques d'amour.

16   Non, rien ne m'inquiète,
Rien ne peut me troubler.
Plus haut que l'alouette
Mon âme sait voler.

17   Au-dessus des nuages
Le ciel est toujours bleu.
On touche les rivages
Où règne le Bon Dieu.

18   J'attends en paix la gloire
Du Céleste séjour,
Car je trouve au Ciboire
Le doux Fruit de l'Amour!

PN 53
Pour Sr Marie de la Trinité

1 Seigneur, tu m'as choisie dès ma plus tendre enfance,
Et je puis m'appeler l'oeuvre de ton amour...
Je voudrais, ô mon Dieu! dans ma reconnaissance,
Oh! je voudrais pouvoir te payer de retour!
Jésus, mon Bien-Aimé, quel est ce privilège,
Pauvre petit néant, qu'avais-je fait pour toi?
Et je me vois placée dans le royal cortège
Des vierges de ta cour, aimable et Divin Roi!

2 Hélas, je ne suis rien que la faiblesse même.
Tu le sais, ô mon Dieu, je n'ai pas de vertus...
Mais tu le sais aussi, le seul ami que j'aime,
Celui qui m'a charmée, c'est toi, mon Doux Jésus!...
Lorsqu'en mon jeune coeur s'alluma cette flamme
Qui se nomme l'amour, tu vins la réclamer...
Et toi seul, ô Jésus! pus contenter une âme
Qui jusqu'à l'infini avait besoin d'aimer.

3 Comme un petit agneau loin de la bergerie,
Gaiement je folâtrais ignorant le danger;
Mais, ô Reine des Cieux! ma Bergère chérie,
Ton invisible main savait me protéger.
Aussi tout en jouant au bord des précipices,
Déjà tu me montrais le sommet du Carmel.
Je comprenais alors les austères délices
Qu'il me faudrait aimer pour m'envoler au Ciel.

4   Seigneur, si tu chéris la pureté de l'ange,
     De cet esprit de feu qui nage dans l'azur,
     N'aimes-tu pas aussi s'élevant de la fange
     Le lys que ton amour a su conserver pur?
     S'il est heureux, mon Dieu, l'ange à l'aile vermeille
     Qui paraît devant toi brillant de pureté,
     Ma joie dès ici-bas à la sienne est pareille,
     Puisque j'ai le trésor de la virginité!...

PN 54
J.M.J.T.

Mai 1897

(Air: "Pourquoi m'avoir livré l'autre jour, ô ma Mère")
Pourquoi je t'aime, ô Marie!

1   Oh! je voudrais chanter, *Marie, pourquoi je t'aime,*
     Pourquoi ton nom si doux fait tressaillir mon coeur,
     Et pourquoi la pensée de ta grandeur suprême
     Ne saurait à mon âme inspirer de frayeur.
     Si je te contemplais dans ta sublime gloire
     Et surpassant l'éclat de tous les bienheureux,
     Que je suis ton enfant je ne pourrais le croire.
     O Marie, devant toi, je baisserais les yeux!...

2   Il faut pour qu'un enfant puisse chérir sa mère,
     Qu'elle pleure avec lui, partage ses douleurs.
     O ma Mère chérie, sur la rive étrangère
     Pour m'attirer à toi, que tu versas de pleurs!...
     En méditant *ta vie dans le saint Evangile,*
     J'ose te regarder et m'approcher de toi.
     Me croire ton enfant ne m'est pas difficile,
     Car je te vois mortelle et souffrant comme moi...

3   Lorsqu'un ange du Ciel t'offre d'être *la Mère*
     Du Dieu qui doit régner toute l'éternité,
     Je te vois préférer, ô Marie, quel mystère!
     L'ineffable trésor de *la virginité.*
     Je comprends que ton âme, ô Vierge Immaculée,
     Soit plus chère au Seigneur que le divin séjour.
     Je comprends que ton âme, *Humble et Douce Vallée,*
     Peut contenir Jésus, L'Océan de l'Amour!...

4   Oh! je t'aime, Marie, te disant la servante
     Du Dieu que tu ravis par ton humilité.
     Cette vertu cachée te rend toute-puissante.
     Elle attire en ton coeur *la Sainte Trinité.*

Alors l'Esprit d'Amour te couvrant de son ombre,
Le Fils égal au Père en toi s'est incarné...
De ses frères pécheurs bien grand sera le nombre,
Puisqu'on doit l'appeler: Jésus, ton premier-né!...

5   O Mère bien-aimée, malgré ma petitesse,
     Comme toi je possède en moi Le Tout-Puissant,
     Mais je ne tremble pas en voyant ma faiblesse:
     Le trésor de la mère appartient à l'enfant.
     Et je suis ton enfant, ô ma Mère chérie.
     Tes vertus, ton amour, ne sont-ils pas à moi?
     Aussi lorsqu'en mon coeur descend la blanche Hostie,
     Jésus, ton Doux Agneau, croit reposer en toi!...

6   Tu me le fais sentir, ce n'est pas impossible
     De marcher sur tes pas, ô Reine des élus.
     L'étroit chemin du Ciel, tu l'as rendu visible
     En pratiquant toujours les plus humbles vertus.
     Auprès de toi, Marie, j'aime à rester petite.
     Des grandeurs d'ici-bas je vois la vanité.
     Chez Sainte Elisabeth, recevant ta visite,
     J'apprends à pratiquer l'ardente charité.

7   Là j'écoute ravie, Douce Reine des anges,
     Le cantique sacré qui jaillit de ton coeur.
     Tu m'apprends à chanter les divines louanges,
     A me glorifier en Jésus mon Sauveur.
     Tes paroles d'amour sont de mystiques roses
     Qui doivent embaumer les siècles à venir.
     En toi le Tout-Puissant a fait de grandes choses.
     Je veux les méditer, afin de l'en bénir.

8   Quand le bon Saint Joseph ignore le miracle
     Que tu voudrais cacher dans ton humilité,
     Tu le laisses pleurer tout près du *Tabernacle*
     Qui voile du Sauveur la divine beauté!...
     Oh! que j'aime, Marie, *ton éloquent silence.*
     Pour moi c'est un concert doux et mélodieux
     Qui me dit la grandeur et la toute-puissance
     D'une âme qui n'attend son secours que des Cieux...

9   Plus tard à Bethléem, ô Joseph et Marie!
     Je vous vois repoussés de tous les habitants.
     Nul ne veut recevoir en son hôtellerie
     De pauvres étrangers, la place est pour les grands...

La place est pour les grands et c'est dans une étable
Que la Reine des Cieux doit enfanter un Dieu.
O ma Mère chérie, que je te trouve aimable,
Que je te trouve grande en un si pauvre lieu!...

10 Quand je vois L'Eternel enveloppé de langes,
Quand du Verbe Divin j'entends le faible cri,
O ma Mère chérie, je n'envie plus les anges,
Car leur Puissant Seigneur est mon Frère chéri!...
Que je t'aime, Marie, toi qui sur nos rivages
As fait épanouir cette Divine Fleur!....
Que je t'aime écoutant les bergers et les mages
Et gardant avec soin toute chose en ton coeur!...

11 Je t'aime te mêlant avec les autres femmes
Qui vers le temple saint ont dirigé leurs pas.
Je t'aime présentant le Sauveur de nos âmes
Au bienheureux Vieillard qui le presse en ses bras.
D'abord en souriant j'écoute son cantique,
Mais bientôt ses accents me font verser des pleurs.
Plongeant dans l'avenir un regard prophétique,
Siméon te présente un glaive de douleurs.

12 O Reine des martyrs, jusqu'au soir de ta vie
Ce glaive douloureux *transpercera ton coeur.*
Déjà tu dois quitter le sol de ta patrie
Pour éviter d'un roi la jalouse fureur.
Jésus sommeille en paix sous les plis de ton voile.
Joseph vient te prier de partir à l'instant,
Et ton obéissance aussitôt se dévoile:
Tu pars sans nul retard et sans raisonnement.

13 Sur la terre d'Egypte, il me semble, ô Marie,
Que dans la pauvreté ton coeur reste joyeux,
Car *Jésus n'est-Il pas la plus belle Patrie?*
Que t'importe l'exil? Tu possèdes les Cieux....
Mais à Jérusalem, une amère tristesse
Comme un vaste océan vient inonder ton coeur.
Jésus, pendant trois jours, se cache à ta tendresse.
Alors c'est bien l'exil dans toute sa rigueur!...

14 Enfin tu l'aperçois et la joie te transporte.
Tu dis au bel Enfant qui charme les docteurs:
"O mon Fils, pourquoi donc agis-tu de la sorte?
"Voilà ton père et moi qui te cherchions en pleurs.

"Et l'Enfant Dieu répond (oh quel profond mystère!)
A la Mère chérie qui tend vers lui ses bras:
"Pourquoi me cherchiez-vous?... Aux oeuvres de mon Père
"Il faut que je m'emploie; ne le savez-vous pas?"

15 L'Evangile m'apprend que croissant en sagesse,
A Joseph, à Marie, Jésus reste soumis;
Et mon coeur me révèle avec quelle tendresse
Il obéit toujours à ses parents chéris.
Maintenant je comprends le mystère du temple,
Les paroles cachées de mon Aimable Roi.
Mère, ton doux Enfant veut que tu sois l'exemple
De l'âme qui Le cherche en la nuit de la foi.

16 Puisque le Roi des Cieux a voulu que sa Mère
Soit plongée dans la nuit, dans l'angoisse du coeur,
Marie, c'est donc un bien de souffrir sur la terre?
Oui, *souffrir en aimant, c'est le plus pur bonheur!...*
Tout ce qu'Il m'a donné Jésus peut le reprendre.
Dis-lui de ne jamais se gêner avec moi...
Il peut bien se cacher, je consens à l'attendre
Jusqu'au jour sans couchant où s'éteindra ma foi...

17 Je sais qu'à Nazareth, Mère pleine de grâces,
Tu vis très pauvrement, ne voulant rien de plus.
*Point de ravissements, de miracles, d'extases
N'embellissent ta vie, ô Reine des Elus!...*
Le nombre des petits est bien grand sur la terre.
Ils peuvent sans trembler vers toi lever les yeux.
C'est par *la voie commune,* incomparable Mère,
Qu'il te plaît de marcher pour les guider aux Cieux.

18 En attendant le Ciel, ô ma Mère chérie,
Je veux vivre avec toi, te suivre chaque jour.
Mère, en te contemplant, je me plonge ravie,
Découvrant dans ton coeur *des abîmes d'amour.*
Ton regard maternel bannit toutes mes craintes.
Il m'apprend *à pleurer,* il m'apprend *à jouir.*
Au lieu de mépriser les joies pures et saintes,
Tu veux les partager, tu daignes les bénir.

19 Des époux de Cana voyant l'inquiétude
Qu'ils ne peuvent cacher, car ils manquent de vin,
Au Sauveur tu le dis dans ta sollicitude,
Espérant le secours de son pouvoir divin.
Jésus semble d'abord repousser ta prière:
"Qu'importe," répond-Il, "femme, à vous et à moi?"

Mais au fond de son coeur, Il te nomme sa Mère;
Et son premier miracle, Il l'opère pour toi...

20   Un jour que les pécheurs écoutent la doctrine
De Celui qui voudrait au Ciel les recevoir,
Je te trouve avec eux, Marie, sur la colline.
Quelqu'un dit à Jésus que tu voudrais le voir.,
Alors, ton Divin Fils devant la foule entière
De son amour pour nous montre l'immensité.
Il dit: "Quel est mon frère et ma soeur et ma Mère,
"Si ce n'est celui-là qui fait ma volonté?"

21   O Vierge Immaculée, des mères la plus tendre,
En écoutant Jésus, tu ne t'attristes pas;
Mais tu te réjouis qu'Il nous fasse comprendre
Que notre âme devient *sa famille* ici-bas.
Oui, tu te réjouis qu'Il nous donne sa vie,
Les trésors infinis de sa divinité!...
Comment ne pas t'aimer, ô ma Mère chérie,
En voyant tant d'amour et tant d'humilité?

22   Tu nous aimes, Marie, comme Jésus nous aime,
Et tu consens pour nous à t'éloigner de Lui.
Aimer c'est tout donner et se donner soi-même.
Tu voulus le prouver en restant notre appui.
Le Sauveur connaissait ton immense tendresse.
Il savait les secrets de ton coeur maternel.
Refuge des pécheurs, c'est à toi qu'Il nous laisse
Quand Il quitte la Croix pour nous attendre au Ciel.

23   Marie, tu m'apparais au sommet du Calvaire
Debout près de la Croix, comme un prêtre à l'autel,
Offrant pour apaiser la justice du Père
Ton bien-aimé Jésus, le doux Emmanuel...
Un prophète l'a dit, ô Mère désolée,
"Il n'est pas de douleur semblable à ta douleur!"
O Reine des Martyrs, en restant exilée
Tu prodigues pour nous tout le sang de ton coeur!

24   La maison de Saint Jean devient ton seul asile.
Le fils de Zébédée doit remplacer Jésus...
C'est le dernier détail que donne l'Evangile.
De la Reine des Cieux il ne me parle plus.
Mais son profond silence, ô ma Mère chérie,
Ne révèle-t-il pas que *Le Verbe Eternel*
Veut Lui-même chanter les secrets de ta vie
Pour charmer *tes enfants*, tous les Elus du Ciel?

25   Bientôt je l'entendrai cette douce harmonie.
     Bientôt dans le beau Ciel, je vais aller te voir.
     Toi qui vins *me sourire* au matin de ma vie,
     Viens me sourire encor... Mère... voici le soir!...
     Je ne crains plus l'éclat de ta gloire suprême.
     Avec toi j'ai souffert et je veux maintenant
     Chanter sur tes genoux, Marie, pourquoi je t'aime
     Et redire à jamais que je suis ton enfant!...

                                   La petite Thérèse...

Poésies supplémentaires

PS 1
O Dieu caché

1   O Dieu caché sous les traits de l'enfance,
     Je vois en toi le monarque des Cieux.
     Je reconnais ta grandeur, ta puissance,
     Au doux éclat qui brille dans tes yeux.
     Si tu voulais, mille légions d'anges
     A ton appel viendraient former ta cour.
     D'étoiles d'or semant tes humbles langes,
     Ils chanteraient ton ineffable amour.

R.1 Je vois sur la rive étrangère,
     Et ne pouvant parler encor,
     Mon Dieu, mon Sauveur et mon Frère,
     N'ayant ni sceptre ni trésor.
     Adorant ce profond mystère,
     Divin Roi, je t'offre mon or.

2   O Roi du Ciel, tu viens sur cette terre
     Voulant sauver le genre humain ton frère.
     Pour ton amour, oh! je voudrais souffrir!
     Puisque pour moi tu veux un jour mourir.
     De tes douleurs je t'offre le symbole.
     Voyant briller ta sanglante auréole,
     Ah! je voudrais te gagner tous les coeurs,
     Divin Jésus, pour essuyer les pleurs.

R.2 Reçois la myrrhe, ô Roi du Ciel,
     Puisque tu veux être mortel.
                         [inachevé]

PS 2
En Orient…

1   En Orient apparut une étoile,
Et nous suivons son cours mystérieux.
Astre bénie, sa clarté nous dévoile
Que sur la terre est né le Roi des Cieux.

2   Le Ciel nous protège;
Et notre cortège,
Bravant pluies et neige,
Suit l'astre brillant!…

3   Que chacun s'apprête!…
L'étoile s'arrête…
Entrons tous en fête,
Adorons l'Enfant!…

PS 3
Depuis cinquante ans…

1   Depuis cinquante ans sur la terre,
Vous embaumez de vos vertus
Notre humble petit monastère,
Le palais du Roi des Elus.

Refrain

Chantons, chantons l'heureuse entrée
De la doyenne du Carmel.
De tous nos coeurs elle est aimée
Comme un bien doux présent du Ciel.

2   Vous nous avez toutes reçues
A notre entrée dans ce séjour.
Vos bontés nous sont bien connues,
Ainsi que votre tendre amour.

3   Bientôt une plus belle fête
Viendra réjouir tous nos coeurs.
Nous poserons sur votre tête
En chantant, de nouvelles fleurs.

PS 4
Le Ciel en est le prix

1   Le Ciel en est le prix.
La matraque sonore
Qui devance l'aurore
Me fait sauter du lit.

2   Le Ciel en est le prix.
Aussitôt qu'on s'éveille,
On voit d'autres merveilles
Que celles de Paris.

3   Le Ciel en est le prix.
Dans ma pauvre cellule
Point de rideaux de tulle
Ni glaces ni tapis.

4   Le Ciel en est le prix.
Rien, ni table ni chaise.
N'être pas à son aise,
C'est le bonheur ici.

5   Le Ciel en est le prix.
J'aperçois sans alarmes
Mes scintillantes armes.
J'aime leur cliquetis.

6   Le Ciel en est le prix.
A moi le sacrifice.
Croix, chaînes et cilice
Mes armes, les voici.

7   Le Ciel en est le prix.
Après une prière
Il faut baiser la terre.
La règle le prescrit.

8   Le Ciel en est le prix.
Je cache mon armure
Sous ma robe de bure
Et mon voile béni.

9   Le Ciel en est le prix.
Si madame Nature
Fait entendre un murmure,
En riant je lui dis:

10 Le Ciel en est le prix.
Jeûner est bien facile.
Cela rend très agile.
Si l'on a faim, tant pis!

11 Le Ciel en est le prix.
Nous ne respectons guère
Navets, pommes de terre,
Choux, carottes, radis.

12 Le Ciel en est le prix.
Jamais on ne s'étonne
Que le soir on ne donne
Que du pain et des fruits.

13 Le Ciel en est le prix.
Souvent avec justesse
Le pain passe, et je laisse
Dans l'assiette les fruits.

14 Le Ciel en est le prix.
De terre est mon assiette.
Ma main sert de fourchette.
La cuillère est de buis.

15 Le Ciel en est le prix.
Enfin l'on se rassemble.
On peut parler ensemble
Des joies du Paradis.

16 Le Ciel en est le prix.
En parlant on travaille:
L'une coud, l'autre taille
Des ornements bénis.

17 Le Ciel en est le prix.
On voit la gaîté sainte
Marquer de son empreinte
Les fronts épanouis.

18 Le Ciel en est le prix.
Une heure passe vite.
Je redeviens ermite
Sans froncer les sourcils.

19   Le Ciel en est le prix.
        Le bruit des pénitences
        Interrrompt le silence.
        On en est assourdi.

20   Le Ciel en est le prix.
        Des coups que je défile,
        Par an soixante-six mille.
        C'est le nombre précis.

21   Le Ciel en est le prix.
        Pour les missionnaires
        Nous nous faisons des guerres
        Sans trève, sans merci.

PS 5
Pour une Sainte-Marthe

Refr.
        Très nobles soeurs du voile blanc,
        Vous fêter nous rend l'coeur content.

1   A soeur Marie d'l'Incarnation
        Nous offrons la navigation
        Et ce joli petit bateau
        Mam'zelle Henriette le trouv'ra beau.

2   Nous offrons à soeur Saint Vincent
        Ce petit roquet tout pimpant.
        Aboyant près de son jardin,
        Il en sera très bon gardien.

3   Nous offrons au très cher Marthon
        Ce ravissant petit cochon.
        De monture il lui servira
        Quand il fera la chasse aux rats.

4   Pour fêter Mélanie Lebon,
        C'est à Baptiste de donner l'ton.
        Il lui présente un petit chat
        Qui lui servira de lèche plat.

5   Comment dire pour offrir ce broc?
        Ah! vraiment nous ne savons trop.
        ....
        Mon p'pa, voilà le Magister.
        Sauvons-nous, il a son grand air!

PS 6
A Mère Marie de Gonzague

J.M.JT.

21 Juin 1897

Moi aussi, Mère bien-aimée,
Je veux dire mon petit mot.
Mais on n'a pas beaucoup d'idée
Quand on ne boit que du lolo!...
Cependant, ma Mère chérie,
Je vous offre avec grand bonheur
Un album à photographie,
Mes toques et mon petit coeur.

Thérèse de l'Enfant Jésus
rel. carm. ind.

PS 7
Le silence est le doux langage

Voilà mon commandement: c'est que vous vous entr'aimiez, comme
je vous ai aimés!... St Jean XVI-12.

1   Le silence est le doux langage
       Des anges, de tous les élus.
       Il doit être aussi le partage
       Des âmes s'aimant en Jésus.

2   Ce n'est qu'au sein des sacrifices
       Que l'on peut s'aimer au Carmel.
       Un jour, enivrées de délices,
       Nous nous aimerons dans le Ciel.

PS 8
Toi qui connais ma petitesse extrême

Toi qui connais ma petitesse extrême,
Tu ne crains pas de t'abaisser vers moi!
Viens en mon coeur, ô blanche Hostie que j'aime,
Viens en mon coeur, il aspire vers toi!
Ah! je voudrais que ta bonté me laisse
Mourir d'amour après cette faveur.
Jésus! entends le cri de ma tendresse.
Viens en mon coeur!

Index of Main Words and Themes

This index is neither a complete concordance or an analytical index; it provides only a few of the key words and themes of the *Poetry*, either from the introductions to the poems or from the poems themselves. (Poems are listed by number and stanza.)

Abandonment: PN 3 intro.; PN 32, 4; PN 52 intro.
Act (— of love): PN 24, 23.
Adoration (eucharistic): PN 21, 3.
Angel: PN 22 intro.; PN 46.
Angelic: PN 47, 1.
Apostolate: PN 35 intro.; PN 36 intro.; PN 47, 6.
Apparel: PN 18, 48; PN 26, 2-3; PN 48 intro.
Baptism (of little children): PN 35, 8; PN 44 intro., PN 44, 10-11.
Beauty: PN 51, 5.
Beg (to): PN 36 intro.; PN 36, 5.
Believe (to): PN 24, 19.
Betrothal: PN 26 intro.
Bird: PN 43 intro.
Blasphemy: PN 17, 11.
Blaze: PN 17, 6.
Blood (of Jesus): PN 25, 6.
Breath: PN 32, 4.
Brother: Cf. Jesus, Sinner.
Captivate (to): PN 18, 37. Cf. prisoner.
Charity (fraternal): PN 17, 8; PN 54 intro.; PS 7.
Child: PN 36 intro. Cf. Baptism. (Thérèse, — of the Blessed Virgin Mary) PN 54, 1-2.
Childhood (virtues of —): PN 13, 5; PN 24, 9. Cf. Little Way.
Choice (divine): PN 3, 11; PN 53, 1.
Church (my Mother): PN 32, 2.
Ciborium: PN 24, 29; PN 29, 14.
Claim (to): PN 44, 11.
Come down (to): PN 22, 14.
Communion: (eucharistic) PN 25 intro.; (— of saints) PN 35, 11-12; PN 46, 1; PN 47 intro.
Console (to — Jesus): PN 20, 2.
Cross: (to bear one's —) PN 16, 1; (the —, a treasure) PN 17, 4.
Cry (to): PN 54, 2.
Death (of love): PN 17 intro.; PN 17, 14; PN 24, 26; PN 51, 5.
Delirium: PN 33, 3.
Dew: PN 1 intro.; PN 24, 21-22.
Disarm (to): PN 34, ref.2.

Draw (to): PN 54, 2.
Dream (to): PN 17, 14.
Elect: PN 19, 2; PN 40, 10. Cf. Fill (to).
Envy: Cf. Jealousy.
Eucharist: PN 25 intro.
Exile: (the Incarnation, an —) PN 13, 9. PN 54, 13.
Face (of Jesus): PN 20 intro. Cf. Holy Face.
Faith: PN 24, 19.
Family (our soul, — of Jesus): PN 54, 21.
Fast (to): PS 4, 10.
Fickleness: PN 5, 4.
Fill (to — heaven): PN 24, 16. Cf. Elect.
Fire: PN 17 passim.
Flower: (sun and —) PN 22, 4; (— for Jesus) PN 24, 30; (perfumes and
    —) PN 34, 2; (smile of God) PN 34 intro. Cf. Jesus (— of the fields).
Fly away (to): PN 22 intro.; PN 43 intro.; (— to God) PN 52 intro.
Fruitfulness (of virginity): PN 3 intro.; PN 24, 21-22.
Furnace: PN 21, 3.
Gaze: PN 32 intro. Cf. Glance, Look.
Glance, Look: PN 8, 5; PN 18, 50. Cf. Gaze.
Glory: PN 24, 1 and 19.
Godless (science): PN 39.
Gospel(s): PN 24 intro. and PN 24, 12.
Grapes (cluster of —): 25, 7. Cf. Vine.
Gratuitousness: (— of salvation) PN 44 intro.; (— of contemplative life)
    PN 13, 15-16; PN 17,1 3.
Harvest: PN 2 intro.
Harvester: PN 24, 15.
Heart: (of Jesus) PN 24 intro. and PN 24, 20; (of Mary) PN 54, 7; (your
    own —) PN 24, 31.
Heaven: (beautiful —) PN 22, 1; (house) PN 18, 55. Cf. Wait for (to),
    Jesus.
Hide (to): (God hiding): PN 5, 13; PN 24, 23; PN 25 title; PN 36, 2; PN
    54, 16. (hiding in the Face of God): PN 5, 6.
Hill: PN 24, 14; PN 54, 20.
Holy Face: PN 3, 55; PN 20 passim.
Host: PN 19 intro.
Humility: PN 24, 19; PN 46, 2; PN 51 ,2; PN 54, 3.
Idea: PN 54 intro.
Instant: PN 5, 1.
Jealousy: (of God) PN 27 intro. and PN 27, 4; (of the angel) PN 10 intro.;
    PN 13, 2; PN 46, 5.

Jesus: (our Friend) PN 53, 2; (Thérèse's heaven) PN 24, 33; (Flower of the fields) PN 13, 7; (our Brother) PN 23, 4; ("my joy") PN 45 intro.; (unrecognized) PN 13, 9; (our Homeland) PN 54, 13); (father of prodigal son) PN 24, 18; (exiled King) PN 13, 9; (our virtue) PN 23, 7. Cf. Lamb, Love.
Joy: PN 45 intro.
Kiss (to): PN 18, 51; PN 26, 6 and 7; PN 33, 2; PN 44 intro.
Lamb (Jesus, only —): PN 18, 35.
Lap (on Mary's —): PN 54, 25.
Lark: PN 52 intro.
Lavishness (of love): PN 17, 5.
Light (child of —): PN 24, 12.
Lily: PN 44, 2; PN 47, 4.
Little (to stay —): PN 11 intro.; PN 11, 3; PN 13, 5; PN 31, 4; PN 44 intro.
Love: (Jesus, only —): PN 34, 1.
Love (to): (to folly) PN 24, 26. (like Jesus) PN 54 intro.; PS 7 intro.; (— Jesus with his own love) PN 24, 31.
Lover: PN 17, 3.
Lyre: PN 3, 25; PN 20, 4.
Mantle (of the Virgin): PN 11, ref.1.
Martyr: PN 35, 10; (— of love) PN 17, 14; PN 31; PN 33 intro.
Maternity (spiritual): PN 24, 21-22.
Meadow: PN 18, 33.
Milk: PN 1; PN 26, 8.
Miracle: PN 24 intro. and PN 24, 13.
Misery: PN 24, 12.
Missionary (— flame): PN 35 intro.; PN 46 intro. Cf. Apostolate.
Name (whisper of —): PN 23 intro. and PN 23, 2.
Nature: PN 10 intro.; PN 18 intro.
Night: PN 13, 18; PN 45, 3. Cf. Trial.
Nothing (poor little —): PN 53, 1.
Ocean (of Love): PN 24, 11.
Passing (ephemeral): PN 18, 32.
Pearl: PN 26, 3.
Penance (instruments of —): PS 4, 5.
Perfume: PN 2 intro.; PN 17 intro.; PN 17, 12. PN 20, 3; PN 34, 2.
Place: (the lowest —) PN 29, 8; (— prepared in heaven) PN 24, 33.
Poverty: PN 24, 8; (spiritual —) PN 51 intro.; PN 54, 16.
Prayer (the — of Thérèse): PN 24, 14; PN 54, 15.
Priest: PN 17, 10; PN 24, 15; PN 40 intro.
Priesthood: PN 40 intro.
Prison: PN 18, 32.

Prisoner: PN 25 title; PN 17, 2; PN 31, 5. Cf. Captivate.
Purgatory: PN 17, 6; PN 23, 8.
Raise (— your eyes): PN 24, 15.
Receive (to — everything from God): PN 44 intro.
Recognize (to): PN 24, 23-24.
Reign (to): PN 10 intro.
Rejoice (to): PN 54, 18.
Remember: PN 8 intro.
Resemble (to): PN 20 intro.; PN 20, 5; PN 32, 4.
Rest: PN 21 title; PN 24, 32-33.
Rest (to — together): PN 13, 1.
Reward: PN 17, 15.
Root: PN 52, 1.   *
Sacred Heart: PN 15 intro. Cf. Heart.
Sacrifice (to — oneself): PN 7 intro.
Sanctuary: PN 32, 2.
Search for (to): PN 54, 14.
Secret: PN 24,12 and 20.
See (to): (desire to — God) PN 17, 15; (desire not to — God) PN 24, 27.
Shadow: PN 19, 1 and 4; PN 24, 27-28.
Shore: (eternal —) PN 21, 4. (other —) PN 33, 1.
Sign: PN 26, 7.
Silence: (— of Jesus) PN 13, 13; PN 24, 5; (— of Mary) PN 54 intro.; PN
    54, 8; (— language of the angels) PS 7.
Sinner: PN 17, 11; PN 46, 4.
Sleep (of Jesus): PN 17, 9; PN 24, 32.
Smile: PN 32, 1.
Soon: PN 33 intro.
Spark: PN 24, 17.
Star: PN 18, 27. (Jesus, Morning —) PN 1, 1; (Mary, Sweet —) PN 5, 11.
Stay (to — little): Cf. Little.
Storm: PN 17 intro.; PN 17, 9.
Suffering: (love and —) PN 17, 4; (joy in —) PN 10 intro.; PN 47, 3; PN
    54, 16; (to hide her —) PN 45, 5.
Sun: PN 22, 4.
Superiority (of humans over angels): PN 3, 85ff; PN 26, 4; PN 54, 10.
Swaddling clothes (God in —): PN 24, 3.
Sweetness: PN 10 intro. Cf. Humility.
Tabernacle: PN 40, 6.
Tears: Cf. Valley.
Thirst: PN 24, 10 and 25.
Thought: PN 54 intro.

Thrill (to): PN 54, 1.

Throne: PN 1, 3.

Touch (to): PN 52, 5.

Treasure: (Jesus) PN 51, 5; (— of Mary) PN 54, 5.

Tree: PN 52 intro.; PN 52, 1.

Trial (of faith): intro. to PN 30, PN 31, PN 32, PN 33, PN 36, PN 45, PN 48, PN 50, PN 54; and PN 32, 1; PN 45, 3; PN 48, 4; PN 52, 13-15; PN 54, 15-16.

Understand (to): PN 54 intro.

Unknown (to live —): PN 20,2 .

Unrecognized: PN 13, 9.

Valley: PN 2 intro.; PN 18, 22; PN 54, 3; (— of tears) PN 32, 1.

Veil: (without —) PN 5, 13; (— of Mary) PN 13,4 .

Vine: PN 5 intro.

Virginity: PN 26 intro.; PN 54, 3.

Virtues: PN 24, 9; PN 35, 3; PN 54,6 .

Wait (to), wait for: PN 17, 9; PN 46, 5; PN 54, 16.

Warrior: PN 36 intro.

Way (little): PN 3, 29-32; PN 11; PN 13 intro; PN 30 intro.; PN 31 intro.; PN 45 intro.; PN 45, 4; PN 46 intro.; PN 46, 2; (ordinary —) PN 54, 17.

Weakness: PN 54, 5.

Will (of God): PN 24, 32; PN 54, 20.

Wings: PN 22 intro.

Wipe (to), to dry: (— the Face of Jesus) PN 17, 11; (— his tears) PN 34, 1.

Word: PN 17,1; PN 24, epigraph. (— of Jesus on the cross) PN 24, 25.